BUSINESS DECISIONS

That Changed Our Lives

BUSINESS DECISIONS

That Changed Our Lives

EDITED

BY

SIDNEY FURST

President, Furst Survey Research Center, Inc.

AND

MILTON SHERMAN

Vice-President, Benton & Bowles, Inc.

Random House   New York

TO

ANNE BETSY FURST

AND

JENNIFER AND JOHN SHERMAN

Preface

This book did not begin in the way that it ended. It began as an investigation of market research and its relationship to the decision-making process. It ended with the decision-making process and its relationship to the changing consumer.

The book was originally conceived as a collection of management case histories in which the role of market research was particularly decisive. Such a collection would demonstrate how market research could be of greater value to management. We also reasoned that the "nonbusiness" reader would like to know how modern businessmen arrive at their decisions.

After pursuing this approach for several weeks, we discovered, much to our professional chagrin, that market research as it is being practiced today really is not playing the decisive role we accorded it in the decision-making process.

Our discussions with various business executives revealed a much more complex and intricate process of decision-making than we had imagined. In effect, we found out that market research has had only a limited value. For today's business executive it performs a confirming role, not a creative one.

With this realization, our book assumed a different character. We decided to record the fascinating experiences we had heard from these business executives in their own words. Many of them volunteered to find time within their busy schedules to write the business decision stories as they recalled them and in many instances experienced them.

What you have before you, therefore, are first-hand accounts of the inner workings of modern business corporations. We did make one specification—that each decision story be told with the awareness that one of the major "characters," if not the central one, was to be the consumer. The decision, in each case, was to relate how it changed consumer habits and behavior—in short, the consumer's life itself.

We cannot say that this collection is an attempt to exhaust all business decisions that have changed consumers' lives. These chapters were selected as examples. They represent a range of decisions and are intended to illustrate the process of innovation.

We wish to gratefully acknowledge the time and effort so generously given to us by the contributors and their associates in relating their innovations from this point of view.

Finally, a most important acknowledgment must be made to Miss Vivien Ranschburg. Her efforts on our behalf supplied the *esprit* as well as the needed follow-through in bringing this book about. In all candidness, she is our "third editor."

NEW YORK, N. Y.   S. F.
NOVEMBER, 1963   M. S.

Contents

Preface   vii

Introduction—THE BUSINESS DECISION
AND THE CONSUMER
The Sociology of the Business Decision

    by Sidney Furst and Milton Sherman   1

1 THE TRADING POST COMES TO THE CITY
The Origin of the Supermarket

    by M. M. Zimmerman, President, Super
    Market Publishing Company and Founder
    and Honorary Life Member, Super Market
    Institute   33

2 A HOUSE IS NOT ENOUGH
The Story of America's First Community Builder

    by William J. Levitt, President, Levitt and
    Sons, Inc.   59

3 PROVIDING FOR ILLNESS IN TIMES OF
   HEALTH
The Creation of the Blue Cross Plans

    by J. Douglas Colman, President, Associated
    Hospital Service of New York   75

4 YOU PRESS THE BUTTON—WE DO THE
   REST
   The First Kodak Camera for Everyone

   by William S. Vaughn, President, Eastman
   Kodak Company   99

5 BUTTON, BUTTON, WHO NEEDS THE
   BUTTON
   The Story of the Development of the Zipper

   by Lewis Walker III, President, Talon, Inc.   115

6 SLOW-OUTS INSTEAD OF BLOWOUTS
   The Development of the Tubeless Tire

   by P. W. Perdriau, President, B. F. Goodrich
   Tire Company   137

7 BETTER TO USE, CHEAP ENOUGH TO
   THROW AWAY
   The Disposable Paper Product

   by John R. Kimberly, Chairman of the Board,
   Kimberly-Clark Corporation   151

8 BABIES ARE OUR BUSINESS
   The Story of Commercially Prepared Baby Foods

   by Daniel F. Gerber, President, Gerber
   Products Company   167

9 CONVENIENCE, EASE AND SUCCESS FROM
   THE OVEN
   The Story of Prepared Cake Mixes

   by Paul S. Gerot, President, The Pillsbury
   Company   187

10 THE GOOD HANDS
The Counterrevolution in the Insurance World

  by Judson B. Branch, President, Allstate
  Insurance Company   203

11 THE SAVINGS ACCOUNTS THAT BUILD
AMERICA'S HOMES
The Growth of the S&L's

  by Warren Lee Pierson, Chairman of the
  Board, Great Western Financial Corporation   227

12 MAIN STREET COMES TO WALL STREET
A New Investment Concept Is Born

  by Walter L. Morgan, President, Wellington
  Fund   251

13 SERVING PEOPLE—WHERE THEY ARE
Food for Thought about Vending

  by Davre J. Davidson, Chairman of the Board,
  and William S. Fishman, President, ARA
  Service   277

14 THE MATTER OF BEAUTY
The Development of the Futurama Lipstick Case

  by Charles Revson, Chairman of the Board,
  Revlon, Inc.   293

15 A BETTER PRODUCT BETTER SOLD
A Winner in the Mass Market

  by Leonard H. Lavin, President, Alberto-
  Culver Company   309

16 SAVE AS YOU SPEND
    The Rise of Trading Stamps in Retail Promotion

        by William S. Beinecke, President, The Sperry
        & Hutchinson Company   329

17 A CAR IS A CAR AGAIN
    The Story of the Rambler Concept

        by Roy Abernethy, President, American
        Motors Corporation   351

INTRODUCTION

The Business Decision
and the Consumer

The Sociology of the Business Decision

BY

SIDNEY FURST
AND
MILTON SHERMAN

I

To speak of business decisions and decision-making is to speak of the nature and process of our free economy and ultimately of the character of our society. In its broadest sense, as used in this book, "the business decision" embodies not only the businessman's activities in maximizing profits and minimizing losses, but more essentially the realization of community and social values upon which our economic as well as our political system is based. The nature of these values and their pervasiveness in our society attests to the importance of studying their vitality and definition in the business decision.

The competitive activity of making and selling is rooted in the individual's right to a choice. Ideally, this right sustains the producer and the consumer. The producer has the right to make a choice among the varieties of commercial activity; the consumer, the right to choose among the varieties of products and services.

The structure of business exists on these rights of choice. These rights motivate its functional and varied activities. They influence the use of raw materials, the production standards, the distribution routes, the information values and finally the concern with consumption satisfaction. These rights, so necessary to the existence of the producer and the consumer—even in our day, when they are being modified and limited—are the fundamental principles of our economy. Without them, our economic and social life would have to assume a different character.

It is the underlying drama of the rights of choice that makes American business dynamic rather than static, that makes its practice a viable discipline open to individual performance and interpretation. Yet in delineating the functions of the businessman and his decision process, we find that the nomenclature itself is too broad to give us a focused view of the dynamics involved. The word "business" today has become syncretistic. It has assumed many qualities that, although relevant to the practices of trade and its complex structure, do not assert the sociological implications it has assumed in our time. To be more exact, the word "marketing" is closer. But it would be far better to invent a word for the phenomenon which is observed in this book. Even the word "marketing" as it has evolved in recent history has been bequeathed, unfortunately, a kind of parochialism by the "marketing departments" of corporations and the "marketing courses" in business schools.

In our economy, marketing is the force, the animating effort, the institutional means by which the choice of the producer and the consumer are made to interact. The competitive capacity of business and the ever-changing character of the consumer no longer permit a simple supply-and-demand relationship. In today's economy, choice, which implies infinite possibilities, has replaced the simple supply-demand nexus; the producer's choice as to what to make and the consumer's choice as to what to buy. No matter how complex and imponderable the relationship between the choices has become, the survival of the business enterprise hangs in the balance. The knowable elements of this relationship define the executive's decision-making role. "Marketing," as Theodore Levitt points out, "is where the customer is, and it is the customer who in the end decides the fate of business." [1]

The word "decision" in this essay focuses on the critical activity of business in our economy today. It is the decision function which epitomizes and characterizes the role of the business executive. His transformation from supplier to decision-maker has been the major trend in this century. In earlier phases of our economy, the entrepreneur's role was limited to the problems of production and distribution of products for existing needs. The relationship between the consumer and the businessman was simple and direct. In most cases he was a small businessman whose span of operations was limited in great measure by his lack of mobility and his need to interact directly with the consumer on a personal basis. He understood what the consumer wanted and spent most of his waking hours trying to fulfill these wants. To-

---

[1] Theodore Levitt, *Innovation in Marketing*, McGraw-Hill Book Company, Inc., New York, 1962, p. 13.

day, this simple relationship of supply and demand has evolved into a very complicated, many-faceted system. Business grew and became incorporated and a new type of man rose to leadership, one chosen not for his understanding of consumer wants, but rather for his ability to co-ordinate and administrate a complex system. This administrator, abetted by the technological advances of his time, solved the problem of production and organization. Although he was successful in this role, he lost his forefather's direct knowledge of the consumer. Today he finds himself at the center of a system beset with the problems of what to produce, when to produce it, how to sell it, and to whom to sell it. The simple demand situation of his forefathers has gone. In its place is the complex maze of critical choices which he must make and on which his success with the consumer depends. It is in this respect that we say that the defining characteristic of the businessman is his role as a decision-maker.

In the context of today's economy, what is a business decision? The answer to this question takes on many forms ranging from administration of the corporation to reaching the end user. There is no single type of business decision that can characterize the sum total of the corporation's business activities. There are decisions which maintain its organization and purpose. There are decisions which involve the efficient inter-relationship of one part to another. There are decisions which impel and perpetuate the organization on its present course. There are decisions which still involve the relationship of men to machines and to each other. And finally, decisions relating the corporation to its ultimate consumer.

It is this last group of decisions which is at the heart of the business or, more exactly, the marketing function. These are the decisions of the greatest uncertainty. These are decisions where the risk cannot be defined by simple probability formulas. These are decisions of ultimate consequence and their ramifications are complete success or complete failure. The business decisions which are recounted in this book by corporate decision-makers concern the relationship of the business enterprise and the consumer. They are decisions in which the whole existence of the corporation interacts with the community. These decisions have consequences far beyond the confines of the corporate entity. They are decisions that have created as well as dissolved business enterprises. These are decisions which are involved in the day-to-day re-evaluation of our social life. Today, they are business decisions of the highest order.

Individual characteristics, psychological predispositions and attitudes play an influential role in many major decisions where the corporation's existence is at a crucial turning point. So much of the literature of organizational theory, so many books about the executive life place the major emphasis on the qualities of leadership and the unique characteristics of the individual executive. But they do not examine the larger social context, the consumer stresses and resistances involved, the stakes and the consequences of a wrong choice.

When we first approached the chief corporate executives whose accounts of major decisions comprise this book, and asked them to recount the major turning points in the history of their corporations, we placed particular emphasis on the evolving or continuing process by which the decision was made. We asked them, in narrating the process of the decision, to illuminate the continuity of the process and their role in it.

There are indeed certain individuals who have the rare capacity of making decisions under situations of extreme risk and uncertainty. We are all aware that the decision-maker and the decision are not wholly separate and independent. However, no decision process can be revealed completely by studying only the motivations and actions of an individual. That would be the psychological study of leadership. As valuable as this would be as a by-product of this volume, it would fail to give us an insight into the dynamics of the decision-making process interacting with the valuative choice of the consumer. It is this last point with which we are concerned in this essay.

II

The business decision, as we conceive it, begins as an innovating, uncharted idea about consumer wants. The process by which this uncharted idea eventually becomes a meaningful part of the consumer's experience is the great phenomenon of our business society. To the extent that the process is unknown, one senses only the competitive manifestations of it in the flood of new products, in the "irrational" switching of consumer loyalties and in the "circus-variety" of advertising and merchandising techniques. To the extent that the process becomes known, one grasps in the form and content of these outward manifestations a meaningful exchange between the producer's idea and the consumer's reality. And in this exchange, one can discover a predictable process by which certain ideas and innovations are accepted and others rejected.

What is involved in the process itself? Essentially, we find that a product assumes a quality which is greater than its use or appearance. This additional value comes from the user. In simple terms this is the process by which the consumer's idea of the product and the producer's "uncharted" conception of the product become one. The product differentiates itself in the market place by reason of a social value which becomes an inherent part of its use value. The product's acceptance as well as its life span is dependent upon the degree to which it embodies the social value, regardless of its ability to perform its use function. In this process the consumer not only responds to the product as an entity, but reacts to the energizing, fulfilling, catalytic function which is attached to the product. The product takes on a meaning and a living function far above its technological and inherent properties. In this process an idea, whether of a new product or a service, a modification or improvement of an existing product, or a new way of looking at an old product, gains acceptance. To borrow a term from the sociologists, the phenomenon we are describing is the institutionalization of an idea, that is, a product becomes the physical manifestation of a social value. In a way, we say, it becomes the "institution" in which the value is represented.

The attempts and the efforts to embody these values in a product are the essence of marketing as we conceive it today. They are also at the heart of the true decision-making function.

For example, consider the experience of Mr. Gerber. He took as his "uncharted idea" a small jar of strained peas, which was not an innovation, and created for it a vast new market for commercially prepared baby food. In this marketing process the product acquired values far more important than the inherent quality of the product itself. The values it acquired were those of pediatric assurance of better nutrition and health. The values it realized in the consumer's life were a new sense of freedom from drudgery in the child's first year, and a new saving of time. This reorientation of the mother's role was accomplished so universally that it is hard to believe that the product ever existed without these other values.

On the other hand, the institutionalization of an entirely different class of values is exemplified by the business decision of the Kimberly-Clark Corporation to market a two-ply piece of paper as a handkerchief. In the marketing process, this product becomes the symbol for cleanliness, manners and convenience and in so doing reorients the American consumer to the permissiveness of disposability and waste.

III

There may be some who see in our interpretation of the primary decision function, a minimizing of the secondary decisions that are carried on in the business organization, such decisions as those that involve finance, plant location and labor relations, among innumerable other activities. These help make the corporation into a healthy organism, but do not necessarily involve interaction with the consumer.

Furthermore, we have left out a whole area of the business community whose products and functions are not directly concerned with the individual consumer, the military-government market, the industrial market and the institutional market. No matter how important these other decision areas and markets have become in recent years, they are not at the core of our economy. It is the free-choosing consumer and businessman, in the final analysis, who occupy that spot and are the enriching source of the vitality in our society.

Whether you are of a Keynesian persuasion or a follower of Adam Smith, you cannot deny the obvious fact that the manufacture of consumer goods and the availability of services direct to consumers annually account for the major share of our gross national product.

The technological capacity and the legal structure of our present society makes it impossible for an innovation to exist for very long without imitators. This has resulted in a growing frequency and intensity of the kind of business decision we are talking about, the kind that results in direct contact with the consumer. The sheer volume of this decision activity has produced a demand for a more thorough understanding of the decision-making process. We are no longer satisfied with "seat of the pants" thinking or the idea of intuitive "flashes." Simple probability formulas indicate that as the number of necessary decisions to be made increases so will the risk of "hitting it right" any one time. In simpler terms, the businessman who now finds himself in the position of making these innovating decisions, more frequently than not, is in a quandary. Driven by anxieties, fears and doubts, he has only a scant understanding of the "intuitional" decision process of his forebears. Chosen for his ability to make a decision, he now finds he lacks the information upon which such ability can be used. He has looked to the universities, the management consultants, and the whole array of related service businesses that have sprung up and appropriated more and more areas of expertise.

The editors of *Fortune,* in their study of "The Executive Life," have taken cognizance of the situation:

An intellectual breakthrough is shedding some light on the process of decision-making. The breakthrough is scarcely recognized as such, for it is occurring in many areas of study, such as mathematics, economics, neurology, psychology, strategy, information theory, communication theory. These bits have yet to be integrated, and they exist for the most part in the form of theories whose connections with reality have not been thoroughly established. Yet the breakthrough is manifest in the sudden preoccupation of hundreds of the country's best academic minds with decision-making as an identifiable aspect of human behavior.[2]

Regardless of which discipline approaches the businessman's constant preoccupation with the mounting volume and the growing import of his decisions, it has not met him on his own terms. It has approached him in his need for clarification and direction and has returned to offer him systems for increasing the efficiency of his routinized activities. He remains in a dilemma. The application of "systems" to the management and organization situation adds a greater efficiency, a new vocabulary, but no greater clarity. Herbert A. Simon, in his book, *The New Science of Management Decision*, exemplifies the situation in speaking of "programmed" and "nonprogrammed" decisions:

> Decisions are programmed to the extent that they are repetitive and routine, to the extent that a definite procedure has been worked out for handling them so that they don't have to be treated *de novo* each time they occur. The obvious reason why programmed decisions tend to be repetitive, and vice versa, is that if a particular problem recurs often enough, a routine procedure will usually be worked out for solving it. Numerous examples of programmed decisions in organizations will occur to you: pricing ordinary customers' orders; determining salary payments to employees who have been ill; reordering office supplies.
>
> Decisions are nonprogrammed to the extent that they are

[2] The Editors of *Fortune, The Executive Life,* Doubleday & Company, Inc., Garden City, N.Y., 1956, p. 164.

novel, unstructured, and consequential. There is no cut-and-dried method for handling the problem because it hasn't arisen before, or because its precise nature and structure are elusive or complex, or because it is so important that it deserves a custom-tailored treatment . . .[3]

But the breach between managing and directing, between efficiency and innovation has become wider in the process. The decision-maker has been freed of the routinized selection among choices and alternatives, but he is still left with the core of his problem—decisions whose success or failure is not measured by the extrapolations of double-entry bookkeeping, but by the enigmatic double jeopardy of the consumer.

IV

Although economists may differ in their interpretation of the fact, most agree that the basic shift in the American economy during the last century has been from one geared to the production of capital goods to one with a much greater concentration on the distribution of consumer goods. You have only to look at the stock market listings of the past thirty years to see ample documentation of this shift. Where once U.S. Steel, New York Central, Standard Oil and large public utilities exemplified the blue chip segment of the market, today these corporate giants have been joined by such companies as Procter & Gamble, General Foods, Standard Brands, Bristol-Myers and National Dairy, to name just a few—companies whose growth, sustenance and essential character are dependent upon the individual consumer. In fact, it has been the consumer's acceptance of their "new products" that has accounted for the enormous growth of these latter companies. But not only have we seen the upsurge of these consumer-oriented companies in our time, we have also noted that major capital industries such as steel, oil, aluminum,

---

[3] Herbert A. Simon, *The New Science of Management Decision,* Harper & Brothers Publishers, New York, 1960, pp. 5-6.

rubber and glass have become increasingly dependent upon the distribution activities of consumer products. In many instances, even where these capital goods companies are concerned only with the ingredients of consumer products, they have nevertheless taken it upon themselves to contribute to the distribution process of the end use products. As Thomas C. Cochran noted in his book, *The American Business System,* "By 1950 half the buildings used for homes were occupied by owners, and 60 per cent of all the durable equipment in the country, which included factories, power plants, railroads, buildings, trucks, automobiles, and similar utilities, was being used directly by consumers for their own purposes." [4]

What are the implications of this shift? The obvious and most apparent one is that the consumer—his behavior, his wants, his desires and his psychological predispositions—is the guts of our new economic stage of development. Today we must paraphrase Alexander Pope and say—the proper study of the businessman is not business but the consumer.

The second implication of this shift involves the basic question: What is this new economic man—this consumer? We have already seen that he is no longer merely the end user who buys the products of industry to satisfy his basic needs of hunger, warmth and protection. He has risen from the primal stage of consumership to the role of a consumer in a highly elaborate advanced stage of civilization. He buys not merely to satisfy needs but to identify himself in this evolving social process.

The world of today's consumer is populated by thousands and thousands of bulging supermarket shelves, gleaming freezers filled with perishable, specially processed packaged foods, massive displays, maze-like aisles for which a directory is needed, individual shopping carts engineered to move easily and designed to hold a week's supply of groceries plus a squirming child. The consumer's countryside is an arterial maze of roads stretching from central city to central city with connecting tributaries into every suburban hamlet and township, tied together at key

---

[4] Thomas C. Cochran, *The American Business System,* Harper Torchbooks, Harper & Row Publishers, Inc., New York and Evanston, 1962, p. 120.

points with cloverleaf intersections, overpasses and rotaries. The consumer's home contains endless modifications of labor-saving appliances, an integrated entertainment center made up of television, record players, radios set amidst all kinds of hobby devices and other recreational equipment.

This environment of abundance, this society of plethora is of his own making. It has come about through the opportunities he has provided for the enterprising businessman who must place his products within a meaningful context in the consumer's life. It is sustained by a constant concern with his freedom of choice. Some have looked upon this situation with complete disdain, seeing it as the bizarre manifestations of a self-pampering, over-indulged society. John Kenneth Galbraith in his book, *The Affluent Society*, sees irony in the abundance, and waste in the process. He calls the rationale for this consumer-oriented economy the Dependence Effect:

> As a society becomes increasingly affluent, wants are increasingly created by the process by which they are satisfied. This may operate passively. Increases in consumption, the counterpart of increases in production, act by suggestion or emulation to create wants. Or producers may proceed actively to create wants through advertising and salesmanship. Wants thus come to depend on output. In technical terms it can no longer be assumed that welfare is greater at an all-around higher level of production than at a lower one. It may be the same. The higher level of production has, merely, a higher level of want creation necessitating a higher level of want satisfaction.[5]

We have heard a lot about the engineering of consumer wants. Galbraith is not among the first to point to this supposed evil in our economic system. There seems to be a basic confusion which can be eliminated only by a more systematic look at just what the engineering of wants involves.

Galbraith, like Vance Packard and Toynbee and many others

---

[5] John Kenneth Galbraith, *The Affluent Society*, Mentor Books, The New American Library of World Literature, Inc., New York, 1958, p. 128.

who have attempted to analyze today's business situation, have thus placed the impetus for our economy's growth:

> The fact that wants can be synthesized by advertising, catalyzed by salesmanship, and shaped by the discreet manipulations of the persuaders shows that they are not very urgent. A man who is hungry need never be told of his need for food. If he is inspired by his appetite, he is immune to the influence of Messrs. Batten, Barton, Durstine & Osborn. The latter are effective only with those who are so far removed from physical want that they do not already know what they want. In this state alone men are open to persuasion.[6]

The major shortcoming of this position is that it takes into account the businessman's activity but does not take into account the consumer. It is as though the consumer is made of some pliable, absorbent material, lacking any inherent form or character of his own, merely reacting to the arbitrary kneading of the persuaders. What is missing from this concept is an understanding of the consumer. It is from this understanding that the businessman gains an insight not only into what he should produce and when to produce it, but also how to distribute his product and communicate its value to the consumer. What is missing from this concept, in effect, is the volatile interaction and modifying force of the consumer choice. Because the consumer is left out, these theories tend to confuse appearance and reality, and their authors are led to make social judgments without understanding the underlying social processes.

Basically, they do not understand the function of the product in our economy. The crucial question to ask is: How do these critics explain the reasons for the failure of so many products and product ideas regardless of the size of the advertising budget? Would they say that the failure lies in the lack of ability of the persuader? Or have they taken such delight in flagellating the persuader as an evil in itself, that they have lost sight of the subject? Like the sixteenth century physicians who insisted upon explaining physical processes of life through "the humours" of the body

---

[6] Ibid.; p. 128.

and took little interest in the physiological causes of disease, these critics are left with an equally superficial explanation of the vitality of product acceptance, and a disinterest in analyzing product failure. But as surely as disease teaches us much about health, so product failure must teach us much about product acceptance and success.

The businessman cannot take such a short-sighted view as these critics. He cannot cavalierly dismiss the consumer or the possibility of product failure. His developing concern with the accountability of his investment in the tools of persuasion make him much more sensitive to its role, its capabilities and its limitations. In his world the story of the failure of the Edsel is a legend— the moral of which must be taught to every young executive. In our time, in fact, persuasion, or more specifically advertising and merchandising, is only the last element in the interaction process between the producer and the consumer. The content, direction and ultimate effectiveness of such means of persuasion depend upon the ability to communicate the institutionalization process by which any product is accepted.

V

The institutionalization process is the way in which a product assumes a meaning in the consumer's life beyond its use value. This new meaning—in a sense we may call it its new value—becomes the expression by which the consumer identifies the change in his living pattern. The product is the "objective correlative"; it symbolizes the shift in the consumer's value.

Let's take the case of the introduction of cake mixes. When the product was first developed it packaged the right measurements of each ingredient, already pre-mixed. The consumer added water, mixed, and placed the batter in a pre-heated oven. The laborious sifting of flour, of separating whites from yolks, of mixing in sugar, baking powder, shortening, etc., of beating until creamy smooth, could become a thing of the past. The housewife was promised a new liberation, a new freedom from the cares, the work and time involved in baking a cake. It meant a change in her role in the kitchen. She had come to regard the care and toils of baking of no value in themselves. The end product—the finished cake—was the thing of value, and that alone.

Yet this product did not "compete" with packaged and bakery cakes. These seemed too impersonal to offer the same rewards as a cake right from the oven. So cake mixes positioned themselves as "competitors" for the housewife's baking activity. To her forebears the acceptance of this product would have meant that a housewife would have to surrender the values she saw in baking a cake —values which placed emphasis on personal preparation, individual expression—and modify her role as the family feeder. She would be surrendering the psychological, almost "religious" rewards of labor spent in baking for a new set of social values that placed approval on the finished product without the time and toil. In this sense the product was the "objective correlative"—the physical symbol of a new social value which awarded satisfaction regardless of the lack of labor involved. In effect it made the baked cake coming from the oven with a minimum of work acceptable. The housewife, conditioned by the traditional belief in the values of labor, had to be reassured that success was possible with a minimum of toil and effort. But Ann Pillsbury, and her competitive imitators, lent the constant assurance and guarantee of success with each box used so that the new housewife's dream of a "perfect" cake without the "trouble" could become a reality.

This switch in values is an example of what we have called the institutionalizing process. It encompassed not only cake mixes but a vast array of similar convenience products. In so doing, it brought about a pervasive reorientation from the puritanical value of work to a new acceptance of self-fulfillment with less effort. Thereby, the housewife was ready to relinquish these values, but she would not do it unless the demonstrable results were guaranteed—results she could point to as her own even though they were accomplished without the amount of work, time and trouble which her mother and grandmother thought was not only necessary but "right."

In this process the role of the business decision is not limited in our time to whether a product such as cake mix can be produced, but whether a product such as cake mix can be accepted within the present experience and orientation of the consumer, or whether this orientation need be changed in order for the product to be accepted.

What we have just described is how the institutionalization process works in the market place. We can now go on to detail this interactive process in some of its varied forms. Although basic, the example above demonstrates just one of these forms. Actually, it is the institutionalizing of social values for a new product that has never existed. However, it can also take the form of reorienting an existing product to a new set of social values and thereby provide a new perception and meaning for the product. Or, the process can be seen working to orient a new product into an existing set of social values.

These variations of the institutionalizing process can categorize all the chapters in this book. However, under closer analysis, we see them not as distinct types but rather as stages in a continuum. At one end is the institutionalization of social values born directly out of a build-up of social needs. This is a direct and simple reaction of the businessman to the needs of the consumer. It is accomplished by a popular mandate, since it is brought about in response to an immediate situation.

The degree to which it successfully meets these needs is directly dependent on the way it achieves its acceptance within the context of existing social values. As we see in the chapter which traces the development of the supermarket, the rising need for economies in food distribution during the thirties, and the concomitant need for a "cash-and-carry" relationship between the retailer and the consumer, called for change in the retailing of groceries. But this change, although foreseen by several perceptive individuals before the thirties, did not become the accepted way of selling groceries until the innovation was adopted by the large retailing chains. Only then did the "fly-by-night" appearance of the early innovators gain status. The process by which this came about was the interaction of the consumer's need for a "bargain" and the values consumers placed on the reputation of the chain. In other words, the "bargain" became anchored in the respectability of the chain's status. This pattern of institutionalization, or in this case gaining respectability for a "bargain," is reflected in the recent evolvement of a "discount" chain which needs the respectability of a Fifth Avenue address.

At the other end of the continuum is a form of the institutionalization process that is more pervasive in our current marketing scene. It is the variety of solutions to the problem of competition among "brands" of the same product category. Some refer to it as *marginal differentiation*. Essentially, it is a matter of gaining for the product a distinguishing identification within an already existing set of consumer values by which preference is achieved. In respect to this process we begin to hear such terms as "product image," "user profile," "specific consumer benefits" and "Unique Selling Proposition." What these terms attempt to describe from various viewpoints is the manner in which competing products differentiate themselves.

The cosmetic market today is a good example of this striving for differentiation within the context of common social values. Charles Revson, in his chapter, "The Matter of Beauty," relates how the decorative refillable lipstick case was introduced. He describes the outspoken objections of some of his colleagues, who were "men of experience and ability" in the cosmetic field; but what Revson saw in the lipstick case was not the cosmetic business but "fashion." In effect, what Mr. Revson did with the lipstick case, as with products that were introduced before and after it, was the institutionalization of the values of fashion within the competitive cosmetic market. Prior to his introduction of this differentiating strategy, the methods of marketing cosmetic products were similar to those of other packaged-goods manufacturers: a standardization of product, inventory control and a wide distribution pattern under known brand names. The packaged-goods manufacturer would consider it insanity to operate on a seasonal basis. It would be incongruous to him to put special emphasis on a particular color or style for one season, change it the following season and not repeat it the following year. These are the marketing techniques of the soft goods merchandiser, not the packaged-goods industry.

This example was taken from "the most competitive area" of this institutionalization continuum. In this area, the values that first established the product category still persist, and the necessary differentiation process becomes one of shifting emphasis. In a sense, the shift of emphasis is a *re-institutionalization* of the same social values in a new context or situation which gives it a new sense of vitality. Such re-emphasis characterizes the process by which a particular brand achieves its distinctive association in the consumer's mind, and its distinctive market position. It is for this reason that at this end of the continuum we see so much concern with packaging, "completeness of line," uniqueness of copy claims, and the like, since this is the way that many marketing men carry out their competitive strategy. However, unless these efforts can help reorient the common social values associated with the product, they cannot be effective. In Revson's case, the values of glamour and beauty were re-institutionalized with new emphases borrowed from the "fashion world."

Thus far we have described the institutionalization process as it operates at the extremes of the continuum. At one end we have marketing situations based on direct consumer wants and needs. At the other end, as we have just seen in the case of Revlon, the consumer demand has already been met and values have already been associated with particular brands. The problem here is re-emphasizing what has already been institutionalized in a more meaningful way. At one end, the consumer creates the direct demand and the problem is to fulfill it. At the other end, the demand has been fulfilled, and the problem here involves consumer resistance to change and apathy to associate the product in another context.

Between the extremes of the continuum we have transitional situations. Here the ultimate objective is to change consumer behavior from gratifying needs directly to fulfilling these needs in a broader social context. To do this, the producer must confront the consumer with a product that has values beyond those demanded by the initial situation. In this transitional phase, the prime concern of the producer is to establish the social value of the new form *within* the use value of the existing one. In this way one product replaces another. And this, in essence, is the mechanism of the institutionalization process.

Looking across the broad span of these transitional situations, we see at work an interaction of product and social forces. This social interaction involves the overcoming of consumer resistances to the new form of the product. This new form incorporates new social values which the consumer acquires as part of the benefit and reward of using the product in its new form. These new values, once acquired, set the stage for all types of new products to incorporate this new value.

This phase of the continuum is exemplified in Mr. Gerber's account of introducing commercially prepared baby foods, in the decision of the Kimberly-Clark Corporation to market disposable sanitary napkins, and in the account of the introduction of Pillsbury's cake mixes.

These examples are all instances of the establishment of convenience and ease as a pervasive social value. Once established, the field is then open to a proliferation of convenience products. Today, one would have to search far and wide to find any product or service area that comes into the life of the ultimate consumer that is not dominated by such products.

VI

The chapters in this book have been ordered to illustrate the continuum. Starting with the development of the supermarket, which responded to a direct need in our social life, we have:

> *Levitt,* and the development of mass-production methods in building houses to meet the acute housing shortage after World War II. The institutionalizing process which altered the homeowner's values from the custom-built, individually-suited home of prewar days to those of the identical mass-

produced houses of the postwar period was the incorporation of communal values.

Blue Cross, and the innovation of prepaid hospitalization insurance, grew out of the economic crisis of the thirties which had drained hospital funds as well as the individual's ability to pay. In meeting this consumer demand, the value of a personal and private relationship with one's doctor was incorporated in the plan. Other hospital plans which did not incorporate this basic value, the free choice of physician and hospital, have had limited acceptance because of the inherent clash of social values.

Moving further along the continuum, we come upon situations where the consumer demand for a product is already being met by other products. In reality, the only way the new product can replace the old product is by embodying a new social value.

Eastman Kodak developed a camera simple enough for everyone to use. The emphasis on this latter feature brought the value of simplicity and convenience to photography, and thereby made the camera a common family possession.

Talon replaced the ubiquitous button and the fastidious hook and eye with a new value of convenience embodied in a mechanism that did the previous job with just a simple "zip."

B. F. Goodrich, in producing the *ideal* tire that no longer needed the inner tube, found that the public would not accept it until the value of greater security and safety from blowouts was established with it, in the consumer's mind. In order for consumers to accept these values, it needed a demonstrable symbol—the now famous spike board.

Kimberly-Clark's development of disposable paper products was accepted by the consumer because it incorporated the social values of health, cleanliness and neatness, which created the permissiveness of disposability and waste.

Gerber, in marketing commercially prepared baby food, provided the needed assurance of pediatric authority that the new product did not compromise the baby's nutritional needs and health. Once accepted on this basis, the new product meant a saving of time and toil for the mother.

Pillsbury provided the convenience of having all the ingredients of a cake pre-mixed for baking. For this innovation to be accepted, it needed the assurance of "perfect results" before the consumer would accept the convenience it offered.

Allstate found that they could not completely eliminate the public's traditional faith in the relationship between agent and customer even if it involved a lower cost. It wasn't until a modified agency system was adopted through Sears' outlets that the value of personal reassurance was added to its traditional method of direct selling. Only then did it get broad market acceptance. Today its policy program has expanded to all forms of insurance.

Great Western Financial Corporation added the values of size, security and stability to savings and loan associations who were unable to command an appreciable share of America's savings despite their higher interest rates.

Wellington Fund's innovation in mutual funds was the idea of balance—a conservative investment program including bonds and preferred stocks as well as common stocks. This provided the additional value of security to the possible inherent growth in stock investment.

ARA Service discovered that it could not fulfill the values of quality and variety in foods by vending machines alone. It had to combine manual preparation with machine distribution. By this combination of values, it was able to fulfill commercial feeding needs by offering variety inherent in manual methods with dispersion possible with vending machines.

Thus far in the institutionalization process we have moved, from one extreme, where innovations are developed to meet built-up needs, to those instances where new products replace existing ones by incorporating new values. Now, nearing the opposite extreme of the continuum, we come to the process of marginal differentiation, of competition within the context of common social values.

Revlon, as we have seen earlier, achieved distinctiveness as a brand by shifting the emphasis of the accepted values of cosmetics. It did this by combining the values of fashion with those of packaged goods.

Alberto-Culver entered an extremely competitive field late. In the hair preparations and toiletries market, the consumer demands had been met by a succeeding variety of products. The values of appearance and grooming had been asserted and reasserted by a continuous array of new brands. When Mr. Lavin decided to enter this market, he did not follow the example of his successful predecessors in extending the varieties of end results achieved by the products. Instead, he reverted back to the product itself as the demonstrable source of the original value. He reasserted the product quality which could best demonstrate the social value—hence a hair spray that can be shown to leave no residue or film makes it a more effective avenue to appearance and grooming.

S&H Green Stamps, achieved widespread acceptance because the things consumers "bought" with the accumulated stamps were products they would not necessarily buy out of their budgeted income, or whose priority was low among planned purchases. The social value which these trading stamps incorporated was the permissibility of the unnecessary purchase by attaching it as a "bonus" to the necessary one.

American Motors, through the Rambler, represents a singular case history in the institutionalization process we have been describing. In effect, it results from a *reaction to the excessive development of a social value.* The competitive striving to express this value led to the overdevelopment of fins, chrome, and the "dinosaur" proportions of automobiles. Rambler changed the physical proportions and reoriented the social value. The automobile was the most expensive possession for the majority of Americans. It bespoke affluence. Rambler

substituted utility and functionality for "showiness." In so doing, affluence took on a "new look."

From these brief analyses of the institutionalizing process
involved in each of the corporate accounts in this book, we
see that a basic premise underlies each situation. This basic
premise, although not explicitly stated, is the beginning of the
decision-maker's encounter with the market. Prompted by some
insight into the social milieu in which he sees the consumer he
wishes to reach, he decides upon a course of action by which to
affect this consumer's living pattern. If, for example, he sees his
consumer as Mr. Levitt did, as highly social and eager to participate in a community, he will fulfill his urgent housing need,
on a mass scale and at the same time integrate the values of communal resources. Or, if he sees his consumer as the Pillsbury
Company did, as a housewife who has been nurtured on the
maxim that anything worthwhile requires toil and time, he will
provide her not only with a package of pre-mixed ingredients but
continually reinforce the assurance of successful results. If he sees
his consumer as skeptical and reluctant to believe the new advantages of his "ideal" product, he will provide persuasive demon-
stration and proof, as the president of the B. F. Goodrich Tire
Company has related. But in each case, before the decision to incorporate his product with the *meaningful* value, he must have
a basic understanding of the nature of the social character involved.

It is our feeling that the nature of social character is as important to the corporation's balance sheet as is the latest piece of
capital equipment. Yet only in isolated instances do we find any
formal attempt to integrate a study of social life into the pre-
requisites of a career in business. As Paul F. Lazarsfeld has posed
the problem in his essay, "Sociological Reflections on Business:
Consumers and Managers":[7]

We can take it for granted that a majority of the sociologists
teaching in American liberal arts colleges will have an ideo-

---

[7] Robert A. Dahl, Mason Haire, Paul F. Lazarsfeld, *Social Science Research
on Business,* Columbia University Press, New York City, 1959, p. 101.

logical bias against business. Aiding the doctor, promoting justice, or supporting the agencies of the law—all these are in accord with accepted norms; helping the businessman make money is not. Even if the goal of business is formulated in broader terms—organizing the productive capacities of the country—many sociologists will doubt whether the contemporary American businessman is on the right track toward achieving it.

But as the need for social understanding grows within the business community, this antipathy described by Lazarsfeld will be overcome. For, in essence, the business decision-maker can offer the sociologist the opportunity of enriching his empirical analysis of behavior, while the sociologist can enlarge the businessman's perspective of marketing as an institution in our society.

No better example of the mutual benefits to be derived from integrating the disciplines of business and sociology can be found than in the work of David Riesman, particularly his seminal study of contemporary America, *The Lonely Crowd*. In his view, the emerging American character is seen as predominantly "other-directed"—that is, the source of direction for the individual is derived from his contemporaries, his peer group—"either those known to him or those with whom he is indirectly acquainted, through friends and through the mass media." [8]

The implications of this observation for marketing are only partially delineated in this concept. Nevertheless, it holds immeasurable value for the decision-maker, in the way it amplifies his more intimate knowledge of the marketing process. For instance, it explains the marketing phenomenon we have seen in the acceptance of the range of "convenience" products. Here we see the "inner-directed" motivation of reward for labor supplanted by the "other-directed" motivation of achieving results without effort. In Riesman's terms, this marketing reorientation was brought about not by the inherent properties of the new product per se, but rather by the values established in the awareness of

---

[8] David Riesman et al., *The Lonely Crowd,* Yale University Press, Revised Paperback Edition, New Haven, 1961, p. 21.

what the consumer believes *others* are accepting and doing. In effect, the complex mechanism involved here relies on the "simple" fact that the end results are demonstrable to others, whereas the product's inherent properties are demonstrable only to the consumer.

In a broader sense, Riesman's thesis of the emerging, "other-directed" character of America documents the social psychology of the institutionalization process in marketing we have been describing in this essay. For, as we have shown, a consumer accepts a product, not for its inherent properties, but for the values this product has come to incorporate. However, there is an essential difference between Riesman's view and the decision-maker's view of this social phenomenon. Riesman is concerned with the mechanism as it affects the individual. Hence his resolution leads to the goal of an autonomous consumer. The business decision-maker, on the other hand, must by the very nature of his function see this social mechanism not in its effect on the individual, but rather as an instrument of bringing individuals into a social consensus. For the businessman, the resolution is in a "greater share of the market."

VII

The process we have described and the documentation which we have provided in the chapters that follow are offered for the understanding of how successful innovations and marketing decisions are carried out. But the reality of this process, as well as the validity of its documentation, can assume depth only if we fully appreciate the elements of uncertainty and risk involved in any marketing decision. These elements point to the necessary condition that explanation of failure as well as of success must be grasped in order to appreciate the implications of the institutionalization process.

The most obvious causes of failure of any innovation is the attempted incorporation of a value for the product which cannot be translated into meaningful terms in the consumer's experience.

Or, similarly, the consumer is not sufficiently concerned with the value to make him seek out the product. In short, he does not want to "buy" the value. This explains why more marketing innovations die from consumer apathy than from any shortcoming in the product.

We find this consumer apathy becoming widespread at the same time marketing activities for new products are becoming intensified. Despite all this intensified activity on the part of marketers, the consumer is still only left with a constant proliferation of "me-too" products—products that claim the same social value. The root of consumer apathy for the imitative product lies in the fact that the original innovating product has vitally continued its association with the social value in the consumer's mind. As long as it performs this role in the consumer's life, only peripheral interest can be generated by the imitator. Some marketing men are misled by thinking that they can get away with giving their product a "new look" through promotion and advertising. These methods may prove to be very arresting, but they fail most dramatically because they do not give the product a meaningful social value. The "look" can be used to communicate the value, but cannot, by itself, substitute for it. These are overt mistakes in marketing that have caused products to fail with distressing frequency.

The seventeen success stories that make up this book give us a profitable perspective from which to view failures. They indicate not only what is lacking in today's marketing thinking, but also provide a methodology by which these costly mistakes can be avoided. Yet these are not "handbook" examples to be followed. It would be a mistake to imitate the marketing strategy of Revlon in the cosmetics field or Kimberly-Clark in the disposable paper products market. The route has been pre-empted. Such efforts cannot be expected to meet with the same success even though they follow the same formula. There are no immutable laws in marketing. There are only principles relative to the situation. Revlon, Kimberly-Clark and the others cannot give us the "secret" of success. They can only tell us how they came to discover it.

We can decipher certain underlying patterns that vary according to the stage of marketing development. The most common and pervasive of these stages is where a brand dominates the market by reason of the fact that it has been able to successfully associate itself with a meaningful social value. In this situation, the most immediate strategy would be to add a peripheral value in order to enlarge on the original value. This process is commonly referred to as *marginal differentiation*. It is marginal because the difference between the competitive brands is really an emphasis on minor distinctions to which the consumer must be educated. In essence, the competitive product is sold the same way as the leading product. The addition of these marginal differences helps to individualize and give distinction to competing brands. Examples of this can be found in most products of mass distribution, such as laundry products, face soaps, breakfast cereals, soft drinks and, until recently, toothpaste.

After this strategy of marginal differentiation has gone on successfully for some time, any further competitive continuation of this pattern tends to lose its effectiveness in terms of the consumer's experience. In this stage a major "breakthrough" is necessary either through technology, or, if that is not available, through a startling innovation in the way in which the product fulfills its basic value. Revlon is an excellent example. Here, technology could offer no basis for product differentiation and it was left to the insight of the decision-maker to bring about the successful innovation. We can best describe this process by the concept of *cross-fertilization*. In essence, it is the process by which the market techniques of one product category are transplanted to another—cosmetics are sold like fashion, beer is sold like a grocery item together with butter and eggs, and a whole area of foods and packaged products become available everywhere in vending machines. In this process, new ways of marketing a product are made possible. The traditional boundaries of particular markets are broken down. All products of one market are subject to the scrutiny of other markets. In recent years this marketing practice has shown immense potential for realizing success even in market stages where traditional brand standings have had a tendency to discourage innovators.

There is a further stage of market development when the competitive strategies of many brands have as their effect a "watering down" of the initial social value of the product by constant emphasis and re-emphasis of minor differences. The marketing men have lost sight of the original purpose for which the product was produced; and have instead created a condition of proliferating products whose only reason for being is a minor variation in the product, in the form of packaging, color, scent, etc. The consumer, on the other hand, maintains a constancy and a belief in the original social value of the product. The marketer can *revitalize* the consumer's constancy in the social value by "going back." In this way a new product is able to capture a high share of a competitive market by no more complicated means than *reasserting its initial purpose*. In this way Alberto-Culver entered the hair spray market late in the game and was able to demonstrate a more effective product in simple, concise terms. Marginal differences were wiped away and we were presented with the original value of the product. In a short time it became the leading product, passing the old and established brand names.

The demands the innovative process make upon the marketing executive call for a new identity for the decision-maker. He must no longer be just an expert in soap, soup or supermarkets. He must know more than the history of his own company and product. He must be an "expert" consumer as well as an informed market strategist. Today's corporate executive must be first and foremost an ubiquitous observer. He must keep up with the marketing problems and practices of many product categories unrelated to his own. He must be a technological, economic and social historian. Only by these means will the decision-maker have at his disposal sensitivity to the values in those markets within which he must effectively guide his products. In short, today's market demands, not the specialist or "expert" in twentieth-century terms, but rather a type of man the Renaissance emulated—a man of varied interests and many skills.

The decision-maker, like the creative writer or artist today, must come to grips with the issues of his time. The writer, especially in America, does this through language, image and character which are the means by which he creates a higher sense of reality and in so doing reorients the reader to a greater insight into the times. The decision-maker, like the creative writer, moves through this very same process. He must create a greater social reality for his product and by so doing confronts the emerging values and the social institutions of his market place.

M. M. ZIMMERMAN

Supermarkets

M. M. Zimmerman is president of Super Market Merchandising, founder and honorary life member of Super Market Institute. He has devoted his life to the study of food distribution in all its phases. On graduating from Yale University in 1911, he entered the commercial field. In 1914, while on the editorial staff of *Printer's Ink,* he made the first depth study of chain store distribution. This study formed the basis for his book, *The Challenge of Chain Store Distribution,* published in 1930. The trade magazine Mr. Zimmerman inaugurated in the early thirties, *Super Market Merchandising,* became a leading spokesman for the infant industry and did much to shape its course during the next two decades. Following World War II, he traveled extensively through Europe as a good-will emissary of the supermarket method of retailing, and in 1950 he founded the International Association of Food Distribution in Paris. For his efforts on behalf of European food distribution, he was decorated by the governments of France, Belgium and Italy. Subsequently he traveled through the Far East, Middle East, Japan and Australia expounding the phenomenon of supermarketing. In 1955, he wrote *The Super Market—A Revolution in Distribution,* which is now being used as a textbook in many marketing courses.

The Trading Post
Comes to the City

The Origin of the Supermarket

BY

M. M. ZIMMERMAN

In the early thirties, two distribution bombshells burst around New York, with the opening in 1930 of King Kullen's first supermarket in Jamaica, Long Island, followed in 1932 by the opening of Big Bear in Elizabeth, New Jersey. So propitious was the moment—economically and psychologically—for the appearance of a new system of mass distribution, that the opening of these two unique markets was hailed as marking a new phenomenon. And the history of the supermarket industry is generally reckoned from this time.

Actually, however, the appearance of these two amazing food retailing operations on the Atlantic Seaboard had been preceded by many experiments in other sections of the country, the various features of which combined to make up the composite operation since glorified by the name "supermarket." Just where the term "supermarket" originated is still a mystery. As far as we can determine, it "just grew." One of the early supermarket pioneers believes that its origin dates back to the early twenties, when the word "super" was coined and used so much by Hollywood motion-picture promoters.

Up to 1932, there were many established supermarket types of operations that did not call themselves supermarkets. The first food company to use the term in its corporate trade name was Albers Super Markets of Cincinnati, which opened its first unit in November, 1933. In those early days, too, we were often asked the question, "What is a supermarket?" Hence, in 1936, when publishing my first article on the subject, I originated the following definition:

> A supermarket is a highly departmentalized retail establishment, dealing in foods and other merchandise, either wholly owned or concession operated, with adequate parking space, doing a minimum of $250,000 annually. The grocery department, however, must be on a self-service basis.

And this remained the basic definition accepted by industry and government alike over the years, changing only slightly as the operation and size of the supermarket itself expanded. The minimum annual volume has, however, been increased to $500,000, even though the average for the industry today is well over one million.

The supermarket represented both evolution and revolution in distribution. Its "heart" was—and remains—self-service. But in 1930, self-service and "cash-and-carry" were not new in this country. Self-service, in fact, is as old as time itself, because ever since barter or trade intercourse started, people have been acting as their own carriers. The bazaars of the world are still the market places where cash-and-carry or self-service, is the rule. Even today we can visit any of the Oriental countries and see people trading as their ancestors did, selecting their merchandise, paying for it, and carrying it away.

However, in this country the introduction of self-service to modern retail distribution was the result of a succession of events, each of which contributed a share in the development of the supermarket as we came to know it in 1930.

If we are to begin at the beginning, we must go back to some historical experiments, which are still remembered. For instance, Stanton W. Davis, president of the Brockton Public Market of Brockton, Massachusetts, recalls that his father told him of the first large departmentalized food store under one ownership, started before the Civil War in Lowell, Massachusetts. It was called the Lowell Public Market. This market was the first, to his father's knowledge, to precut meats before they were put on display. This practice proved so successful that it was imitated shortly after by three other food companies in Lynn and Worcester, Massachusetts, and Providence, Rhode Island.

In 1896 Frank Munsey, publisher of the *New York Sun*, dissatisfied with the kind of service grocery stores furnished, decided to open a new type of store, calling it the Mohican. He threw open its doors to the fanfare of a new style of food store advertising. Featuring an overwhelming variety of items under one roof, it was built on very large proportions. Its advertising for those days was sensational. The store was highly departmentalized, offering many non-foods as well as foods. It featured price marking, extra customer service (in addition to some self-service), money-back guarantees, and stressed its "bigness" as evidence that patrons could get maximum values. Free delivery was offered, but the ads emphasized the economy of cash-and-carry savings. Despite its showmanship, values and one-stop shopping idea, the project was ahead of its time. Housewives of that leisurely era just didn't appreciate the many-stores-under-one-roof concept. Not until the supermarket idea had finally taken hold did the Mohican Company begin to profit from its early experience.

One of the most colorful figures in the development of self-service and probably the first to introduce the turnstile and checkout counter—definite features of the supermarket—was Clarence Saunders of Piggly Wiggly stores, who called his later ventures "Clarence Saunders, sole-owner-of-my-name" stores, "Keedoozle" stores, and "Foodelectric" stores. No book on food distribution can be written without discussing Saunders, who made a definite contribution to the supermarket through his Piggly Wiggly stores.

Mr. Saunders, born in Amers County, Virginia, on August 9, 1881, left school at the age of fourteen to take a position in a general store, where he clerked for four years at a salary of two dollars per week and board. In 1900 he took a job with a wholesale grocer in Clarksville and at nineteen was a traveling "drummer," making his rounds of rural merchants by horse and buggy. In 1904, seeking larger fields, he went to Memphis as a city salesman for Shanks-Phillips & Company, a wholesale grocery firm.

His dealings with retail grocers soon convinced him that the failure of so many small grocery stores was due to their heavy credit losses and high cost of operation. In 1915 he organized the Saunders-Blackburn Company, a wholesale grocery that sold for cash only and encouraged its merchant customers to do likewise.

About that time, his idea of the Piggly Wiggly was born—a self-service grocery store, in which the customer would select his own merchandise from display counters and pay cash. The secret of the operation was a turnstile at the checkout counter. In 1916 his first self-service Piggly Wiggly store was opened at 79 Jefferson Street, Memphis, Tennessee, with colorful ceremony, including gifts of roses to red-haired women and a brass band. Here was born the turnstile idea later used in countless supermarkets throughout the United States. Other successful Piggly Wiggly stores soon followed. At the peak of the company's success, there were 2,660 Piggly Wiggly stores scattered throughout the United States, with an annual sale in excess of $180 million.

At the height of his success, Mr. Saunders built himself a new home—a pink palace—now a Memphis landmark and museum. But Clarence Saunders never got to occupy his dream castle. Early in 1923, when "bear" interests in Wall Street attempted to hammer down the value of Piggly Wiggly stock, Mr. Saunders boarded a train and went to New York to personally stem the attack. A report, never verified, said he carried one million dollars in cash in a small handbag.

Piggly Wiggly shares were as low as $39 when Saunders

launched his buying campaign. On the first day, he bought 30,-
000 shares, and the price shot up to $77. He continued to buy
until he held orders for 196,000 of the corporation's 200,000 outstanding shares—and the price rose to $124.

But the New York Stock Exchange declared that a "corner" on
the stock existed and granted five days for delivery of the stock,
instead of the usual twenty-four hours. At the expiration of that
time, Mr. Saunders received his stock in full, but its value had
crashed—and Clarence Saunders was beaten. His financial disaster was complete. As a result of these misfortunes, he was soon
forced out of the presidency of Piggly Wiggly. His voluntary pe-
tition in bankruptcy quickly followed.

"If it had worked the other way, I would have cleared forty
million dollars," he said later, "and I would have won, if some of
my former friends had continued to stand behind me and hadn't
gotten scared and sold their stock."

The hundreds of Piggly Wiggly stores that dotted the nation
soon passed into other hands, the fifty-seven in Memphis being
acquired after a relatively short period by the Kroger Company.
His "Clarence Saunders sole-owner-of-my-name" stores, which
followed as his second major venture, flourished for a time and
then faded from the scene.

In 1945 he opened his robot "Keedoozle" store, in which, by
complicated electrical and mechanical apparatus, merchandise
was sold from glass-fronted display cases without the aid of clerks.
The venture gained its unusual name because the customer
carried a large "key" and turned it in the locks of cases containing the items he or she desired. An automatic conveyer system
tumbled the merchandise from stockroom shelves into a traveling
belt, which carried it to the checker's counter, properly identified
by the key number.

Mr. Saunders confidently envisioned a vast chain of Keedoozle
stores throughout the United States, automatically selling merchandise ranging from food items through hardware. The intricate mechanism, however, proved too costly, and this third venture folded shortly after it began.

Mr. Saunders had planned to open his fourth venture, the first

"Foodelectric" store, during the latter part of 1953, but he died on October 14, 1953. He is remembered as an amazing genius in food distribution.

Throughout the country there were in the twenties other pioneers who had opened large stores and were operating them along the same lines as present-day supermarkets, but they were thought of then primarily as large combination food stores. However, it should be emphasized that because the psychological moment had not yet arrived, or because the movement still needed the impetus of a depression to accelerate its growth, it was not until the thirties, with the opening of King Kullen and Big Bear, that the nation-wide movement known as the supermarket industry truly got under way.

It might even be said that the real predecessor of the supermarket in American merchandising was the old trading post or general store, which in so much of this country's early history was an important part of the American way of life. The supermarket, to a startling degree, is nothing more than the general store of yesteryear grown to Gargantuan proportions.

To understand the real parallel between the modern supermarket and the old trading post, one must try to visualize the significance of those old-time centers of retail trade and social exchange. The trading post was generally situated in the center of a rural or frontier settlement and was usually the hub of a community's existence. The proprietor of such a store rarely made an effort to entice or lure trade or customers. The store's presence in the neighborhood was presumed to be a blessing in itself. Its goods were there for customers to take or leave. Service and delivery were unheard of; fitting rooms or even a mirror were luxuries beyond realization—a woman bought a hat or a dress as she might buy a ham. In an unbelievable mélange was to be found everything a purchaser of those good old days could desire: calicoes, bustles, horehound candies, cans of lard, harnesses. From the ceilings hung frying pans, trousers, farm implements, animal traps. Nevertheless, the general store was a wondrous emporium —men, women and children from all over the countryside looked forward with pleasure to a visit to its cheerful chaos. Whole families piled into the buckboard or family buggy, lunches were carried aboard—and off went the entire clan. Sometimes they would drive ten or fifteen miles, or even more, for what was in those days an exciting experience.

The early supermarket smacked of the same atmosphere. A kind of picnic air pervaded its vast interiors. Like the trading post of old, the supermarket drew no lines in the variety of wares it featured. But the very diversity of the goods provided allure, as had the counters in the old-time store. And when these heaping gondolas also appealed to the customer's saving instincts because of their good values, the combination proved irresistible. Since large numbers of supermarket customers in the early days were drawn from many miles away, the comfort of free and easily accessible parking was a plus item in the buyer's psychology. Hence, though the hitching post gave way to the parking lot, and oats were replaced by gasoline, the social and economic significance of the shopping process was still pretty much the same—the family saw it as a pleasurable event. They came to stay for a while and enjoy themselves, to shop at leisure, to see and touch the bargains on display, to sift the values, and to buy.

Before we continue to evaluate properly the contribution the supermarket as we know it today has made to distribution, it is essential to turn the clock back to 1920-30 and review the food retailing pattern at this time.

The retail distribution picture in those days was in a state of flux. The corporate food chains had made progress in slowly taking over a substantial slice of the retail food business, due to the backwardness and inefficiency of the independent. In the 1920's, when Mrs. Consumer wished to buy her groceries, meats and produce, she generally had to visit three different shops. Such items, for example, as baby foods, fruit juices and most ready-to-eat cereals were nonexistent. Frozen foods were not even heard of. Soap chips were scooped up from twenty-five- or fifty-pound drums and coffee was purchased in bulk and ground to order, usually by hand. Cookies and crackers came out of the big cracker barrel or box.

Did the merchant know how much it cost him to do business?

How much profit he made? No statistics were kept—there was no measuring stick—and overhead expenses were considered only in connection with rent, light, paper and ice. In the average retail grocery store, the proprietor's family supplied the labor. In fact, a large family was often an important requisite for opening a grocery store. Many men who did not have large families could not be grocers because they could not afford to hire labor. A well-lit store was a luxury. Stores were usually rather dim. Heat was unheard of. No heat was the rule in meat markets, and it took zero weather to make the proprietor swing his door shut. All meats were cut to order. Plattered meats were a rarity, because customers would not buy them.

Merchandising was only a word in the dictionary to the average grocer, whose sole idea of merchandising acumen was suggestive selling: when a customer bought one item, the clerk suggested another related item. All items of stock were behind the counter. The customer had to ask for what she wanted. Whatever displays were made were on the counters or in the windows, although sidewalk displays were also quite common. It was only when a butcher and a grocer (they were usually located next to each other) decided that it would be to their advantage to cut a hole in the wall between them and combine forces, that a certain consolidation of foodstuffs took place.

Toward the end of the twenties, grocers began to handle what they termed "hard" produce—potatoes, onions and cabbage. Potatoes were the only items sold by the bag. On their part, the chains had already begun to popularize the combination food store and to promote the one-stop shopping facility. They had introduced newspaper advertising around 1927, and the chief feature of their copy was several below-cost items. It was about this time, too, that the chains introduced interior floor and counter displays on a small scale.

Still and all, the lot of the independent merchants continued to grow worse. They were steadily losing sales to the chains and many were forced out of business. In desperation, the independents turned to their politicians, locally and nationally, to introduce legislation. Many such legislative measures were introduced into municipal and state legislatures. But all of them were ultimately declared unconstitutional. Meanwhile, much needed leadership sprang up within the ranks of the independents. The voluntary and co-operative chain came into being, operated by wholesalers and the more aggressive and successful independents. These were the first efforts which created co-operative buying and advertising, thus enabling the independent to operate under a definite plan and program. This effort proved helpful—at least for the time being—and restored to a great degree the morale of the independent merchant. Later this movement was to grow and expand among the voluntary groups which developed management and merchandising programs that compare favorably with the chain organizations.

While all these innovations were being introduced and developed, the great Depression of 1930 fell upon the country. The nation's economy descended to its lowest ebb. Our national income was $41 billion. Total employment was 36 million. Unemployed numbered 14.5 million. Our farmers were in dire straits. There was no market for their products. They were uprooting their crops and letting them rot in the fields. The hog farmer was forced to kill his little pigs and bury them. There was little or no market for agricultural products. The prices that the farmer was offered were not enough to pay the interest on his mortgage.

The processor and manufacturer were in a similar plight. Their plants were at a standstill. Inventories were glutting the warehouses. Whatever they managed to sell was frequently at a loss. The retail distributors naturally labored under the same burdens. Buying power was reduced to the barest minimum, and pennies were hoarded. The most prominent retailer in many cities at that time was the apple vendor on the street corner. We were living in an era in which, as President Roosevelt aptly described it, one-third of the nation was "ill-fed, ill-housed and ill-clothed." The entire grocery and combination store volume was $5 billion. Wholesalers and retailers were burdened with large inventories but lacked the know-how, dynamism, or imagination to introduce new methods or ideas to move these surplus stocks. In other words, they were unable to meet the challenge of the moment: to reduce prices to meet the shrunken pocketbooks of the consumer.

Such was the national picture before the supermarket entered the field. Thus, by 1930, the distribution stage was divided between chains and independents and voluntaries, and was set up for the supermarket.

Michael Cullen—or "King Kullen—the world's greatest price wrecker," as he advertised himself—threw the initial bombshell when he opened his first market in Jamaica, Long Island, in August, 1930. The blast he created reverberated around the country and was heard by everybody in the food world. He heralded such low prices in his opening advertisements that he startled consumers and retailers alike. Soon he had customers from fifty, seventy-five and a hundred miles away stampeding his store, and merchants from all over the country were coming to see what the big noise was all about. Many of these retailers came—saw—and were so impressed that they returned to their own home towns to emulate King Kullen by opening supermarkets in abandoned garages, factories and warehouses. Before long, supermarkets became the talk of the nation and were being patronized heavily by hundreds of thousands of economy-minded shoppers.

In the history of supermarket development, Mike Cullen's story stands out as one of the most romantic. Years before making his initial success with the first supermarket in Jamaica, he was dreaming of supermarket development. Even while he worked for large chain organizations as a food merchandiser of unique capacity, he was preaching the gospel of a new era in mass merchandising—one which would dwarf the effort of any existing chain organization. Nor did he keep the idea to himself. He talked of his new development to everyone, because it was not so important to him that he be the one to develop it as that food distributors see the handwriting on the wall.

In 1930 Cullen was working for the Kroger Grocery & Baking Company, in charge of a branch in Herrin, Illinois. Aware of the limitations of his position, which offered no great future, he addressed a letter to the vice-president of the Kroger Grocery & Baking Company, in Cincinnati, in which he set forth his idea of the future supermarket. In the light of the anti-chain propaganda against the corporate chains, he predicted that the then-existing structure of the corporate chain, with its small stores and limited volumes, would remain static unless the chains exploited the movement for a revolutionary change in food retailing. Because his letter was so prophetic—because it called practically every shot in the coming evolution of mass retailing—it remains a historic document.

Among other things, Mike Cullen pointed out to his employers that chains were facing a crucial situation, both because of growing sentiment against them in favor of the home merchant, and because the system of the chain was beginning to be obsolete. In support of this contention, he pointed out that the efficacy of the system of cash-and-carry had already been demonstrated by Henry Krohl, who had been able to build up a substantial chain in New Jersey.

Cullen asked Kroger to make a trial of his proposals by opening up five stores, to be known as the Cullen Stores, anywhere in the United States or Canada, except in the South. He wrote:

> About every 20 years, the grocery business changes. It is time now for another change . . . I want to open these five stores anywhere in the United States . . . These five stores that I want to open will be monstrous stores, size of same to be about 40 ft. wide and 130 to 160 ft. deep, and they ought to be located from one to three blocks out of a high-rent district with plenty of parking space, and same to be operated as a semi-service store—twenty per cent service and eighty per cent self-service.

His figures and statements seemed fantastic to an industry which was then averaging $500 to $800 in stores of about 500 to 600 square feet. Today his figures would be regarded as conservative.

Mike Cullen had thought out his project to the last detail. In his letter, he outlined costs and projected returns. Evidence of how accurately he hit the target is seen in the following quotations from his letter:

My grocery equipment would cost two thousand five hundred dollars. My meat equipment would cost about $4,500 complete. A total outlay of $7,000 for equipment and a $23,000 stock of merchandise in each store. In other words, I would have an investment in each store of $30,000. My operating expenses would be as follows:

1 Grocery Manager	$ 50	per week
1 Fruit Man	25	per week
1 Assistant Fruit Man	18	per week
1 Assistant Grocery Manager	25	per week
2 Male Clerks $18	36	per week
1 Cashier	15	per week
3 Lady Clerks $12	36	per week
1 Male Clerk	15	per week
12 Extra Saturday Clerks $2.50	30	per week
Total Salaries	$250	per week

I expect to do a grocery business of $8,500 per week, per store, a fruit and vegetable business of $1,500 per week, per store. In other words, the kind of stores I have in mind should do a grocery business of $10,000 a week and a meat business of $2,500 per week. On the grocery business, including fruit and vegetables, I can operate on a gross profit of nine per cent. My complete operating expenses on a $10,000 a week grocery business would be as follows:

Help	$250	2.50 per cent
Rent	58	.58
Investment on Money	30	.30
Insurance	10	.10
Light-heat-water	7	.07
Taxes	10	.10
Depreciation	10	.10
Supervision	20 $\frac{1}{5}$ (5 stores)	.20

Paper, Bags, etc.	75	.75
Income Tax	30	.30
Hauling	20	.20
Advertising	50	.50
Buying	40 ⅕ (5 stores)	.40
M. J. Cullen	40 ⅕ (5 stores)	.40
	Total	6.50 per cent

Our meat department sales per store would be at least $2,500 per week, and we would make a new profit of at least three per cent on this meat business. This is the kind of cut-rate Chain of Wholesale selling direct to the public that I want to operate:

> I want to sell 300 items at cost.
> I want to sell 200 items at 5 per cent above cost.
> I want to sell 300 items at 15 per cent above cost.
> I want to sell 300 items at 20 per cent above cost.

I want to gross nine per cent and do a grocery, fruit and vegetable business of $10,000 per week, and make a net profit of 2½ per cent on the grocery department, and three per cent on the meat department.

You need have no fear regarding the present overhead of the Chain Stores. My buying, advertising and hauling expense of $110 per week per store is more than enough to take care of the buying under my supervision; and this could be reduced twenty-five points after I had my fifth store opened.

I would bill all merchandise to the stores at cost, and adopt a cash register check system, so that stealing or dishonesty would be impossible. I would inventory these stores every month at cost and their stock gain less all current expenses would be our net profit per month per store.

It would be a little difficult to begin with to buy for my first store, but after my fifth store was opened, I could buy the minimum shipments and ship eighty per cent of same FOB to the store direct, thereby eliminating entirely a warehouse, which is not necessary when these monstrous stores could show a turn-over such as I would get.

Can you imagine how the public would respond to a store of this kind? To think of it—a man selling 300 items at cost and another 200 items at five per cent above cost—nobody in the world ever did this before. Nobody ever flew the Atlantic either, until Lindbergh did it.

When I come out with a two page ad and advertise 300 items at cost and 200 items at practically cost, which would probably be all the advertising that I would ever have to do, the public, regardless of their present feeling towards Chain Stores, because in reality I would not be a Chain Store, would break my front doors down to get in. It would be a riot. I would have to call out the police and let the public in so many at a time. I would lead the public out of the high priced houses of bondage into the low prices of the house of the promised land.

I would convince the public that I would be able to save them from one to three dollars on their food bills. I would be the "miracle man" of the grocery business. The public would not, and could not believe their eyes. Week days would be Saturdays—rainy days would be sunny days, and then when the great crowd of American people came to buy all those low priced and five per cent items, I would have them surrounded with fifteen per cent, twenty per cent and in some cases, twenty-five per cent items. In other words, I could afford to sell a can of milk at cost if I could sell a can of peas and make two cents, and so on all through the grocery line.

The fruit and vegetable department of a store of this kind would be a gold mine. This department alone may make a net profit of seven per cent due to the tremendous turnover we would have after selling out daily and not throwing half the profit away, which is done at the present time in twenty-five per cent of the Chain Stores throughout the land.

Then the big meat department. This would be a bee hive. We would have the confidence of the public. They knew that every other grocery item they picked up they saved money on same, and our meat department would show us a very handsome profit. It wouldn't surprise me if they could not net five per cent in this department.

How long are you and your Company going to sit by and kid yourself that in a few weeks this Henderson Radio Stuff and Home Owned Retail Store propaganda will pass by?

The reason that I know that this proposition can be put over is that I have already put over a similar proposition right here in Southern Illinois. I operated Bracy's Warehouse store in West Frankford before Bracy bought out Limerick, and did as high as $19,000 per week, $9,000 on groceries, $3,000 on meats, and made a net profit of $15,000 on this one single store year before last, 1928, and I did this in a mining town of 15,000 people, mines only working half time, with A&P in the same city and Limerick doing a big business in this same city.

I was never so confident in my life as I am at the present time; and in order to prove to you my sincerity and my good faith, I am willing to invest $15,000 of my own money to prove that this will be the biggest money maker you have ever interested yourself in.

A salary expense of 2½ per cent, I know seems ridiculous to you. You perhaps think this is almost impossible. I have had a great many stores under me in the past, and their weekly salary was only three per cent, with less than $3,000 sales. So this 2½ per cent salary basis on a $10,000 weekly business is not only reasonable but is practical.

Again you may object to my locating two or three blocks from the business center of a big city. One great asset in being away from the business section is parking space. Another is, you can get generally the kind of store you want and on your own terms. The public will walk an extra block or two if they can save money, and one of our talking points would be, the reason we sell at wholesale prices is that we are out of the high rent district.

My other per cents of store expenses, I believe you will agree, are not excessive. If anything, I am a few points too high.

Don't let the buying worry you in any way whatever. I can handle the buying in fine shape. I could buy goods, ship them direct to my stores, three per cent cheaper than you could buy them, store them in a warehouse, and put them all through the red tape that all Kroger items go through before they are sold. If this proposition appeals to you, there is not a question but that Reock and I could work together. It would be an asset, but what I am trying to bring out is, I would put this over without any assistance from Reock.

Before you throw this letter in the wastebasket, read it again and then wire me to come to Cincinnati, so I can tell you more about this plan, and what it will do for you and your company.

The one thought always uppermost in mind—How can I undersell the other fellow? How can I beat the other fellow? How can I make my company more money? The answer is very simple: by keeping my overhead down, and only by keeping this overhead down can I beat the other fellow.

What is your verdict?

The verdict was a turndown. Michael Cullen was not permitted to see the president of the Kroger Company!

Tired of trying to peddle his ideas, Cullen set out to prove his own theories. He opened a supermarket himself—which gave immediate impetus to the growth of the supermarket industry. Today the industry as we know it comprises some 28,000 super-markets doing a volume over $39 billion in food and general merchandise sales—75 per cent of the nation's total grocery store business.

It is interesting to examine the concept Cullen used in his ad-vertisements. They were unorthodox, contrary to what any ex-perienced advertising man considered good copy, but he caught the attention of the people around Long Island. His catch line, "King Kullen—the world's greatest price wrecker," captured the fancy of the consumer to the degree that his first week's volume was phenomenal. It wasn't long before he opened a second and much larger store, and then a third. He began to add leased departments, or concessions. As fast as he could find room for a new one, whether it was ladies' wear, shoes, house furnishings, furniture, or cosmetics, he took it on.

When Mike Cullen came to a new community, he opened with a blaze of advertising—two-page spreads, four-page sections, with prices that his competitors dreaded to look at. His copy had no elaborate layouts; instead, it carried homely messages to reach the hearts and the pocketbooks of the people. For example, in introducing himself at the opening of a new store in a new community, he would have this feature, in bold type:

Who is King Kullen? Is that his right name? Is he this or that? What kind of man is he? Thousands have asked this question . . . Well, folks, here I am. King Kullen is none other than Michael Joseph Cullen, born and brought up in Jersey. Been in the grocery business all my life. Been with some of the big chains for twenty years or more and finally decided to try it by myself because I want to test out my own theories of merchandising. I opened my own little store on a shoestring and sold everything I could lay my hands on for cost or slightly above cost. People came to my first store for miles and miles. The grocery world was dumbfounded with my low prices. All agreed I could not exist. Today, my sales run into the millions. The big interests call me the wildcat, the banks call me a miracle man. But who cares what they all say. It's you folks I want to please. I want to serve and save money for you. The public is my boss, my judge, my jury . . . Are you with me? . . . What is your answer?

(signed) KING KULLEN

By 1935 King Kullen had fifteen large units in operation, and his volume ran into the millions of dollars. He was now ready to reach out on a national scale, to open many more large markets, and, at the same time, organize a King Kullen franchise operation, bringing in the smaller independents under a voluntary chain plan. But he never lived to fulfill his ambitious ideas. He died in 1936 at the age of fifty-two. His family and his associates said he had worked himself to death. It is not unbelievable.

While Michael Cullen was progressing in Long Island, two other pioneers appeared on the horizon in 1932 with equal faith in the future of mass retailing. Robert M. Otis and Roy O. Dawson, both experienced department and chain store promoters and merchandisers, started their experiment in New Jersey by persuading a Hoboken wholesaler to join them in leasing, for a nominal rental, the vacant Durant automobile plant at Elizabeth. Their plan was to convert it into a huge supermarket which would feature food and household merchandise. They expected to attract consumers from a much wider area than shoppers customarily traveled for food and other necessities.

Utilizing only the first floor of the factory building, comprising fifty-thousand square feet, they converted it into a circuslike emporium, with a food department as the hub, surrounded by eleven other specialty concession departments. Only 30 per cent of the total space was devoted to the food department. Everything about the place was of cheap construction, but it had a bazaarlike appearance. Inexpensive pine board tables were loaded with mass displays of merchandise. Baskets were supplied at the entrance and customers were left free to walk about and help themselves. Then the customers went to a cashier's booth, paid for their purchases, and left.

On December 8, 1932, huge ads with eye-catching streamers appeared in the newspapers of the neighboring towns and communities, heralding the grand opening of "Big Bear, The Price Crusher." With such captions as "Big Bear Crashes into New Jersey," "Big Bear Drives Prices Down," "Big Bear, World's Champion Price Fighter," the market immediately attracted the public's gaze. When housewives saw advertisements featuring their favorite brands at ridiculously low prices, they naturally flocked to buy them. For example, the first ads featured Quaker Oats at three cents; Lifebuoy at four cents; Maxwell House Coffee at twenty-two cents; pork chops at ten cents a pound; Scottissue at six cents; Squibb's and Listerine toothpaste at fifteen cents. The opening day made history in food distribution. All records were shattered for attendance and volume.

What was the result? Big Bear made headlines in newspapers from coast to coast. Women flocked to the market in even greater numbers than the promoters had dreamed possible. Here indeed was the second confirmation of King Kullen's dream about the type of retail distribution that was more powerful than the best organized chain system and that was destined to revolutionize the entire system of food selling.

To appreciate what this change meant, let us cite some figures: In the first three days after Big Bear opened, customers paid $31,861.71 to the cashiers. When told about the thousands of customers who had come and the amount of money they had left in the jingling cash registers, skeptics who had predicted that few people would patronize Big Bear still asserted that these first customers were merely "curiosity buyers."

Yet these same buyers returned the next week and loaded up their cars with bargain merchandise to the tune of over $75,000. They kept coming back in hordes week after week. Many of them drove from more than fifty miles away. They bought not only food, but radios, hardware, paints, and other products. At the end of the first year's operation, Big Bear had taken in $3,873,280, of which 57 per cent represented grocery sales. The gross profit from the grocery department was $262,800, while net profit amounted to a little over $80,000. Rental income from the tenant-operated departments totaled some $86,400, and net profit for the overall operation was $166,500.

Naturally, consternation spread in the camps of the independents and chains. For the first time the two groups held meetings together. Every effort was made to halt Big Bear and the other supermarkets in their tracks. Bulletins were flashed to all retailers throughout New Jersey pointing up the menace which Big Bear and the other supermarkets represented to the future conduct of retail business. Letters were sent to all wholesale grocers demanding that they refuse to sell to the supermarkets. A half-dozen wholesalers were blacklisted for not abiding by the request. Newspapers were threatened with economic boycotts if they continued to accept Big Bear ads. Legislation was introduced in the New Jersey Assembly to outlaw selling at or below cost, and a U. S. Senate resolution was introduced on March 6, 1933, to investigate supermarkets.

Everyone—except the consumer—was up in arms, and the more the organized trades tried to stop the supermarkets, the louder Big Bear heralded its powerful slogan, "Big Bear, The Price Crusher." And it kept on doing a land-office business.

In the light of the ultimate evolution of the supermarket industry, it is curious to note how few economists or distribution experts really understood the significance of both King Kullen and Big Bear. Retailers continued to clutch at the wishful belief that the supermarket was only a novelty which was sure to disappear; but inwardly they were also fearful of the harm it might do to their position in the meantime.

Chain store executives, especially those who had devoted many years to reducing their pattern of cash-and-carry almost to a science, could not understand why the supermarkets—particularly the barren structures located in outlying community areas, with price as their only appeal—received such consumer acceptance. To the high-powered chain executives, these crude operations were the very antithesis of their scientific retailing, which had prevailed for over two decades and had by then captured more than 45 per cent of the country's food volume. Only shortly before this, the chain store spokesmen had boasted that the time was not far distant when these multiple-store operations would control 75 per cent of the nation's food store business.

But the chains, with their vaunted efficiency, didn't know their customers. In the supermarket, for the first time, the American housewife had found a type of store where she was left on her own. All merchandise was openly priced. She could accept or reject any article without interference or pressure. She was her own boss and could determine, free from the influence of the clerk or the proprietor, whether or not she could afford the item. It was a new freedom for her and she enjoyed it beyond measure.

That was an important reason why consumers in the early days flocked to the supermarket.

Without question, the success of King Kullen and Big Bear stimulated the imagination of the food world as their predecessors had never done. Wholesalers, retailers, and even chains flocked to see the new wonders and to glean all possible information about them. Many tried to emulate them. Some failed. But the rank and file of merchants who opened similar operations were successful from the start.

There were practically no statistics or records on the growth of the supermarket in those days. What little was obtainable had to be pieced together from all possible sources, and there was no way of checking authenticity or accuracy. But what information there was indicated a vigorous trend. A spot survey made by the author in 1934 disclosed that there were by then ninety-four markets in twenty-four cities. Two years later, a similar check in eighty-five odd cities disclosed some twelve hundred supermarkets. The snowball had begun to roll and was daily gaining momentum. First in the East and then in the Middle West new markets began to open, with such dynamic names as Giant Tiger, Bull Market and Great Leopard.

Like King Kullen and Big Bear, these early supermarkets put emphasis on price, self-service, and mass displays of nationally known brands. Little thought was given to the store's physical appearance. Fixtures were of the crudest type. The buildings were mostly vacant factories, garages, and the like. As a matter of fact, the cruder the building, the greater was its appeal to the public, since it suggested economy to the consumer. And so the procession started across the country.

A & P was among the first of the giant organizations to enter the supermarket field. At first its approach was cautious. It concentrated primarily on the large type of combination food markets. But by 1937 a definite supermarket program got under way. Part of the program embraced new buildings which were contracted for on a leasehold basis. A & P now moved swiftly, and with its vast resources and large experienced organization, it was not long before daily and weekly announcements began to appear in the newspapers across the country of new A & P supermarket openings.

Kroger opened a number of Pay'N Takit supermarkets in and around Cincinnati to compete directly with the Albers markets, which were setting the pace with their promotions of national brands, and also opened up many units throughout the Middle West. By 1935 the firm was operating some fifty stores in the supermarket classification, six of which had parking lots.

Many other chains—North, South, East and West—were following in A & P's and Kroger's footsteps. Some gained immediate success; others had their problems. Most of the chains still clung to their small neighborhood stores, and the big headache was how to maintain the higher markups in their neighborhood stores, yet sell at lower prices in their supermarkets. It wasn't easy.

All in all, by 1937 the sprawling young industry was taking shape. It needed the impetus of a co-ordinating force to give it a sense of direction which would ultimately enable it to change the retailing pattern of America's economic life. This impetus was provided by the founding of the Super Market Institute and its first convention, held in New York City in September, 1937. Undoubtedly, this was one of the most important events in the history of the supermarket industry—perhaps second only in importance to the opening of Michael Cullen's first supermarket.

That any convention was possible at all for an industry still in the amorphous stage in which it found itself in 1937, was remarkable. Yet this single event gave notice to the distribution world that there was a dynamic new movement afoot, and a new industry for the world of distribution to reckon with. It was a significant fact that at a time when nearly all the operators then in the supermarket business were strangers to each other they had sufficient incentive to form an organization to help fight the many problems, particularly legislative ones.

The history of the Super Market Institute is to a great degree the early history of the supermarket industry. Over the years it has grown and flourished, until today the Institute is one of the shining lights in association work and a powerful spokesman in the world of food distribution.

In conclusion, it may be well again to evaluate what the supermarket has actually accomplished during its brief history. Its most important accomplishment has been a slashing of food distribution costs, from the retail gross margins of 25 to 30 per cent prevailing in the early thirties to about 18 to 20 per cent today. When one considers that the industry at the end of 1962 controlled over $39 billion in sales through its more than 28,000 mass retailing emporia, one sees that a saving of 10 per cent, or even 5 per cent, in Mrs. Consumer's food bill can have an important effect not only on her budget but on the overall national economy.

WILLIAM J. LEVITT

Levitt and Sons

WILLIAM J. LEVITT, president of Levitt and Sons, Inc., pioneered the post-World War II construction movement to bring modern mass-production techniques into the antiquated home-building industry. He attended New York University, but being eager to get into the business world, left shortly before graduation. After service as a lieutenant in the Seabees during World War II, he returned to a peacetime America that was "home hungry and house poor." At the head of the family construction firm again, he worked out and put into practice the famous Levitt technique for mass-producing homes. The company now has seven branch operations in four eastern states, Paris, and Puerto Rico. All projects, except those in Paris, are pre-planned residential communities. In Paris the firm is active in high-rise and garden apartments, but here, too, residential communities are now on the drawing board.

A House Is Not Enough

The Story of America's First Community Builder

B Y

WILLIAM J. LEVITT

Afterwards, people were to write that we started our own revolution during the early days of World War II.

That's a catchy way to approach it. But what happened was this: as war spread over Europe, and as America keyed up its defense efforts, the Federal Housing Administration wrote Section 603 into its regulations, and the War Production Board set priorities on private housing. Four months after Pearl Harbor, the War Production Board stopped all private construction not serving essential war needs, and a month later, in May, 1942, Section 608 was added to the National Housing Act to stimulate the construction of low-cost rental housing for war workers.

We were then, as now, a house-building firm—Levitt and Sons, Inc.—my father Abraham, my brother Alfred, and myself. From the company's beginning in 1929 we had built luxury homes on the North Shore of Long Island, sometimes as many as 200 houses a year. But in the mathematics of that first war year, 603 plus 608 equaled zero of the kind of houses we had been building. Those two necessary, wartime measures meant Levitt and Sons, and virtually every other home-builder as well, would have to shut down operations until the war's end.

Unless, of course, we chose the alternative. We could try to build the kind of houses—and in the staggering numbers—that the country desperately needed to meet the wartime emergency. And so we agreed to take on a job to build 750 low-cost houses to rent to Navy officers in Norfolk, Virginia. Seven hundred and fifty houses! Many of our friends, old-timers in the business, chuckled over their morning blueprints, sure the project wouldn't come off. And the chuckling was understandable, for house-building in America was a catch-as-catch-can kind of thing back in those days, with thousands of builders each putting up only a handful of houses a year.

And like everything else in those months, the deadline for completing them was "yesterday." Friends asked us why we were willing to tackle the Norfolk job. Its size, the press of time, and the industry's history of slow, piecemeal production certainly gave no reason for optimism. We argued the same point among ourselves, and still felt we had no choice. It was sink or swim. The times and circumstances prevented us from building the kind of luxury homes we had built up to that time. We couldn't permit ourselves to tread water until the war's end. So we did what had to be done.

"What had to be done" was to change our entire concept of building. We couldn't even fall back on that comfortable cliché, "The difficult we do immediately; the impossible takes a little longer." We had to do the impossible immediately.

The Norfolk houses, to be sure, would in no way compare to our Long Island "Strathmore" homes. But even at our best pre-war pace, it would take us more than three years to build that many houses. In retrospect, our acceptance of this challenge was the turning point in our business life. It was a decision that was ultimately to affect directly the lives of a good many Americans —several hundred thousand, in fact! Norfolk was an about-face for Levitt and Sons. We had to build an unprecedented number of houses in an impossibly short period of time, and it was something foreign to us. We were used to being delighted with the completion, and sale, of *one* house.

Our family interest in building and real estate probably began even before we were a family, when my father was a second-year student at New York University School of Law. The course that seemed to give more students trouble than any other was real estate law, and so Father, mostly as a gesture of helpfulness to his friends who were having trouble with the course, wrote a book on the subject. Before he knew it, he had a successful book to his credit, and it continued to sell so well that it was to provide more income for him than he earned from his law practice in the first years after being admitted to the New York Bar.

As time went on, his interest in real estate broadened, and he came to have a share in a tract of land in Rockville Centre, Long Island. It looked ideal for development, and the plan was to sell it to a builder for home sites. Adjoining the tract was beautifully wooded acreage which, it turned out, belonged to the then State Assemblyman of Nassau County, Edwin K. Wallace. Rockville Centre decided it needed a new sewer system and therefore a new sewage disposal plant. The best place for the plant, the engineers said, was a three-acre tract apart from the residential district at the lowest elevation in the village, where land was available for relatively little—$1,000 an acre.

But at that point Assemblyman Wallace decided to sell his land, and the village, over public protest which we led, bought not three, but twenty acres of Wallace's land in the middle of the residential district, next door to our holding. The additional seventeen acres were required to screen the sewage plant itself. And the village paid not $1,000 an acre for the land, but $10,000 an acre—$200,000 in all.

We fought the sale at a public hearing, and of about 3,000 votes cast, we lost by exactly 159. No matter how close the vote, we did lose, and with a sewage disposal plant going in next door, the land no longer appeared ideal. Our parcel of land was suddenly without a future. The others who had interests in the property sold out to us, with audible sighs of relief. We owned the land, but we knew we couldn't sell it to a developer as originally planned. In self-defense we built a house on the property, sold it, and the company was formed. Our first reaction was surprise. Our second reaction was encouragement, and we started two more houses. Before they were completed, we sold them and had orders for two more. Our first year's building record: eighteen houses. Years later, our crews would build eighteen houses every morning before knocking off for lunch, then come back and build seventeen more before calling it a day.

The Depression may have been an unlikely time to start a business. But after we sold our first house, we were committed. Even during the bleak "Bank Holiday," we had no trouble securing loans. From 1929 through 1941, we built and sold about 2,800 houses, most of them in the "Strathmores" on Long Island's North Shore, but some in Westchester County, as well.

In Norfolk, however, the most pressing problem was neither a bank loan nor a community sewage disposal plant. In Norfolk the problem was time, or more precisely, the lack of time. In the beginning, the building crews worked as they had in the lazy pre-war days, and the various crews weren't tightly co-ordinated. But given freedom, contractors and the craftsmen who worked for them began to find new ways to do old jobs. As the job grew, so did confidence, and ingenuities blossomed.

Framing crews that began with the "normal," time-consuming procedure, soon found they could build framing sections on the ground more quickly, then raise them into place, with the finished work every bit as good as that done the old way—perhaps even better. Individual sewage disposal units were first built of concrete blocks in an operation that took half a work day. It was the most difficult part of the Norfolk job, because soggy ground conditions made the installation difficult, lengthy and, at best, less than completely satisfactory. An ingenious Levitt engineer put the problem to a friend of his, a builder of burial vaults. With a little adjustment, he converted his products into pre-cast concrete septic tanks which made possible rapid and completely satisfactory installation. In the time once required to install two or three concrete block tanks, the mortician's friend was able to install fifteen to twenty.

Levitt and Sons built the 750 individual houses, and since things went so well, the Government gave us priorities to build 1,600 row houses for shipyard workers. In an eighteen-month assault, we built both the 750 bungalows and the 1,600 row houses. The second job of 1,600 houses was completed ahead of schedule; the budget was kept. The spinach farmers whose land had been bought for the project were happily settled in other places. Everyone should have been pleased, but something was missing.

People were missing. The people who were to occupy the houses were the figment of some planner's imagination. The 1,600 houses were planned for workers at the St. Helena annex to the Norfolk Navy Yard at Portsmouth, but St. Helena never was activated. Later, however, additional workers were brought in to the sprawling Navy operations near Norfolk and the houses eventually were occupied.

People or no, the Norfolk job proved a point, although in the period of national crisis few—except our unbelieving friends who said it couldn't be done—paid much attention to it. Levitt housebuilding would never be the same again.

In Norfolk we had for the first time all the ingredients we needed to put mass-production of houses to its first test. We had demand. We had materials and financing. We had crews and craftsmen blessed with imagination. Strained as we were for time, the Norfolk job offered us little more than practical exposure to the test of mass-producing housing. But the greatest results of the job were two: it proved to us what we had long suspected —that houses could be mass-produced in the field; and it infected us with the fever of mass building. To build our "better mousetrap," we realized the need for precision planning on a scale foreign to the whole house-building tradition. Norfolk proved that mechanically the revolution was possible, that it was one step closer to realization; and it made us hungry for a fullblown, unhampered try at mass-producing houses. But our revolution would have to wait. At the conclusion of the Norfolk project, the Levitt firm suspended operations until the war's end, and I went into the Seabees.

During the wartime building hiatus, we planned and even dreamed a little. Paradoxically, we saw house-building both in larger and in smaller terms than before, with a tract of land as a giant factory, turning out low-cost houses as its product. We designed a basic house, reduced its construction to twenty-six major steps, calculated the shape and size and quantity of materials needed for the construction of that house, down to the last two pounds of four-penny finishing nails; and we envisioned small crews of men, each trained to do one job in the building process, moving from lot to lot in a reversal of the assembly-line procedure. Later, we expanded this idea beyond the construction of houses to the construction of an entire community. It was a king-sized dream. And in the America of 1947, it was going to be tested.

To flex our muscles after the two-year shutdown, we began construction of a thousand houses on Long Island in the first postwar year (still the semi-custom houses on the North Shore). While we built, we collected land in the flat belly section of Long Island's Nassau County, east of the Strathmores that had given us both our beginning and our reputation. Looking back, Levittown probably was born years before. We knew all along we could mass-produce houses. All that is needed is size plus organization. But housing isn't like the proverbial "better mousetrap." Even if you can turn out a better product, at a lower cost, other things have to be going for you or it won't work.

By 1947, those "other things" were going for us. House-hungry GIs, doubled up with in-laws in crowded apartments, were clamoring for homes. The Government, faced with a decision of building the housing itself, or of making mortgage conditions such that private industry would undertake the job, chose the latter, and mortgage money became plentiful. Two of the three ingredients of success were there—the demand for housing, and the availability of money.

The only thing missing was the product, the house. And that's where we came in—walked in, you might say, in twenty-six steps.

The confusion of 1947 was summed up by *Fortune* magazine this way:

> To anyone unfamiliar with the housing industry, the incredible news of 1947 is that home construction is in the doldrums. In the first five months of the year, in spite of the worst housing shortage since the James River landing, the industry showed no appreciable gain over 1946 except in the price of its product, which advanced enormously. In 1946 every conceivable shortage and, by testimony of builders, every obstacle that willfully evil bureaucracy could design stood between the homeseeker and a house. Now materials are comparatively plentiful, government regulations only a vestige—and the industry is perilously close to falling on its face . . . Any reasonable schedule for filling the nation's housing need (in 1947) would call for at least twice as many houses as now are being built, at prices a whole lot lower than now.

In the America of 1947, house-building was, according to *Fortune,* "the industry that capitalism forgot." Home-building was disappointingly out-of-date in the world's most highly industrialized nation, and nothing indicated change was imminent. Optimists, most of them outside the building industry, hoped the day of change had come. Some method had to be found to build housing for "typical Americans" in big and profitable batches. But like weather control, nobody really planned to do much about it.

In this climate, we moved onto three hundred acres of potato farms we had purchased near Island Trees, New York, a Long Island settlement too modest to have been included in the United States census. Four years later it would have a new name, an international reputation, and 68,000 residents.

In the beginning no one, including ourselves, knew how big Island Trees would become. In early 1948 we still planned it as a 1,400-acre development of 6,000 houses. But as we polished our building techniques, as we watched the literally endless line of eager buyers, Island Trees became Levittown, and Levittown became a national institution, the grandfather of the pre-planned community.

Looking back, the most un-Levitt thing about Levittown, Long Island, was that it began without a comprehensive plan. We set out to build houses, and we intended to keep at it until the land ran out. Our concept was to build lots of houses in one place. And our problem was how to build them quickly, economically, and well. Solutions didn't come in flashes of blinding light. They came as a result of planning and thinking. Something evolved.

It was the combination of planning and a little boldness that made the Levitt approach work. In the early post-war days, supplies hadn't always caught up with demands and to a company on the move nothing is more frustrating, nor more damning, than a lack of supplies. We wouldn't let ourselves be stopped by shortages. When cement was unavailable in this country, we chartered a boat and brought it in from Europe. When lumber was in short supply, we bought a forest in California and built a mill. When nails were hard to come by, we set up a factory in our own back yard, and made them ourselves. The supplies rolled in, and the houses sprang up.

Mass-production of housing could not fit the mold of the constantly cited example, the auto industry, simply because the home-builder cannot prefabricate the land. He cannot make the land one of the ingredients on the assembly line inside a factory, since a house, no matter where it is built, must eventually be set into the land. Factory production cannot be the whole answer to mass-production of homes.

The land was our factory. We found it quicker, less expensive, and more efficient to move crews of men in standardized operations over the site, than to move the house itself along a factory assembly line. Success of our system depended on the most minute breakdown of operations. Those twenty-six construction operations, starting with digging house footings and ending with painting the exterior trim, were subdivided into simple standardized steps, each handled by a specifically trained crew. The breakdown extended even to such details as installing the washing machine: one man did nothing but fix the bolts in the floor, another followed to attach the machine. Steps were differentiated also according to the degree of labor skill each required. One crew, for example, put up wall framing; another, more skilled, framed the roof and made the special rafter cuts which determined the five façade variations employed in the house. It was estimated in those days that the average building worker spent 25 per cent of his time figuring out what to do next. In our operation that percentage was close to zero.

Although our Levittown was dotted with about a million dollars' worth of power-driven equipment, ranging from trenching machines to spray guns, the building crews did not use one of the craftsman's most basic tools, the hand saw. Shop pre-cutting of all house parts and shop pre-assembly of plumbing and heating units were basic to the system. Freight cars loaded with lumber went directly into a cutting yard where one man with a power saw cut parts for ten houses in one day. These were bundled into packages, each one containing all the lumber parts for one house, and picked up by fork-lift trucks for reloading and delivery by truck to the house lot.

Next to the cutting yard freight cars unloaded plumbing parts at one side of a building; out the door at the other side went fifty plumbing trees a day. Copper coil for the radiant heating was measured by wrapping it around two barrels set a few yards apart, then pre-shaped and bundled. Two concrete hoppers kept a fleet of transit-mix trucks running. From warehouses, workmen rolled out bathtubs, washers, refrigerators, to be delivered one by one at each house door. All these operations were timed so that each component of a house arrived at a precise time and a precise spot—with no margin for error.

From the beginning we had thought of the houses we built as "complete." We still did. No Levitt house was ready for occupants until the kitchen appliances and automatic washer were in. Early Levittown houses even included Venetian blinds and built-in television sets. And there was the landscaping, the special concern of our far-sighted father. He called it neighborhood stabilization, and the decision to include landscaping in the Levitt package was made with the decision to build that first house back in Rockville Centre. Plantings enhance the value of a property; they are insurance against the effects of time. In Levittown, Long Island, Father was a modern Johnny Appleseed. Sometime about midway through the first Levittown, we stopped building numbers of houses and began building a community.

We began with a house. We ended with a city.

The Levittown house was a Cape Cod, a four-and-one-half-room bungalow. By the fall of 1948, six thousand of them had been built in Levittown, and the FHA, which had underwritten the mortgages, began worrying about "Market Saturation." We had been busy collecting all the surrounding land we could get our hands on, and we felt, quite understandably, otherwise.

During the year before No. 6,000 was completed, the firm had been working on the redesign of the Cape Cod. By redesigning we did not—and do not—mean rearranging lines on paper. We designed by building, ripping apart, and building again. The 1949 house in Levittown, Long Island, was torn apart more than thirty times, and we spent upwards of $50,000 before we were satisfied with the plan for a house to sell at less than $8,000.

The result was an open floor plan, with the symmetrical façade which stands for the Cape Cod abandoned. The expansion attic of the earlier model was retained. The Forty-niner had the living room at the back of the house, with the front door boldly opening into the kitchen. With the living room at the rear, a wall-size double-glazed window (until then a feature found only in higher cost houses) was a natural step. We figured out one day that a house wall—shingles, paper, insulation, plaster board, and so on, was worth twenty-five cents a foot, exactly the cost of double-glazing, and this figuring was responsible for the introduction of this prestige feature into a low-cost house. A two-way fireplace became the central pivot of the plan. Circulation was plotted around the chimney, and the kitchen was made a control station from which the housewife could easily reach any part of the house.

The new house was full of built-in equipment, beginning with the kitchen. The master bedroom had a storage wall to replace bureaus, and a movable wall section near the front door provided a pull-down desk. The Cape Cod had that rarity in a low-cost house, a guest coat closet. It was difficult to say whether the washing machine or the two-way fireplace did more to endear the house to the buyers' hearts. At any rate, when the new model was opened, not an inch of advertising space was bought. The only heralding was a sign in the front yard: "$7,990—$90 down and $58 per month—Veterans Only." In a three-day period, three thousand veterans lined up to compete with each other for the privilege of making a down payment on a house that did not exist.

This was despite the fact that the industry as a whole was gripped by the uneasy suspicion that the "seller's market" had reached its easily predictable, post-war end. The situation prompted *Architectural Forum* to report: "To any member of the long-embattled and much maligned house-building industry this unpalatable miracle (3,000 buyers in three days) was immediately clear: it was only those Long Island wonder boys, the Levitts, at it again." So well-received was the Levitt house of 1949— the one with a Levitt price tag of $7,990—that *Architectural Forum* reported by the summer of 1950 that "more than 4,000 non-Levitt, Levitt Types will be built or under construction in Boston, Philadelphia, Wilmington and Washington, and other eastern cities." The "non-Levitt" Levitts ranged from $500 (without the Levitt fireplace) to $2,300 above our price.

That was the kind of house built in Levittown. But houses alone, no matter how excellent each one is individually, are not enough. A house is only 30, at the most 50, per cent of a home. In addition to the house you need streets and utilities, shopping centers, schools, churches, parks, playgrounds, and swimming pools. That's one of the reasons factory prefabrication of houses can never be the answer. That kind of approach isn't home-building, it's 50 per cent home-building. In Levittown, nine community swimming pools and seven neighborhood shopping centers were built. Playgrounds were established, and a regulation-sized community baseball diamond was built. Land was set aside for churches and schools. Toward the end of the building in Levittown, residents said things would be a lot more convenient if they had a community center, a meeting place for the hundred or so organizations that had sprung up with the new city. So we built a $250,000 building and gave it to the town for Christmas.

As the last of our Long Island land was filled with houses, the "revolution" clearly was successful. It had begun, really, when we chose not to sink when we knew we could swim. It progressed through the mass-production of painstakingly designed and re-designed houses, and it ended with the building of a city of 17,447 homes covering 7.3 square miles. *Fortune* looked over what we had done, and wrote, "If Levitt and Sons is still not the Ford of the building industry, its influence on housing is almost impossible to exaggerate."

Essentially, there are two lessons to be learned from Levittown. First, we builders learned the meaning of the word "community." When you build an entire community, you cannot stop with the delivery of a thousand—or twenty thousand—good homes. The community builder has a responsibility to plan for the social, rec-reational, religious, shopping and educational needs of his town. Access to a swimming pool or a baseball diamond is as important a part of what a purchaser buys as solid walls or a strong roof, be-cause he's not just buying a house, he's buying a way of life. A community builder who faces up to his responsibilities is not only a good citizen—he's a sound businessman.

The second lesson is for the home-buyer. Whether a community grows and increases in value—or falls apart—is strictly up to him. That the home-buyers of Levittown assumed their responsi-bilities is clear. Fifteen years later, the homes sold by us for $7,990 were selling at $13,500, and that's for those few homes which had not been expanded or remodeled. It's not unusual to see price tags of $20,000 to $23,000 on homes in Levittown, Long Island.

After Long Island, we moved to Bucks County, Pennsylvania, to build a 17,311-house Levittown—the first entirely pre-planned community since Washington, D. C. In New Jersey, between Phil-adelphia and Trenton, a third Levittown was begun in 1958. In 1960, the company broke with its thirty-one-year tradition and announced that it would build at more than one location at a time, and by the middle of 1963, we had become active in seven metropolitan areas in the United States, the Caribbean and Europe.

With Levittown, New Jersey, still under construction, Levitt and Sons established branch offices and began building in suburban Washington, D. C., in northern New Jersey and in the New York metropolitan area. The fourth Levittown was started near San Juan, Puerto Rico; high rise and garden apartments were begun in Paris, France; plans were announced for a new Long Island community near Stony Brook in Suffolk County; and Levitt announced it was starting a new community near Cape Kennedy, Florida. More communities, in this country and abroad, are in the offing.

Over the years, the Levitt techniques have been refined. Houses have changed, grown larger and more spacious, with more appliances and equipment; community planning has been broadened. By the most conservative estimate, a quarter of a million Americans have lived in Levitt houses.

J. DOUGLAS COLMAN

Associated Hospital Service
of New York

J. DOUGLAS COLMAN graduated from Cornell University in 1932 with a degree in mechanical engineering. However, during the Depression years, he took on the responsibilities of manager of the Medical, Hospital and Dental Division of the New Jersey Emergency Relief Administration from 1932-35. As executive director of the Hospital Service Plan of New Jersey, he developed the state's Blue Cross program. From 1937 to 1951, Mr. Colman was executive director in Baltimore of Maryland Hospital Service, Inc. (Blue Cross) and Maryland Medical Service, Inc. (Blue Shield), associations which he organized. From 1951 to 1957 he was vice-president of Johns Hopkins University and Johns Hopkins Hospital. Mr. Colman became vice-president and secretary of the national Blue Cross Association in 1957. He was elected president of Associated Hospital Service of New York on April 6, 1960, and took office on May 1 of that year.

Providing for Illness
in Times of Health

The Creation of the Blue Cross Plans

B Y

J. DOUGLAS COLMAN

One human intellect struggling for a "yes" or "no" when the choice will affect the course of human events, is the usual image of a "great decision." There are such moments in history. Eisenhower deciding when to launch the Normandy invasion comes first to mind. But such moments are rare. They may even be the exceptions that prove the rule that the course of human events is changed most often and most significantly by gradual processes shaped by many minds and hands.

Certainly this is true of Blue Cross. Any attempt to portray its vast growth and substantial accomplishments as the inevitable result of great decisions would be inaccurate. My willingness to attempt to chronicle some of the events along the way, and to describe some of the forces which shaped them, stems from two simple facts. First, I was asked. Second, only a relative handful of people have been a part of and lived through the events of these past thirty years as a relatively simple idea became a significant social force directly affecting almost 60,000,000 Blue Cross subscribers and, to a greater or lesser degree, all of the patients in the nation's 6,000 general hospitals.

As the country sank into the great Depression of the nineteen-thirties, one of the more unhappy effects of its economic illness was felt by those citizens who had the misfortune to be ill themselves, physically. Many, living on reduced incomes or none at all, simply could not afford hospital care. Their frustration built a bottled-up force, as did the complementary frustration of hospitals lacking the resources to do their job of healing as well as they knew how.

As various methods were tried, the prepayment one (budgeting for illness in times of health) seemed to work the best. A scattering of individual hospitals experimented with it, most successfully the Baylor University Hospital and the Methodist Hospital, both of Dallas, Texas. Among the interested observers of these early experiments was a former college teacher named C. Rufus Rorem, a Ph.D. who became aware of the problem as a staff member of the Committee on the Costs of Medical Care and later became first director of the national Blue Cross Commission. Dr. Rorem added his vision of how people's hospital service needs could be met realistically and, with the force of his logic and the strength of his convictions, patiently began to enlist the support of civic leaders across the country. Thanks largely to his work, the prepaid health service idea began to be tried in a few localities on a broader scale than first envisioned. This expanded conception provided the catalyst previously missing from the mixture. The yeast of community-wide attack upon a common problem began to work to lower the economic barriers separating hospitals from the public they existed to serve. This ferment, sweeping from place to place, created Blue Cross Plans as we know them today.

How phenomenal all this was can be judged by the position Blue Cross occupies in the nation's life today, a mere thirty years later. Spreading out from nuclei in Newark, New Jersey and St. Paul, Minnesota (where all the hospitals in an area first joined forces to offer prepaid hospital service through a single community service agency), Blue Cross has become a group of 76 community service organizations, with a United States' membership of close to sixty million persons. Annually, it provides $2.1 billion worth of hospital services to 8,000,000 patients each year through 6,000 member hospitals.

Reviewing its explosive growth, one is struck especially by the number of climactic situations that could be met only by fresh new solutions. Each seemed "the thing to do" at the time, but in retrospect, their consequences in both human and dollar terms make them "great decisions." Dr. Rorem was as outstanding among the decision-makers as he had been among the movement's originators. At his initiation, the American Hospital Association established in 1933 a number of criteria, which largely influenced the form Blue Cross was to take.

EMPHASIS ON PUBLIC WELFARE

Group hospitalization is intended primarily for the general public who use the hospitals. It is a method of assisting employed persons to budget hospital bills rather than a plan for providing revenue to hospitals.

NONPROFIT SPONSORSHIP AND CONTROL

Representative groups in the community should sponsor and control hospital service plans rather than private investors who are primarily concerned with personal gain. No individual or group should be allowed to assume the risk of financial gain or loss, although employed persons (i.e., employed by the plans) should receive reasonable incomes for necessary services. Financial gains from operation of the plan should accrue to the subscribers, either through reduction of subscriptions or increase in hospital benefits, or both.

ENLISTMENT OF PROFESSIONAL AND PUBLIC INTEREST

Advice and counsel should be enlisted from the medical profession, hospital trustees, and other qualified persons or groups interested in the health of the people.

FREE CHOICE OF PHYSICIAN AND HOSPITAL

Subscribers should be free to choose among several hospitals at the time of illness, and no provisions should interfere with the subscriber's choice of physician and surgeon. Subscribers should be hospitalized only while attended by a physician and upon a physician's recommendation. Opportunity should be given for all institutions of standing in each community to become participating hospitals. In this way, the administrators and trustees of the member hospitals will be able to throw their influence behind one hospital service plan rather than to dissipate their energies in competition. Free choice of hospital also avoids interference between the subscriber's relationship to his physician and the physician's relationship to the hospital.

[Limited as they were to individual hospitals, early prepayment experiments did not accomplish this result. Hence, a number of patients and doctors were excluded and the plans' growth was inhibited.]

LIMITATION TO HOSPITAL SERVICE

The Council of the American Hospital Association approves plans which cover services provided by hospitals only, and do not include the services of private physicians or nurses rendered to subscribers during hospitalization.

[With his command of fact and his patient lucidity, Dr. Rorem gained broad acceptance for the idea that all general hospital services should be available to subscribers and, most importantly, that hospitals guarantee the delivery of the services offered. This last fact obviated the need to raise large amounts of capital which, in the 1930's, would have been impossible. He espoused the idea of payment in service benefits rather than in cash. Previous to the Baylor experiment, commercial insurance companies, employee benefit associations, and other enterprises based on the idea of risk predictability, had undertaken to shield a participant against illness. What they were interested in, however, was protection of his income rather than the provision of health services. Much of the unique character of the Blue Cross plans lay in their offer to exchange small, regularly budgeted amounts of cash for hospital service when needed. The public appreciated the distinction, for the cash benefit method often fell short of the hospital bill; besides, when a man becomes ill, he usually is more concerned with being treated than with being paid. But service-for-cash, as opposed to cash-for-cash, does not lend itself to long-range projections, so responsible insurance companies were shy of it. At least at the start, they were inclined to leave the field pretty much to Blue Cross.]

ECONOMIC AND ACTUARIAL SOUNDNESS

Compliance with legal requirements of each state is essential, and each plan should be economically sound with regard to subscription rates, benefits, payments to hospitals, eligibility of subscribers and accumulation of reserve.

DIGNIFIED PROMOTION AND ADMINISTRATION

The plans should be introduced in a dignified manner, in keeping with the professional ideals of hospital service. The cost of administration should be as low as is consistent with efficient control, and all public relations should emphasize the advantages of group budgeting rather than the merits of individual hospitals.

As I repeat these principles and their explanation thirty years after they were laid down by Dr. Rorem, I find them astonishing. They anticipated and comprehended so much that was to happen, inviting the good and forearming against the bad.

But again I must remind the reader that the decisions these principles generated as they were applied and put into action were not made by one man nor one group of men. Nor were they applied uniformly in all parts of the country.

More than anyone else, Dr. Rorem recognized the need for guiding principles, distilled them from his wide experience and gained acceptance of them. However, these decisions were made by many different groups in hundreds of cities throughout the country. In Essex County, New Jersey, Washington, D. C., New York City, Rochester, Cleveland, and many other places, it was the local Council of Social Agencies, a hospital council, or some similar group that first took responsibility. Then the boards of thousands of hospitals had to ponder the wisdom of incurring the potentially large liabilities of the new idea.

The annual meeting of the American Hospital Association in 1932 triggered some of the plans, including New York's. That year, after having been casually tabled the year before, the developments in Dallas were discussed. They caused a stir, and Homer Wickenden, who was present as general director of the United Hospital Fund of New York, carried home a report of the discussion. As he had in so many other health and welfare activities, Mr. Wickenden saw a need and a way to meet it, and he put the leaders of New York's health and welfare agencies to work. A month later, in October, 1932, Frank Van Dyk, executive secretary of the Hospital Council of Essex County, New Jersey (where he started the first of the present multi-hospital plans), delivered an address on the subject to the Hospital Conference of the City of New York.

After remarking that "the operation of the plan under the auspices of a group of hospitals, such as our Council, offers the best and fullest advantage," Van Dyk went on to concur in a number of Dr. Rorem's other findings, such as that only employee group applications be solicited, that only hospital service be offered, and that nonprofit operation seemed to promise the greatest success.

Since they were typical, more or less, of what was going on in other parts of the country, I shall briefly describe the decisions prompted by the Wickenden and Van Dyk reports which resulted, two years later, in the establishment of what became the largest of all the plans, The Associated Hospital Service of New York.

The United Hospital Fund started things by setting up a committee to study the problem. After consulting with hospital administrators and representatives of the medical profession, the committee next turned its attention to the various methods of operating a group hospital plan: by a commercial company, by individual hospitals, or by the Fund itself. It finally decided that the best method would be by a separate nonprofit membership corporation.

By February, 1933, a tentative plan had been drafted toward this end and was submitted to the hospitals and to the Superintendent of Insurance of the State of New York.

Numerous decisions affecting the development of Blue Cross dealt in matters for which no precedent existed. An example is the reaction of the Superintendent of Insurance to the UHF blueprint. The Insurance Law, in his opinion, was not broad enough to cover so anomalous a proposal; he recommended that the law be amended. The necessary legislation was prepared and unanimously passed by the Legislature. But the Governor (Herbert Lehman) refused his signature on the ground that the bill was ambiguous and might be taken advantage of by unscrupulous parties.

A newly drafted bill included the provision that the rates to be charged to members be approved by the State Insurance Department. It also stipulated that the rate of payment to hospitals be approved by the State Department of Social Welfare. This version was passed by the Legislature, again unanimously. It was signed by the Governor in May, 1934. The money needed to put the plan in operation ($30,000) then was obtained from the Commonwealth Fund and the Josiah Macy, Junior, Foundation, and the Associated Hospital Service of New York was incorporated.

Subsequently, forty other states followed New York's example in adopting "enabling acts" for Blue Cross plans. These acts recognized the essential differences between insurance companies and nonprofit hospital service plans, in both objective and method of operation.

As I tell it now, all of this sounds very orderly and inevitable. But to really understand the events described, one must recapture some of the climate of the times.

In some communities, 20 per cent of the population was on relief. A few hospitals, struggling to pay creditors, decided to let the future take care of itself and closed their nurse training schools. Ordinary citizens, business executives and hospital boards were all so consumed with meeting the problems of the moment that the idea of paying now to provide for future needs was accepted slowly, often only when human tragedy underscored the consequences of unpreparedness.

"Employer contributions" to the cost of health benefits were the rare exception. There were few large employee health and welfare funds. Enrolling subscribers was not always the dignified order-taking that phrase implies. It meant meeting with milkmen as they started their predawn runs. It meant coffee with newspaper press operators as they closed down presses in the early morning hours, explaining, convincing, persuading. Finally, in city after city across the land, a new idea had taken root and began to have a life of its own.

In May, 1935, a truly major decision, influencing the whole Blue Cross movement, was made in the Essex County, New Jersey, plan. After tabulating the incidence of hospitalization of a pitifully small cross section of its membership—then 4,800 persons in all—and despite the dire predictions of some actuaries, the decision was made to extend coverage to wives and children of employees.

Since the family is the economic unit that must deal with a hospital bill incurred by any of its members, this innovation met with instant response.

Some personalization of these cold facts may help illustrate the step-by-step evolutionary process by which Blue Cross has grown. When viewed over the sweep of thirty years, these steps have taken us a long way. While no individual step seemed epoch-making at the time, many proved to have long-range significance and most were repeated over and over with different people in different states. To illustrate, let me describe the events that swept Frank Van Dyk and me into the first "family" rate.

The dire predictions of the actuaries were based on the assumption that with no job to go to and no wage loss when they went to the hospital, wives and children would use unreasonable amounts of hospital care and were "uninsurable." But we decided to challenge this assumption with whatever facts we could accumulate.

We found some case workers from the local relief administration who agreed to spend some of their evenings interviewing employed Blue Cross subscribers. They canvassed five hundred who were married and would tell about their family's total use of hospitals during the past three years.

This information was then put on punch cards, and I found an opportunity to sort and tabulate it on some IBM equipment after regular working hours.

When John K. Gore, then one of the country's leading actuaries and a board member of the Essex County Blue Cross plan, saw the work sheets and the consistency of the data, even for this small sample, he encouraged us to go ahead with the offer of a combined rate for the entire family.

Just a few months later, Frank Van Dyk went to New York to start the New York City plan. Having succeeded him in Essex County, and as a very new, young and somewhat quivery corporate executive reporting to his board of directors for only the second time, I urged the board to authorize the introduction of the family plan.

At about the same time, the newly organized plan in North Carolina took similar action. Various plans across the country followed suit, adopting various ways of offering family membership. Some allowed discounts for a subscriber's dependents, some partial coverage, some individual rates, duplicating the subscriber's own, and some full coverage. The most usual pattern was a single rate for the employee, his spouse, and all children under nineteen. Again a new tool had been forged to cut hospital bills down to manageable size.

The phrase "all children" deserves notice. It will be recalled that the first of the American Hospital Association's criteria for plans, the "Essentials," as they were called, stressed public welfare. And certainly public welfare, rather than the welfare of hospitals, was uppermost in the minds of the plan leaders who first offered family benefits. It was a risky thing to do, for it substantially broadened the plan's liabilities with only fragmentary experience as a guide.

Dr. Rorem's comment on the matter is interesting and typical:

> From the point of view of social usefulness, it appears justifiable to charge single persons and those with small families proportionately more for protection than the person with many dependents. The mutual principle applied in this way is to be justified on the basis of the long-run objective of hospital service plans, namely, to provide the general public with adequate hospital care.

His words touch upon some of the most delicate decisions Blue Cross has made. They affect the relationships between the separate plans and member hospitals.

It is said in some quarters today that the plans are merely agencies of hospitals. This criticism underlies much of the natural resistance to the rate increases necessary to preserve service rather than cash benefits in the face of rising hospital payrolls and the ever broadening scope of hospital care. If the plans are agencies of hospitals, it is argued, how can they help but favor the hospitals over the public?

As explicitly stated in its 1933 Essentials, the American Hospital Association views group hospitalization as a service to the public, not as a device "for providing revenue to hospitals." This attitude, which is reflected in Dr. Rorem's remarks on family rates, has prevailed throughout the history of Blue Cross. It appears in many plan aspects, including the composition of most boards of directors. At the time of its incorporation, for example, the Associated Hospital Service of New York had a board of directors consisting of eleven members, most of whom were trustees or directors of member hospitals, as required under the then relevant article of the State Insurance Law. Later the law was revised, and today the New York plan's board is made up of twenty-six members, six from the medical profession, six representing hospitals, nine representing subscribers and five from the public at large. The preponderance, in other words, favors the public. All serve without pay, although under them, the plan's working staff receives salaries commensurate with the responsibilities it carries.

Summarizing other public safeguards in the operating of the Associated Hospital Service of New York, William C. Breed, Jr., who helped draft the New York State enabling legislation, has written:

> Contracts with the hospitals are service contracts, and the success of any hospital service plan necessarily rests on the willingness of the hospitals to provide the care to subscribers.
>
> Rates of payment to hospitals are approved by the State Department of Social Welfare as to adequacy and by the Insurance Department as to reasonableness; rates charged to subscribers must be approved by the Insurance Department.
>
> AHS is, therefore, a semi-public corporation in which the interests of the public are properly protected.

The phenomenal growth of the plans placed pressures on many of them to behave and think nationally in addition to locally, as they were designed at first exclusively to do. Both factors have forced some weighty decisions.

In 1937, for example, Blue Cross enrollment first topped the million mark and everyone was astonished, including the enrollers. Obviously a thing of such size needed, despite its local orientation, some kind of central co-ordinating bureau. But what kind? The answer seemed to lie in an association of the local plans, so one was set up and called the Blue Cross Commission. It was established as a trust within the structure of the American Hospital Association. Of its fifteen members, twelve were elected by the plans from each of twelve districts in the United States and Canada and three were appointed by the President of the Association. (Canada was considered a district by itself, with the eleven United States districts conforming roughly to the boundaries of the Federal Reserve districts.) The Commission was charged with administering minimal dues contributed by the plans toward five well-defined objectives:

1. The widest possible public acceptance of the principle of voluntary, nonprofit prepayment health service.

2. Development and acceptance by the plans of joint action programs.

3. Exchange of information on matters of common interest.

4. Research.

5. The providing of comprehensive data and recommendations to assist the Association's Board of Trustees in determining compliance with Approval Standards.

The last point needs some explanation. After adoption, the AHA list of Essentials, enumerated above, was incorporated into a set of Approval Standards. In order to receive Association accreditation, it was decided the various plans must meet these Standards; otherwise they could not expect support of their local voluntary hospitals and thus would have no product to offer. The plans submit annual applications for reapproval and their content determines whether or not a plan continues to be accredited.

The Blue Cross emblem became an essential part of the Approval Procedure. A very early leader in Blue Cross, the late E. A. van Steenwyk, had a greater influence on events than anyone, with the possible exception of Dr. Rorem. He created the Blue Cross emblem in 1934, a year after he had been named first executive of the Hospital Service Association of St. Paul, Minnesota. A young teacher, he early saw the great need for prepaid health service and devoted his energy, wisdom and imagination to its development throughout his all too short working life. He began using a blue cross on the literature distributed by his association. So, without any formal search for a "corporate image," the Blue Cross symbol, first used by van Steenwyk as a part of a poster design in St. Paul, began to be used by plan after plan as its corporate mark. Its value today is inestimable. Here again is an example of the fortuitous circumstances that time after time throughout Blue Cross history have made its accomplishments seem almost foreordained.

It is an example, too, of another unique characteristic of plans that still contributes to their success and strength. Each plan operates in a sharply defined geographic area. Hence, there is no selfish hesitancy about helping each other.

In the early days of the Maryland Plan, an associate, who had been a newspaperman, and I produced an annual report of which we were very proud.

Then one morning he came into my office with fire in his eyes.

"Look at this," he said, holding out a poor photocopy of our beloved annual report. In his hand was the annual report of another Blue Cross plan with art work, text and layout obviously "borrowed" from us.

"Those hillbillies have done nothing but insert their own data. We'll have to copyright everything we do from now on."

I had to explain to him that much of the material we were using in Maryland had been adapted from that used in New Jersey, St. Paul, etc., and that another plan's putting our material to good use simply added to our total effectiveness. This sharing also occurred in ideas and in statistical and other information. It soon formed the basis for the many inter-plan operating programs that now enable them to function with national effectiveness.

Responding to the growth of the plans, the Blue Cross Commission made a number of decisions beyond the scope of any one plan. Among the most important was that of supplementing and revising early enrollment practices.

The custom had been (and still generally is) to invite the enrollment of subscribers in groups organized, as a rule, at their places of employment, rather than as individuals. It was reasoned that, if individuals were allowed to enroll freely, many would wait until they or members of their families became ill and then hurry to sign up in order to have the hospital bill paid for by Blue Cross. Should anything of that sort happen, the rate of member hospitalization would reach excessive heights, of course, and the saving effected through prepayment would vanish.

When, on the other hand, large numbers of employed persons were enrolled together during limited periods, the plan was likely to obtain a representative cross section and the predictability of the number of hospital cases would approximate that of the general population.

Furthermore, with millions of persons enrolled, it was considered inefficient for Blue Cross plans to bill and collect fees from every subscriber every month, or even every year. The required paper and administrative work would have cost so much that the prepayment idea's chief appeal, its economy, would have suffered. The preferred method, it was decided, would be for the plans to collect a single payment each month or quarter from the employer on behalf of the enrolled employees; then the employer would compensate himself at regular intervals through deductions from the employees' paychecks.

This method was adopted and has resulted in an extremely low collection expense. On an average, less than five cents of every dollar paid in to Blue Cross plans is spent for all administrative expenses. This is phenomenally low compared to similar enterprises.

However, there inevitably arose the problem of what to do about the increasing number of subscribers who were losing, quitting, or changing jobs. Should they be encouraged to continue on the rolls as individuals and families, or should their benefits cease until the possible day when they would enroll again with another group? The former course was chosen, and no other single decision has contributed more to Blue Cross' status as a community service organization.

People between jobs or reaching retirement were not only permitted but encouraged to maintain their membership. Twenty-five years later, this became a requirement of law for all companies doing a group business in New York State, but most Blue Cross plans, since inception, have had as their goal, "Once a subscriber, always a subscriber." As a result, they now protect at standard rates more than 5,000,000 persons over sixty-five years of age. Without fully anticipating the future importance of their decisions, Blue Cross plans, thirty years ago, began the first large enrollment of the aged whose health needs now command such national attention.

Meanwhile, subscribers were also showing an increasing tendency to travel and seek hospital service in areas distant from their home plans. To meet this situation, the plans first of all entered into a reciprocal service benefit agreement. This soon matured into the present Inter-Plan Service Benefit Bank, through which subscribers to one plan are treated by another and its member hospitals as though they were local subscribers. Through this clearing-house, more than a hundred million dollars' worth of hospital services each year is provided to Blue Cross members needing hospital care away from home.

One of Blue Cross' major tests came in 1950. The United Steelworkers and the steel companies, led by Bethlehem and U. S. Steel, negotiated a contract which called for uniform hospital service benefits for over 300,000 workers and their families at uniform subscription rates at all of the companies' locations. In a few months, thousands of hospitals, hundreds of plan employees and board members, and regulatory agencies in many states had to make adjustments in their accustomed way of doing things to achieve the required uniformity. As other companies and unions also applied for mass enrollment, Blue Cross proved that its strong and varied local roots could support a national growth.

At that time I was responsible for the plan in Maryland, where some 35,000 Bethlehem Steel workers were located. With their families, they comprised more than 100,000 persons, many of whom had previously relied on the wards of the teaching and municipal hospitals for free or below-cost care. The company-union contract called for an effective date of February 1. But it had been signed so recently, that none of the formalities of the multimillion dollar agreements between the company and the plans and their member hospitals had been completed. Nevertheless, everyone was infected with the drama of this new "first."

State insurance departments, plans, hospitals, the company and the union had all been kept informed of the lightning progress of events. So, at midnight on January 31, all Bethlehem employees and their dependents who were in the hospital, began to have their bills covered under the new program in amounts piling up at the rate of more than $14,000 each day, even though no legally binding documents were completed for weeks afterward.

The decision to incur the heavy, unknown and unsupported liabilities associated with the February 1 effective date might have become something less than a noble achievement. But the whole development of the program had been so sound that I had to regard its final "signing and sealing" as a formality, which it turned out to be. One of the happy recollections is a thank-you note from the mother of a baby born shortly after the midnight start of the new program.

Much earlier, in 1941, the United Auto Workers and the General Motors Corporation established a pattern for enrolling employees through local plans serving the various General Motors locations. This was new and pattern-setting at the time, even though it did not require the inter-plan fiscal and legal structure of the steel enrollments. A few of us chipped in to buy a wristwatch for the man who had done most of the work to bring about the enrollment as a part of his regular salaried job.

In an even more massive sense, Blue Cross national capabilities have been proven by the services rendered the United States Government. In 1959, the Federal Employees Health Benefits Act came into being. Under it, the Civil Service Commission was authorized to recommend to government workers a list of reliable health insurance agencies, and this it did, to the number of thirty-seven, of which Blue Cross was one. Part of the cost of each subscription was to be borne by the Government, the rest by the subscriber himself. The general purpose was to regularize previously helter-skelter practices in the choice of health protection.

The results have been highly gratifying. More than half the total number enrolled under the program chose Blue Cross in preference to all other agencies, and a whopping 65 per cent of new subscribers annually is making the same selection. These employees comprise the largest single employee group ever enrolled by any health-care protection agency.

Another Blue Cross undertaking for the Federal Government is called Medicare, a name officially adopted before the press began applying it to health care for the aged. Inaugurated in

December, 1956, Medicare provides hospital benefits to the immediate families of men and women in active military service. The program, administered by Blue Cross in thirty-three states and the District of Columbia, by now has provided more than five million days of hospital care to more than one million patients.

As each year passed, the problems needing solution became more national and the solutions, within the framework of individual state insurance law, became more complex. To comply with local law in each state while still preserving the nonprofit character of Blue Cross, another unique instrument was forged in 1948. In that year, a stock insurance company, Health Service, Inc., was formed to seek licensure in every state. Its stock, however, is held not by private investors but in trust by the national Blue Cross Association, thus achieving the unique result of an insurance company with all its usual powers operating as a nonprofit community service agency. If a Blue Cross plan is unable to provide any part of the service asked for by the industrial groups it deals with, Health Service will write the benefits. This company also offers special types of coverage not included in individual plan contracts, and has initiated experimental programs in new types of coverage, such as comprehensive health and medical benefits.

This widening of Blue Cross' horizon has been mirrored in the short but significant history of the Blue Cross Association. At first passive, merely fulfilling its unique function of making Health Service, Inc., a truly nonprofit stock company, it also served as the base for the retirement benefits program for Blue Cross employees. In 1957, the Association was greatly strengthened. It expanded to undertake enrollment, public relations and administrative functions, the Inter-Plan Service Bank, Medicare, Subscriber Transfer, Private Wire Service (thousands of miles of private telephone lines which speed service to subscribers away from home), as well as research, education and planning responsibilities in partnership with the American Hospital Association.

In this new role as the plans' official channel for national expression and as their co-ordinating agency, with headquarters in Chicago and several regional offices, it replaced the former Blue Cross Commission.

High on the list of decisions confronting Blue Cross today are those associated with the continuing increases in hospital costs, the wise use of hospital facilities, efficient methods of hospital payment, regional planning for hospital service, quality of patient care, and other aspects of the give-and-take among hospitals, plans and the public they both serve.

Just as the growing use of electric power resulted inevitably in the inter-system linkages between local electrical generating and distribution companies—and as the nation's independent banks are linked together to serve their depositors through clearing-houses and the Federal Reserve System—and as great marketing and merchandising units in various cities have joined to enhance their efficiency through bulk purchasing and mass distribution—so is the growth of prepayment producing an inter-relatedness among the nation's hospitals that may become Blue Cross' most significant contribution.

Anyone in the 1930's predicting that Blue Cross would have enrolled 50 per cent, 60 per cent or 70 per cent of the population, as it has in many of the populous northeastern states, would have been classified at least as a visionary, if not under one of the more serious psychiatric diagnoses. I remember talking with a middle-aged man in Maryland when we had about 10,000 persons enrolled. He was considering coming to work with us and was wondering what kind of future it held for him. When I said our job would just begin when we had 250,000 persons enrolled in Maryland, his look of disbelief was obvious and he decided to cast his lot elsewhere.

It is not surprising that little time could be found in those critical early days to contemplate the opportunities for expanded service and the differing problems that large, geographically concentrated public participation would bring with it. To a degree, this is still true. Blue Cross' full potential for improving the quality and minimizing the cost of hospital service is just becoming recognized and used effectively. The important decisions of the next decade will be made around these issues.

Even more clearly than before, one can anticipate the impact of circumstance upon the outcome. Flowing through the Blue Cross system daily is the largest volume of uniformly recorded data about hospital service yet known. Increasingly, it will be used by hospitals, by the medical profession, by Blue Cross and by other public agencies, first to understand and then to improve the totality of care given to the population.

Clinical medicine must have the individual patient as its primary focus. There are, however, some problems of hospital service which become apparent only as one looks at the care given by an individual physician to all patients or by an individual hospital to all its patients, or to all the patients in a geographic area.

For example, will it be possible to bring the full fruits of modern medical science to all the residents of an area if the continued building of small general hospital units, of, say, one hundred beds, is permitted? The natural urge of patients, their physicians, and even of town fathers trying to demonstrate the "up-and-comingness" of their town, is to want a structure labeled a hospital somewhere in town not too far from Main Street. Against this natural attraction of convenience and prestige must be balanced the less obvious advantages that can come from larger units of three hundred or more beds serving a wide geographic area, relying more on transportation and providing a workable economic base for the broad range of specialized services that a truly general hospital can offer but which cannot be supported economically if used only occasionally for a small number of patients.

Regional planning for hospital services by organizations with competent, full-time, professional staffs is being undertaken in a number of areas throughout the country, often with strong support and active participation of the Blue Cross plan of the area. Here again, Blue Cross' expanded opportunity came not so much as a result of a great decision, but as a natural response to an unfolding opportunity. Almost the only decision that could have been fatal would be to decide determinedly to do nothing new or different.

One of the most delicate and significant areas in which Blue Cross has been called upon, and will increasingly be called upon to make decisions, is that of quality of hospital service.

Quality, however, is a difficult thing to measure, let alone provide unvaryingly. Efforts to enhance and maintain it usually involve an attempt to eliminate obviously bad practices, an attempt to improve the overall average and, occasionally, attempts to raise sights as to the peak performance possible. Enforcing a minimum standard, upgrading the general level of practice and demonstrations of excellence, all have their places in improving quality.

Without doubt, the tap root of quality of medical care is the standards which medical education in this country have largely imposed on itself. Supplemented as these are by our postgraduate medical education program in hospitals, the best medical care available in the United States is probably close to the best humanly possible in the light of current medical knowledge. But this is no cause for complacency. There is evidence that a significant portion of medical care is at levels below the best available.

Nowadays, an increasing proportion of medical care is rendered in, and in association with, hospitals. For that reason, and because hospitals have an established pattern of relationship with medicine, the most immediate results in improving quality probably can be achieved by the medical staffs, administration and boards of hospitals.

The hospital may expect to be and should welcome being held accountable for responsible performance. Increasingly, it may expect such accountability to be asked of it by standard-setting agencies, by prepayment agencies and by public regulatory bodies. If informed public servants or responsible legislators become convinced that these institutional responsibilities for quality of care within the institution are undischarged, they will find large segments of the public ready to be aroused to punitive action.

For the public is becoming more informed about and concerned with the quality of medical care. This public concern represents a social force of considerable magnitude, which with irresponsible or uninformed leadership can lower the quality of medical care, or with constructive guidance can improve it. Action undoubtedly will be taken on a number of fronts: legislative, regulatory and voluntary. There is much that physicians, hospitals and prepayment agencies can do beyond what is being done now. Our limited resources of time, energy and money can best be devoted to bringing fact and objectivity into full play in making the value judgments inherent in judging quality and, having arrived at these judgments, *in acting on them.*

The matter of improving quality is one, but not the only one, of the goals toward which Blue Cross is now striving. In addition, ways are being explored to provide patients with care after the acute phase of hospitalization—for instance, in their own home or a nursing home, on an ambulatory outpatient basis, and through visiting nurse services. Under study, too, is the feasibility of providing coverage for the cost of prescription drugs, dental needs and more care for mental illness.

While this book was conceived as an exploration of the results of the decision-making process, one cannot escape the conclusion from the Blue Cross experience that there is an ebb and flow of forces in enterprises involving large human populations. The management function then, is not only to make decisions and seek compliance with them, but, perhaps more importantly, to recognize and put to constructive use the human forces in a democratic society that are beyond the reach of anyone to control by law or regulation. As we have proved so often in the United States, our strength is in people, not in paper work.

WILLIAM S. VAUGHN

Eastman Kodak Company

WILLIAM S. VAUGHN, president of the Eastman Kodak Company, has been associated with the company since 1928. He is a director and a member of the executive committee. Before joining the Eastman Kodak Company, Mr. Vaughn received a B.A. degree from Vanderbilt University, and a B.A. degree from Oxford University, England, where he studied as a Rhodes Scholar. He also received an M.A. degree from Rice Institute in Houston, Texas. Mr. Vaughn began work in the development department at the Kodak office in Rochester. In May, 1930, he was transferred to the accounting department. From 1930 through the 1950's, Mr. Vaughn progressed through the various departments and divisions of the vast camera corporation including: Camera Works and Hawk-Eye plants in Rochester; Kodak Limited, London; Tennessee Eastman Company, Texas Eastman Company, and Eastman Chemical Products, Inc. Mr. Vaughn was elected president of the Eastman Kodak Company in May, 1960, and in 1962 was made director of Kodak-Pathé and a director of Kodak Limited.

You Press the Button—
We Do the Rest

The First Kodak Camera for Everyone

BY

WILLIAM S. VAUGHN

In one of his very rare published interviews,* George Eastman told of his early encounters with the art or the ordeal of photography in the 1870's.

In those days one did not "take" a camera; one accompanied an outfit of which the camera was only a part. I bought an outfit [anticipating a trip to Santo Domingo—*Ed.*] and learned that it took not only a strong but a dauntless man to be an outdoor photographer. My outfit, which included only the essentials, had in it a camera about the size of a soap box, a tripod heavy and strong enough to support a bungalow, a big plate holder, a dark tent, a nitrate bath, and a container for water.

---

* By Samuel Crowther in the old magazine *System.*

The glass plates were not in the holder, ready for use. They were "wet plates"—that is, glass which had to be coated with collodion and then sensitized with nitrate of silver in the field, just before exposure. Hence the nitrate of silver was something that always had to go along, and it was perhaps the most awkward imaginable companion on a journey. It was corrosive, so the container had to be glass with a tight cover; silver nitrate is not a liquid to get intimate with. The first time that I took a silver bath away with me, I wrapped it with exceeding great care and put it in my trunk. The cover leaked; the nitrate got out and stained most of my clothing.

The actual taking of photographs outdoors was an elaborate and painstaking ordeal. One had to set up the dark tent (as close as possible to the scene to be pictured) and coat and sensitize the plates. This was not only a tedious undertaking but one that required considerable skill. In fact, I could do nothing with my first outfit until after I had paid a professional photographer in Rochester $5 to give me lessons. The knowledge was all empirical and the chemical reactions in the nitrate of silver bath were complicated; the coated plate would sometimes most unexpectedly and awkwardly fail to function at all. The procedure was intricate and cumbersome. And the expense considerable; hence people took it for granted that every man who owned a camera made a living out of it. Amateurs were all but unknown. There were only two in Rochester.

Eastman was a bank clerk in those days, a quiet, frugal young man. His superiors at the bank regarded him with favor; given time and seasoning he would assuredly make a good banker. True, he was showing some interest in photography, but it seemed a relatively harmless hobby which did not interfere with work. And it would undoubtedly lose its appeal as young Mr. Eastman's responsibilities at the bank increased.

Somehow photography's appeal did not slack off. For with his appreciation of its difficulties came the conviction that it could be made considerably easier. And if it could be made less onerous it would certainly become far more popular, more useful.

Eastman, who had no scientific training whatever, took to reading everything he could find on the subject of photography. Most of the literature on the subject came from London, with enough more from Paris and Berlin to make the study of French and German worthwhile. So he acquired a smattering of those languages, plus the sort of overall awareness of what was going on that characterizes the true amateur in any area.

The first real glimmer of hope that photography might be made less of a chore came in reports, from Britain and France, that something called a *dry* plate was being evolved. A dry plate could be coated and sensitized ahead of time, loaded in a plate holder in the convenience of a home or studio dark room, and—after the actual picture-making foray—brought back to the dark room for development. If a dry plate could be made to work reliably, it would do away with the need for a dark tent, for coating, sensitizing, and developing in the field, and for hauling around what Eastman called a pack-horse load of fragile, heavy, and trouble-prone impedimenta.

It would, in short, make the use of a camera outside a studio a reasonably civilized operation. Eastman decided to find out about dry plates for himself. Out of his savings he bought some basic chemical equipment and went to work in his mother's kitchen. The idea was simple enough. A clean glass plate was coated with a thin solution of gelatin in which silver salts were suspended. But actual achievement of a workable dry plate was considerably complicated. There seemed to be imponderables involved which baffled even trained scientists and technicians. Eastman was neither, but he *was* curious, he *was* methodical, and—once started—he would *not* give up.

In the midst of his efforts, which occupied all of his after-business hours (including many all-night operations), he read of a specific dry plate formula in the British *Journal of Photography*. He studied it, made a few changes which his experience seemed to suggest, and finally achieved a dry plate that worked well.

So far, so good. He made all the dry plates he needed for his own use, and distributed a few to professionals and amateurs in the Rochester area. In England, however, two or three companies were actually making dry plates for sale. And they were selling. They were even long-lived enough to be imported to the United States and sold through the very few existing photo materials dealers.

Eastman lifted his sights. If he could make dry plates on a small scale for private use and distribution, why not make them on a large scale—and sell them! The market existed. He sounded out his uncle, Horace H. Eastman, on the matter of financial backing, for money would be needed. But Uncle Horace, having reached the age of discretion (70-plus), declined. In doing so he pointed out that he had not the slightest doubt of his nephew's integrity; he had merely decided not to put any money into any project he could not reasonably expect to survive. This was in the winter of 1877-78.

George did not argue. He could guarantee nothing, certainly nothing immediate. But he continued to experiment, to make plates, to expose them, to record his procedures and results, and to keep on at his work in the bank. Incredibly, his status at the bank held up. The bank officers noticed that he was thin and often tired, but they had no real reason to complain of his work. Somewhat over a year after Uncle Horace's kindly refusal to put any of his money into George's project, George withdrew a whopping four hundred dollars from his savings account and headed for England, ostensibly vacation-bound. But he took along something more than vacation gear; he had an idea, a plan. For as he had studied and cooked emulsions and spread them on glass he had come to the conclusion that quantity production of dry plates, to be sold on the open market, required some sort of machinery—a machine which would coat a dozen or a hundred dozen plates uniformly and well. So he designed such an apparatus, worked it out in detail, and set out for England—the unquestioned capital of the photographic world.

Apparently in Queen Victoria's era things could be accomplished quickly. Eastman got a patent on his plate coater at once, interested the editor of the *Journal of Photography* in it and in his plate-making procedures, and began negotiations to sell the British rights for his machine to one of the three commercial plate makers. Mission accomplished, he returned to Rochester.

By April, 1880, he was ready to go into business. He rented a loft above a paint store in downtown Rochester (near the bank), hired two or three helpers, trained them, arranged to market his product through a New York photo-supply house, and started to produce Eastman Dry Plates. By Christmas he had made and sold enough of his product to be convinced that it could support a profitable business. But real volume production would be necessary; in no other way could he achieve the uniformity he knew was necessary nor the low unit cost which would spell profit.

Eastman's mother, who had been widowed for almost twenty years, maintained a very respectable, very genteel small boarding house on the north side of town. One of her roomers was a portly, prosperous buggy-whip manufacturer named Henry Strong, who—with his wife—made the Eastman house a sort of *pied-à-terre* between trips. Strong recognized in Eastman a comer, a young man who might very well amount to something. So, when Eastman told Strong of his hopes and beliefs, showed him what had been done and what reasonably could be done, Strong was interested. He put up a thousand, Eastman matched it, and the Eastman Dry Plate Company, a partnership, was ready to go with the new year, 1881.

Strong's influence on Eastman is difficult to describe. For he had neither knowledge of nor interest in photography (he "discovered" snapshooting many years later with glee and a kind of how-long-has-this-been-going-on? attitude); he was neither mechanic nor tinkerer, and his acumen as a businessman was no greater than Eastman's. But he was loyal, helped when and as he could, and was one of the very few to whom Eastman freely unburdened himself. His eagerness to have the business succeed was important, but Eastman truly needed no help in that direction. It was probably in his role as father confessor that Strong made his greatest contribution. For Eastman—to whom his business was central, dominant, and all-absorbing—sometimes felt alone. He was no joiner, no exuberant extrovert; he needed no casual social life. But he did need a few good friends. Strong was one of them.

The Eastman-Strong partnership started out with a few back orders for plates, and basic supplies of gelatin, glass, silver, chemicals, and equipment. Eastman had patented his first plate coater in the United States as well as in Great Britain, and had evolved a totally new machine for the same purpose, on which another patent was obtained. For he had to have volume, had to have uniformity. The partnership also had a market. Most of it was supplied through the New York firm of E. & H. T. Anthony, but word of Eastman's plates had spread abroad and dealers there asked to be let in.

In the autumn of 1881 Eastman resigned from the bank. His plate factory was prospering; he could no longer find time or energy enough for a schismatic life. And he had a hunch that photography had just begun to grow.

So the winter of 1881-82 was spent in getting in shape to meet the expected demand of the spring. For photography was violently seasonal in those days; only a few professionals thought of picture making in the dreary days and long nights of winter. But when spring came there was a rush to the suppliers for plates and processing chemicals and all the rest.

Eastman's little factory busily coated and shipped new quantities of plates. And everything looked rosy for a while but then, from users all over the country, came loud wails. The plates were no good; nobody expected much of last season's plates but the new shipments were the real villains. They should have been good, and they weren't.

Eastman recalled as many of the recent shipments as he could locate and promised to make good on any others that failed to function. He stopped production for sale and launched on a long series of experiments to discover where the trouble lay—and what could be done about it. His little business gasped for breath. Even Strong turned to, and worked along with Eastman and the crew of "veterans," making new batches of sensitive emulsion, coating plates, and testing them. The formula Eastman considered "standard" simply refused to work. So Eastman tried others, or improvised. It was slow, hard, exacting work, with long periods of inaction while new batches of emulsion were cooked and cured. After 454 batches had been made and tested, there was a ray of hope; the tests were better. By the time batch #472 was reached, things looked positively promising. And then its container broke, and the batch went down the drain.

Eastman and Strong put on their hats and coats and went to England. Surely someone there could explain their tragic plight. Incidentally, the way Eastman used to sail for Europe—a two-week voyage each way—is a revelation of his character. If the trip was important to his business, he took off; time and distance and cost simply didn't matter.

Again London came through. For there Eastman learned enough to suspect that his troubles were not in his formula or his procedures; they were, much more probably, in the all-but-ignored gelatin which was supposed to serve only as a kindly if inert vehicle for the light-sensitive silver salts. Eastman and Strong returned to Rochester, obtained a new supply of a superior grade of gelatin, and went to work. After some sixteen batches, the tests started running consistently good. When further tests continued to hold up, Eastman began shipping again. And high time; for he was badly in need of money. He went six hundred dollars in debt on a short term loan. Much more importantly, he decided on a kind of quality control for in-coming supplies, a control which was eventually to become a do-it-yourself program for his company. If, he argued, he couldn't get materials and supplies of known purity and quality from outside sources, he would make them himself. This is what happened, ultimately, in such diverse supplies as—among many others—gelatin, paper, optical glass, sensitizing dyes, and synthetic chemicals.

He had proved his first point; that a wagonload of heavy, hard-to-handle paraphernalia was not necessary to outdoor picture making. Photography had perked up noticeably with the advent of the dry plate (Eastman's and several others'). But glass was heavy, it was fragile, and it was expensive. If photography was ever to be a truly popular medium, something far lighter, less fragile, and less costly would have to be found. It was simply unreasonable to expect the average citizen (whose numbers constituted an admirable market) to show unstinted enthusiasm in the heavy, complex equipment used by the relatively few dry-plate photographers.

Eastman put his conviction on the back burner and concentrated on making better dry plates. He had to move into larger quarters, add new machines, increase his staff, and eventually, build a plant for his own company's use. (It stood where Kodak Tower now stands.) But he never forgot. A light, simple, easy-to-use camera, loaded with some sort of light, non-fragile photographic material was his goal.

By 1884, when the partnership with Strong was succeeded by a corporation, The Eastman Dry Plate and Film Company (Strong was president and Eastman, by preference, treasurer and general manager), the goal was more clearly defined. It would be achieved in terms of "film"—flexible, rollable, un-fragile film. But just exactly what would constitute film Eastman did not know.

For several years in the middle eighties it appeared that *film* might well be *paper*. Paper rolled, paper held a photographic emulsion reasonably well, paper was light, and paper was relatively cheap despite the fact that the only good paper for photographic purposes had to be imported from France or Germany. The only really significant problem lay in the fact that paper was not really transparent. It could be made pseudo-, quasi-, semi-, almost transparent by rubbing it with oil or glycerine or other after-ointments. But, at best, the oil paper negative showed, on being printed, some trace of the felted fibers of which it was made.

Paper, however, had such definite advantages that Eastman decided to try to use it as a negative support. First, some sort of device had to be designed which would transport rolled paper through a camera and hold it flatly in position while the exposure was made. With William H. Walker, then secretary of the company, Eastman worked out the details and construction of such an apparatus. Logically, it was designed to fit the existing view cameras, in place of the usual plate holder.

The Walker-Eastman Roll Holder was a great success, for it permitted the photographer to make a score or more exposures with considerable convenience. No more heavy glass plates, no more tragic breakage of irreplaceable negatives. And, even though the paper negatives showed more or less paper grain, many photographers willingly accepted the fault; after all, a discreet show of grain could be deemed "artistic."

Eastman, of course, knew better. If photography was to be what he was sure it could be, "almost" wasn't good enough. But a rollable negative medium was clearly the thing to shoot for.

In 1886-87 he took the next step. He continued to make Walker-Eastman Roll Holders to fit existing cameras but, in addition, began to work toward a camera which would incorporate the roll-holder principle. He discovered that cameras were tricky things to make. But despite delays and frustration he let it be known that his company was about to produce a "Detective" camera. The word was, for its era, what "Candid" was for the 1930's and '40's; it simply meant a relatively small, inconspicuous box camera. Ultimately he discarded his "Detective" camera in disgust; it simply wasn't good enough. Of the very few of these cameras produced, one can be seen at the Smithsonian Institution and another at the George Eastman House of Photography in Rochester. They are definitely collector's items.

Simultaneously, his paper film went through another stage of development. Called "American Film," it was coated and exposed and developed much as before, but after the negative on the paper base had been fully "fixed," the thin, delicate emulsion layer was transferred to a sheet or skin of transparent gelatin. The process was intricate, but the final result was sufficiently good to encourage Eastman in his continuing search for a really transparent, durable, impervious film base which could be relied on in the camera, in processing, and in printing or enlarging.

In 1888-89 things came to a boil. With the lessons learned from the fiasco of his Detective camera, Eastman decided on a totally new camera. It would use "American Film" sufficient for many exposures, it would have a minimum of gadgets or adjustments to go wrong, and it would be part of a system which put the emphasis on the pleasures of picture making, with the technicalities left for the people in the factory, both in camera manufacture and in picture processing.

For this drastic concept he needed a name, a name which meant nothing specific in any language, a name or word which would be easy to say, to use, and—to remember. Because he liked the sharp, clean sound of the letter K he began playing anagrams with combinations of letters, beginning or ending (or both) in K. Ultimately he hit on KODAK. It met all his specifications. And when the few he tried it on said, "Yes, fine! But what does it *mean?*", he said nothing, implying that time would tell. In memos to colleagues in the company he referred cryptically to the forthcoming camera as "the K camera" and reserved public use of the magic word for the announcement and presentation of the actual, finished, and successful camera in mid-summer, 1888.

When that announcement was made, at the convention of the Photographers Association in Minneapolis, it created an unbelievable sensation. Some photographers viewed it, understandably, as a threat, but the great and eager public saw in it the realization of a desire that had gone unexpressed because it seemed so obviously impossible.

For, imagine! With a compact, boxlike camera, devoid of mechanical contraptions other than a string (one pulled it to set the shutter), a button (one pressed it to release the shutter), and a film-winding knob, anyone could make pictures, remarkably good pictures. The camera came loaded with enough American Film for a hundred pictures. When they had all been exposed, one merely sent the camera back to the Eastman plant in Rochester whence, in due course, it was returned, re-loaded with fresh film, along with the finished pictures of the previous loading.

Photography, in terms of George Eastman's long-cherished goal, had become democratic. And his "system" was realized, a system which forever banished the pack-horse concept of picture making. Within a year the new Kodak cameras had achieved incredible and worldwide fame. The trade-mark word KODAK had proved its worth by its acceptance in a dozen countries; invariably it meant an Eastman-made camera with a somehow special personality or character.

And when Eastman summarized the system in 1889 in the line, "You press the button—we do the rest," he formalized a totally new concept of photography, the concept of picture making with all the technicalities kept backstage—in the factory, in the processing laboratories—and all the pleasures and benefits out front where they belonged. Incidentally, in 1889 final freedom from a paper film base was achieved in a truly transparent, flexible, and inert cellulose compound.

From that day to this, Eastman's basic decision to free photography from its old bondage to drudgery has been honored and maintained by the company he created. Since that time, Kodak has made innumerable and far better cameras, films, lenses, prints, and all the rest. But the objective of keeping the pleasures and satisfactions of photographic picture making—with the sweat, tears, and frustration left out—has been sustained. In its continuing effort to simplify the *means* of photography so that the *ends* could be better, more easily attained, and more useful, Kodak has had to be flexible. It has had to abandon many a good, workable, lucrative product or process in favor of something better—and do it without a reluctant backward look.

Eastman himself set this pattern. Along in 1892-93, when the first Kodak cameras were basking in the limelight of unprecedented acclaim, when the slogan "You press the button—we do the rest" had so tickled the fancy of the whole world that it entered the language and emerged in music-hall patter and operetta lyrics (Gilbert and Sullivan's "Utopia" included a number featuring both cameras and the slogan), Eastman produced a new camera which was a radical departure. It was a smaller camera designed for (relatively) easy film loading by the user, without recourse to a dark room. The shorter rolls of film did not have to be sent to the factory for unloading and processing; the user or a local photographer could do the developing and printing, usually at a material saving in time. For a little while the famous slogan was amended to read "You press the button—we do the rest—or you can do it yourself." But because this was obviously un-singable and diffuse, it was promptly abandoned. Incredibly, the original slogan persisted in the public's memory and is familiar even today to thousands who have no notion of its original connotations.

Incidentally, the marketing of the "day-load" cameras served to create a wholly new industry—photofinishing. At first, naturally, users of the new cameras tended to have the developing and printing done by the local professional photographers. But as the trade grew, established photographers found that the volume of routine "d and p" orders was interfering with their regular portrait work and defacing the image of their profession. They were artists, and this messing about with amateur button pushers was undignified. Inevitably there arose a new group, untroubled by considerations of prestige or status and quite willing to make money. For years photofinishing was a riotous, disorganized, unpredictable affair, but with Kodak and Kodak's competitors providing technical know-how and materials and merchandising advice, it grew up. Today, the photofinisher is an established businessman, skilled, well equipped, and well organized. And he does a prodigious business.

Flexibility was, and is, one of Kodak's great assets. And it has led to a series of serendipities which, in turn, have given Kodak a degree of diversification which even Eastman could not have foreseen when he decided to do something about pioneer photography's deplorable plight.

Back during World War I America's supplies of synthetic organic chemicals, ordinarily obtained from Europe, were cut off. In 1912 Eastman had set up a formal but uninhibited research laboratory and staffed it with skillful, imaginative people. So when needed chemicals were unavailable, the research laboratory, working with a state university, proceeded to do, on a crash program, what the chemical houses of Germany had been doing commercially for generations. And in the process, Kodak was catapulted into the chemical business. Today, the huge installations of the Tennessee Eastman and Texas Eastman Companies provide not only most of the chemical needs of their parent company but market a bewildering variety of chemicals, dyes, plastics and man-made fibers (including the cellulose tow for billions of cigarette filter tips) which other manufacturers use for their own purposes.

Kodak got into the vitamin business by way of a serendipity. Film shipped to the tropics suffered because of heat and humidity. So an Eastman laboratory man was asked to investigate means for film's protection. Vacuum packing seemed a likely answer. But the available pumps weren't exactly right. So a variant was evolved, and it proved so good that, out of curiosity, other uses for it were investigated. Would it serve as part of the process of distillation of vitamins from fish oil? It would. It did. And Distillation Products Industries, a division of the company, began to evolve and prosper. D.P.I. itself diversified and ultimately was neck-deep in many other projects far, far removed from photography—additives for animal feeding, for example.

But for all that Kodak's enterprise has led it into unpredictable areas, most of which have been reasonably successful, Kodak has remained largely a photographic business. It is still working on George Eastman's basic assumption—picture making need not be drudgery. And it is still doing something about it. The Instamatic camera with cartridge loading, a 1963 achievement, exemplified not only tenacity of purpose but a surprising flexibility and capacity for change-of-pace. With dramatic suddenness Kodak introduced a wholly new concept in film for amateur still cameras. One didn't thread or arrange film in a camera; one merely popped it in, flicked a lever, and started making pictures —pictures which, depending on the film one used, could be color prints, or color slides, or black-and-white snapshots. And, despite the fact that the company was operating in implicit conformity with Eastman's precepts of quality, quantity, uniformity, economy, and massive merchandising, the Instamatic camera practically blew up in the corporate face. For more people wanted more of the new cameras and new film loadings than even the least cautious of Kodak's market analysts dared dream. The resulting crisis induced vast quantities of sweat. But very few tears.

In 1926 George Eastman, on his way to a safari in Africa, wrote home to his associates in Kodak Park's Pioneer Club: "The world is moving. If the company should content itself with its present accomplishments, it would soon fall behind. As you grow old, don't grow logy. Keep the pioneering spirit."

There is very little evidence that it has been lost.

LEWIS WALKER III

Talon, Inc.

LEWIS WALKER was born in Pittsburgh, Pennsylvania on April 26, 1913. His grandfather, Colonel Lewis Walker, was founder and first president of Talon, Inc. Lewis Walker joined the company after finishing college in 1936. Except for a three-and-one-half-year tour of duty with the U. S. Navy during World War II, Mr. Walker has spent all of his adult life in the affairs of Talon. Since 1939 he has served as director of Talon, Inc., and since 1944 he has been president of the corporation. In addition he serves as a director of Talon's foreign and domestic subsidiary companies.

Button, Button, Who Needs the Button

The Story of the Development of the Zipper

BY

LEWIS WALKER III

In 1923 a streamlined rubber galosh of revolutionary design made its debut in the American market place and became a sensational best seller overnight. Nobody had ever seen a rubber galosh like this before, because the traditional bulky and unwieldly ladder buckles had been completely eliminated. Instead, a neat section of tiny chain ran up the instep of the boot and could be opened and closed by the sliding action of a small metal pull. People were fascinated by the easy convenience and neat appearance of this new closure, and in trying to describe it to interested friends, they referred to it as a "zipper." They called it a zipper because the boot in which it was used was sold under the name "Zipper Boot." That's how the "slide fastener" became known as a zipper and that's how zipper became a new word in the American language.

The appearance of the zipper solved an age-old problem. But the slide fastener, as its developers first called their product, did not come into being in a sudden blaze of ingenuity. Like most inventions which finally prove to be successful, it emerged out of a long, patient struggle with difficulties. The significance of this record of experimentation lies in the fact that at last there came to be a precise mechanism for doing well something which centuries of human beings had had to settle for doing badly. The zipper closes expertly things that for dreary ages had continued to sag and gap and pop. It brought to its function the beauty of exactitude, replacing the ugliness of the clumsy.

Today the article has come to be regarded almost as a universal necessity. No doubt in the communes of China there are men and women who have never put their fingers to the pull of a zipper. In Russia it has only now made its debut as a symbol of progress. But in Western civilization it has long been an important item of a way of life—the way of modern technology. It is impossible to think of living without zippers just as it would be impossible to think of living without a motor car or a TV set.

The story of the zipper revolves about three men—Whitcomb L. Judson, who invented the original zipper idea; Gideon Sundback, who perfected the idea; and Colonel Lewis Walker from Meadville, Pennsylvania, who provided the inspirational and motivating spark that made the zipper dream a reality.

From the very moment he first saw Judson's crude closure idea to the time of his death, Lewis Walker was the central figure in every chapter of the zipper story. He was the one man whose faith in the usefulness of the slide fastener kept the idea alive through thirty discouraging years of failure and frustration. It took twenty years to develop the zipper into a marketable product, and another ten years to persuade people to use it.

Legend has it that Whitcomb L. Judson invented the zipper when he could no longer endure the nuisance of bending over to lace his boots. There is an element of truth in this legend because the zipper idea actually came about as a result of Judson's compulsion to perform a necessary task more efficiently than it had ever been performed before. Judson was an engineer of the self-educated kind, and his interests were limited to the application of known principles of science to practical uses. He differed from many another inventor of limited background and unlimited faith in his talents chiefly in that his range was wide and his appetite for experimentation prodigious. On the menu of projects that he attempted to digest were ones having to do with combustion engines, variable speed transmissions, clutches for automobiles and traction wheels applicable to vehicles for desert travel. In sixteen years of strenuous activity he was granted thirty patents. Fourteen of these covered various features of his designs for pneumatic street cars; ten were scattered among his many other interests; six were concerned with the design and manufacture of slide fasteners.

The zipper idea was born on August 29, 1883, when Judson was awarded a patent on a shoe closure device which he described as "a clasp locker or unlocker for automatically engaging or disengaging an entire series of clasps by a single continuous movement." The mechanism was provided with a "movable guide" for performing the operation. This movable guide was the counterpart of today's slider and the series of clasps the counterpart of the teeth or chain of the modern zipper.

The first person to see the Judson clasp locker was Judson's business partner, Harry Earle. The second person to see it was Colonel Walker. He fell immediately under the spell of this article and believed even then that it would have a brilliant future. He had a pair of clasp lockers put on his own shoes and became a missionary for the device. A sense of history made him keep those shoes, and they repose today in the archives of Talon, Inc.

In the fall of 1894, the Colonel, Judson and Earle began doing serious business together. On November 7, the Universal Fastener Company was organized in Chicago to market the new product. Colonel Walker was elected a director at that first meeting. He owned 291 of the original 3,000 shares of stock. Judson meanwhile had done further work on what was now being called not a clasp locker, but, as the name of the new organization indicated, a fastener. Two more patents were applied for in 1894 and were issued on March 31, 1896.

The question of who was to use the fastener, and for what, gave Judson, and more particularly Earle, constant concern. They considered a wide range of possibilities. The improved model still looked heavy and suggested rugged uses. Judson, always ready for new possibilities, suggested mail bags. Harry Earle went out to look for new backers. He found them in the town of Catasauqua, Pennsylvania, near Bethlehem. A group of its citizens agreed to finance experiments with the new application. The work was begun in the shop of the Bryden Horse Shoe Company at Catasauqua.

Theoretically it was successful. Specimens of the mail bag application still exist to demonstrate its engineering efficiency. In April, 1896, government experts examined the model and agreed that it had met every test. The Second Assistant Postmaster General gave an order for twenty pouches to be equipped with fasteners and "go into active service."

But the organization of the new company was awkward. Judson stayed in Chicago; Harry Earle was in New York; machinery for large-scale manufacturing was being developed by the firm of Blake and Johnson in Waterbury, Connecticut; work was going ahead at Catasauqua. By the end of 1897, it had become clear that twenty mail pouches do not make a business. No big contracts with the government had materialized. The experiment seemed to be moving toward a dead end of apathy, and the Catasauqua backers began to fade away.

Still Harry Earle was not discouraged. Another of his friends, George H. Ely, was promptly persuaded to come in. Ely was a banker, a sound man of affairs in the Ohio town of Elyria, which was named for his pioneer ancestors. Ely's idea was to put the device into leggings. Colonel Walker was delighted. He had always regarded the kind of coverage worn by himself and the other officers of Governor Beaver's Pennsylvania honorary guard as an insult to military smartness. Here was a chance to improve the business outlook and the appearance of soldiers simultaneously. George Ely wanted also to make "overgaiters," a kind of elongated spat of cloth or leather popular in the nineties. The prospect seemed promising, and Colonel Walker became more active than ever before in the affairs of the fastener.

The base of operation was moved to Elyria. Judson became a salaried employee under contract to "perfect the details" of the new application. The machinery that moved in from Waterbury did not function well, and the inventor was sure that he understood better than anyone else what was needed. He went to work and designed a new press. He developed a device called the slide bender. He revived old plans for applying the fastener to shoes and developed new ones for putting the device into corsets. The minute book of the Universal Fastener Company reports hopefully the completion of Judson's design for a "new starting device for such articles as have to come apart at both ends." Samples of this fastener were actually made, but there was no market then for an article so far ahead of its time.

In the meantime Judson came up with a revolutionary departure from his original clasp idea and that was the use of cotton tape instead of chain to which the fastening teeth elements could be clamped. Simultaneously, several processes were simplified. The elements themselves could be formed by stamping operations; machinery for making the fastener required far less complicated design; and, finally, the finished product could be attached to a garment by sewing machine. Gone was the tedious necessity of having to sew each link of the old chain fastener to a garment by hand.

C-curity was the name given to the new model. Its place in the evolution of the modern zipper is apparent and, in the examples shown in the early advertising copy, the resemblance of the closed fastener to the familiar ones of today seems to be close, lacking only their delicacy and refinement. Actually, there was a major difference. Illustrations of the open C-curity expose the sharp little hook reaching out for its mate, the eye on the other side. It is not difficult to understand why these aggressive-looking, almost threatening objects gave trouble. Despite the joy with which C-curity was greeted by its sponsors, the hook-and-eye principle, as applied to the fastener, never ceased to be a complete nuisance, and it was only when it was replaced by one much more imaginative as well as more functional that the fastener achieved real and lasting success.

C-curity directed its appeal especially to women. Early leaflets describing its operation were all addressed to women. Indeed, the second name of C-curity was Placket Fastener. The word "placket" meant "woman" when it first came into the language. Later it was applied to the slit made in a garment to facilitate putting it on, and in that sense it is still used by the trade. "A Pull and It's Done," boasts the copy recommending C-curity. But it wasn't as easy as that. A leaflet printed in March, 1906, tacitly confessed to many difficulties. The instructions for applying the fastener were wordy and complicated. The sponsors of C-curity betrayed their own lack of security by stating, "Customers will confer a favor on us by reporting any difficulty in applying fastener, in which case we will send more detailed instructions." The "instructions for using" were not merely wordy, but worried. The almost prayerful document ends with a testimonial from a dressmaker which reported that "all patrons are 'simply delighted' with the fastener. These ladies frequently remark that their skirt is sure never to open without their knowledge."

The truth was that C-curity betrayed all the claims made for it by popping open at the most inconvenient moments. Worse, when such an accident occurred, the slider became locked in its position at the end of the chain. The only way to get the garment off was to cut it off or cut the fastener out. It is not difficult to understand why women decided to forego the convenience of C-curity.

In the summer of 1906, a significant turn took place when Judson agreed that only a highly trained mechanical engineer could design the machine they had to have. That man turned out to be Gideon Sundback, a Swedish electrical engineer who had come to this country to work for the Westinghouse Electric Corporation. Sundback was at first reluctant to join such a small and hazardous venture, but finally succumbed to the challenge of the fastener idea and took on the job. It was Sundback who, after years of struggle, succeeded where Judson had failed. He must be recorded as the creator of the modern slide fastener. As he once wrote, he became "immediately and fully saturated" with the problem. Certain autobiographical notes confess that in moments of stress he often lay awake half the night "trying to find a way out." It was because he brought this kind of intense, creative concentration to the job that he was able to master its quirks.

The first thing to be coped with was C-curity's trick of popping open. Sundback contrived an oval-shaped eye extension which completely enclosed the hood and held it firmly in place. Plako was the name given to the new product. Sundback applied for a patent, and received it as No. 1,060,378 on April 29, 1913. This new fastener made its debut on the market in 1908 even before the patent application had been filed. C-curity had damaged the company's prestige and the Colonel was eager to replace it quickly. A contract was signed with a New York sales organization for the entire production. Women were no longer the only customers. There were Plakos for men's trousers as well. "Buttons, hooks and clasps are disappearing before Plako," advertising copy proclaimed. But once more the announcement of a new era in fastenings proved to be premature. Plako was no more trustworthy than C-curity. It developed a grand total of one steady customer. Colonel Walker's mother loyally wore such fasteners to the end of her life.

Meanwhile, Whitcomb Judson, who had retired from Chicago to Muskegon, Michigan, died there on December 8, 1909, and the outlook for the fastener company, now called the Automatic Hook and Eye Company, was indeed bleak. Debts piled up; stores of raw material were exhausted; there were few sales; and the company faced bankruptcy. Sundback drove his attention and all his skills into a complete reconsideration of the possibilities of the fastener. What he developed was a radical departure from all previous forms that the device had taken. The great need was to eliminate the hooks, which had always proved troublesome to the point of being, as the uncompromisingly realistic Sundback said, "fatal." To one side of his new model he now put spring clips or jaws which clamped around a beaded edge into the opened jaws. The jaws then snapped around the bead—and exit the hook.

Walker was delighted. The samples, made by hand, fascinated him as none of the predecessors had done, and he himself offered a name for the mechanism. The "hidden hook," he called it.

In the meantime, the Colonel worked steadily at a reorganization project, which he knew must be undertaken before the early patents ran out. The final moves followed quickly. At the annual meeting of Automatic Hook and Eye Company held on April 28 in Hoboken, the shareholders voted to have officers of the company execute a contract under the terms of which all of its assets were to be transferred to Lewis Walker in exchange for $50,000. On May 10 the Hookless Fastener Company applied for a charter. Its certificate of incorporation was approved on May 15, 1913, and the charter bears that date.

The Hookless Fastener Company was set up in business in Meadville, Pennsylvania and now, for the first time, operations were closely concentrated and interests well integrated. In one of the fantastic early periods (1901), the company's organization chart (if the phrase can be considered applicable to the situation) placed its mechanical staff in Waterbury, Connecticut, its superintendent in Chicago, its secretary in New York and its general offices in Jersey City. Colonel Walker wanted no more of that. He had all the affairs of the fastener brought home where they belonged.

And so, two decades after the invention of the "clasp locker or unlocker" fastener, the degree of faith that the device inspired in its sponsors was still the most noteworthy thing about it. Sundback demonstrated his devotion by spending his days and nights attempting to solve its engineering problems. Colonel Walker was no less assiduous in his determination to master its financial problems. Year after year he tried to sell stock in whatever company was then trying to make the fastener to everyone he met. With persistence as uninterrupted as was his mannerly poise, he pursued business associates, friends, neighbors. These soft-footed approaches became famous; they also became something to avoid if possible. Walking down a street in Meadville, a man would feel his arm tugged suddenly by his companion. A sibilant order would follow: "Cross over quickly. Here comes the Colonel. He'll try to sell us shares in his gadget." Many wish today they had not been so successful in making such escapes. But the Colonel was not dismayed. With a gallant kind of self-induced myopia he failed to see rebuffs. When he ran out of neighbors he began meeting trains at the depot to pick up any prospects he might have missed.

The new beginning in Meadville was modest enough. It was still one to be classified as a pioneer enterprise. The physical setting was a little barn on Race Street near the railroad tracks. The Colonel, with his usual optimism, told his associates in Hoboken that they would find it more convenient "in several ways" than the old factory had been. "The south side of the floor downstairs is practically level," he wrote, "and the downstairs floor is on a good foundation." The assembly room upstairs he was sure would "work out finely." There might be some vibration, but there was comfort in the thought that "the construction was heavy . . . for as old a building as it is."

No ribbons were cut, no toasts were drunk to mark the coming of the Hookless Fastener Company to Meadville. This was not because the community was indifferent to business activity or unaware of its importance to community welfare. On the day of Hookless' arrival a page one story in the *Evening Republican* reported that a Meadville firm had received a big contract to build a water works plant at Jamestown, Pennsylvania. Another feature, with a three-column headline, also on page one, was concerned with the fact that the McCrosky-Reamer Company had just completed a fine new plant. It was into the building just abandoned by McCrosky-Reamer that Hookless had moved. But no mention was made of that modest, perhaps even a little forlorn, debut. It seemed to be of little significance that an obscure company, engaged in the manufacture of an unfamiliar gadget, had come to town.

The press did preserve its reputation for alertness by reporting on the same day that Branch Rickey, formerly a coach at Allegheny College, had signed as manager of the "St. Louis American Baseball Team." It may be said that Meadville's editorial eye had perfect vision; it covered the field of the obvious. But it cannot be credited with clairvoyance. In neglecting the debut of Hookless, it failed to perceive that, within twenty years, the existence of this enterprise would be one of the community's chief points of civic pride and, what is more important, one of its chief means of support.

As soon as the machinery from Hoboken had been, in Sundback's phrase, "rigged up" on the practically-level floor of the new factory, the inventor set to work on improving it for the manufacture of the new hookless fastener. As he had constantly to explain to the over-eager, it was comparatively easy to let the imagination run riot and elaborately put together a device which could be marketed profitably only at the price of a dollar or so. What was really difficult was to provide the mechanical means of making a commercial product at a reasonable price. This was a problem as important as that of creating the fastener itself. It was the difficulty that had blocked one after another of Judson's impetuous forays and left him completely defeated in the end. Sundback, whose faith was in precision, whose gospel was practicality and whose daily discipline was thoroughness, did not propose to be hurried. He set about redesigning his machinery, making innumerable experiments and again lying awake at night creating the whole process anew. However, the first product of Sundback's new principle—it was to be remembered without gratification as Hookless #1—proved not to have the right answer after all.

While the 1913 Meadville debut of the Hookless Fastener Company was at first clouded in the gloom of the failure of Hookless #1, it marked the most significant point in the zipper's history. It was at the end of 1913 that Sundback announced that he had successfully produced Hookless #2. He might well have added "Eureka!", for indeed, as events turned out, Hookless #2 was destined to be the world's first successful zipper.

What Sundback had accomplished with his Hookless #2 was a radical departure in principle from the design of earlier slide fasteners. He himself described the new method by saying that it was "built up of nested, cup-shaped members." These members were essentially like the ones that lock the present-day fastener. Each has a projection on one side and a recess on the opposite side. In the closed position the projection of one member fits snugly and securely into the recess in the adjacent member. The slider guides one member after another into interlocking relation. A stop at one end and another at the top complete the mechanism. Simplicity, precision, security—the trinity so long sought—had finally been achieved. And simplicity had been accomplished, at least potentially, in the machine for making the device, as well as in its operation. The interlocking members could be stamped out of metal in one process. Eliminated at last were the treacherous complications of the Judson principle of the hook and eye. The former has become, in the course of evolution, "merely a dent stamped into metal" while the latter had become "the corresponding bump on the other side of the dent."

This was the product whose birth Sundback announced to Walker in December, 1913. In a fragment of autobiography the inventor commented on his response. He had never known a man, he said, "to take anything so calmly." But he understood the reason well and he added, "Failure of a fastener had never discouraged the Colonel." The reason was quite simple. Walker had never questioned the workability of the fastener any more than he would have questioned the usefulness of electricity. To him it was another kind of natural phenomenon, and he waited with the calm of complete confidence for Sundback to get it under control.

On July 3, 1914, Sundback thought he had it. There it stood, perfect in theory as far as the exacting eye of the inventor could see. The Colonel had planned a great party to be held at the Country Club next day. The occasion was only in part to celebrate the anniversary of their country's independence; the little group from Race Street may be excused for thinking of it primarily as a celebration of their own victory over circumstance and possibly also of humanity's freedom from inadequate closing devices. So on the day before the Fourth of July they turned on the power, confidently expecting their small miracle. But as

Sundback remembered later with his familiar blunt candor, "The fool machine wouldn't work." It ran out two inches of the product and mulishly halted.

No bells were rung or firecrackers lighted at the Country Club that Independence Day. Instead Sundback trudged back to the factory, this time through the summer heat, and began all over again. He scrapped the recalcitrant machine and started, with a fresh sheet of drawing paper, to make an entirely new design. And this one worked!

Colonel Walker and all the other men of the company were well aware that, with the appearance of Hookless #2, a comparably improved approach must be made to the development of a market. No one in the company had been content to see Plako offered merely as a novelty item in a peddler's pack; yet that was what it had been. Hookless #2 was far too good for that fate. The new product must have a dignified career. A commodity hawked at a county fair like a cure-all nostrum, or pressed one item at a time into the more or less reluctant hand of an individual buyer, could never become an object, as Sundback once pointed out, of "legitimate business." Therefore, a new policy was agreed upon. Hookless #2 was to be sold directly to manufacturers who were in a position to put it into use on a large scale. No longer would the company countenance the sale of its product only to have it laid away on a shelf, as far too often Plako had been.

The problems of the new approach were many, as Colonel Walker had pointed out to his stockholders. First, a demand had to be created and then manufacturers of garments and other objects of common use had to be persuaded that the fasteners had become a necessity to them. The demand may be said to have existed for a long time in the unconscious minds of people who were tired of buttons that came off and snaps that wore out and buckles that rattled. But it lay buried under such a dead weight of custom, such a scattered, elusive, unmanageable overburden of inertia that it was frustratingly difficult to get at. Manufacturers were positively hostile. They wished to ward off an innovation the introduction of which involved many challenges of redesign, of drastic changes in methods of manufacture and, most particularly, of additional cost.

Colonel Walker also realized, in this moment of decision when Hookless #2 was being made ready for the market, that he must have new men about him—salesmen who were capable of being missionaries, deputies with the temperaments of disciples. Such men are not easy to catch by fishing at random, or even with expert knowledge, in the common labor pool. Big fish among salesmen are always understandably reluctant to be caught for speculative projects. Fortunately for him, the Colonel did have two such men in his own family, his sons, Lewis Walker, Jr. and Wallace Delamater Walker. They, he knew, would be representatives whose field reports could be trusted, not merely for honesty, but for insight; they would be concerned not merely for their own good, but for the good of the company as well.

The first samples of the Hookless #2 were sold on October 28, 1914—four of them for a dollar. Wallace Walker took the dollar home to Meadville and gave it to Sundback, who had the bill framed as a souvenir. Its value in that way was infinitely greater than its mere value as currency, for it represented the consummation and justification of more than eight years of continuous effort.

Lewis and Wallace Walker now reached out for the mecca of garment manufacturers, where 90 per cent of the trade was concentrated, and New York became the headquarters for their campaign to beat down resistance. Their program settled into a routine which proved to be one of frustration. Broken appointments, hours of being kept waiting on seats that were not so much anxious as isolated in oblivion. The familiar pattern of the "brush-off" was presented to them monotonously day after day and month after month during 1915. A report of Wallace Walker's calls made in the month of February reads like a chant of doom:

Can't see increase in cost of garments . . . too much trouble to take up with pant makers . . . trouble with shop people over fastener . . . want more money for applying it . . . Union will take up matter . . . Price too high . . . couldn't see him . . . Busy . . . Out . . . Not interested . . .

As Lewis Walker, Jr. later recalled his garment district days without fondness: "We were thrown out of all the worst places in New York."

This new pattern of disappointments obscured the prospect of success up to the period of America's entry into World War I. But in the long view, it may be seen as an inevitable stage in the development of an operative device. Sundback had produced the ideal fastener—in theory. It worked perfectly and could be produced en masse at a reasonable price. But it still had to be tested in the laboratory of continuous use in the hands of consumers. That test came in January, 1918, when an enterprising young designer applied the fastener to a money belt which was sold successfully by leading New York retail merchants. This was followed by interest on the part of the military as they sought to improve the functionalism of such things as aviation suits, life preservers, and fuselage covers. During the year 1918, a little more than 90,000 fasteners were sold for approximately $28,500. And so the special conditions of a world war revealed the value of the device and the long awaited breakthrough of acceptance for the fastener had come. The timing was just right because Sundback had in the meantime perfected the production machinery to such a degree that the Hookless Fastener Company was now ready to meet the "big demand."

In January, 1919, there appeared in the New York office of Lewis Walker, Jr., a "nice little chap" wearing an army uniform. M. A. Berger wanted to talk about using the fastener in tobacco pouches. Simply for his own convenience he had applied one to his own pouch and it had been admired by fellow soldiers. More frugal of leisure than many members of the armed services ever have been, he had spent his time on leave making up such articles for sale. He could, he believed, have disposed of thousands through camp stores. Berger was an able young man in a hurry. Though he had not yet been released from the army he wanted to get into immediate production. He had interested the F. S. Mills Company, leather goods manufacturers of Gloversville, New York, in making the pouch. He himself was ready to act as superintendent of the special project.

Lewis Walker, Jr., reported the interview to Meadville with the air of a man who left no stone unturned, though he had no great hope of finding treasure under this particular one. He realized, he said, that orders for "these short fasteners" might be more of a nuisance than they were worth, but in the circumstances he thought it "would be a mistake not to take care of the demand."

It would have been a mistake, indeed. For years this modest interest kept the Meadville factory busy. By one of those miraculous transformations, familiar in the world of business, a tobacco pouch became bread and butter. By July the pouch, called "Locktite," was in the windows of the United Cigar Stores across the country. Their agents reported that it was selling better than any such article they had ever offered. The Hookless Fastener was identified by name in advertising literature printed by the manufacturer of the pouch and it was also on a tab attached to the article itself. The Hookless Fastener became familiar to thousands of well-pleased customers, most of whom never had heard of the device before. By January, 1921, orders for pouch fasteners took 70 per cent of Meadville's entire production. The problem had now become one of rationing demand to keep all buyers satisfied. In addition to these regular orders, there were many from new customers who wished to apply the fasteners to bathing shoes, dust bags for vacuum cleaners, hip-pocket closures, purses, "rubberall" suits, automobile camp tents, bathing trunks, fliers' hoods.

This wave of increased demand had not, of course, washed Hookless into a cozy harbor of profit, as Colonel Walker pointed out to the stockholders:

> We have made decided progress and can prove it. While we have not as yet made any dividends, we believe we are learning to do that very thing also. Ten gross orders do not excite us greatly as they once did. They now come to us in 50 gross blocks and customers ask us to deliver at our earliest convenience.

The awaited big demand for fasteners did begin to be heard loud and clear in 1921. Twice, while it struggled energetically for a place in the great markets, the fastener had made small advances by association with objects of homely use—first the money belt, and then the tobacco pouch. Now a third article, also of a kind to which the application of a fastener was not a completely obvious possibility, became the ally of its progress toward success. It was the use of fasteners in galoshes that brought the first orders of really impressive size. In July, 1921, Meadville received a request for a few fasteners from a new customer, the B. F. Goodrich Company of Akron, Ohio. The order excited Wallace Walker very little. He was chiefly concerned to make sure that it did not disrupt other business. Perhaps, he suggested to his brother, some of the men could be persuaded to provide what Goodrich needed by working at time and a half for a few hours in the evening. Two days later Goodrich made another request. This one Wallace Walker characterized as a "stunner." Akron wanted to know if Hookless could deliver 170,000 fasteners "within the near future for use on rubber galoshes." This number exceeded the entire output of the factory for the previous year.

Dazzling prospects for the future did not blind the men of Meadville to present opportunities and responsibilities. A pleasant foment of activity kept them busy distributing all the product that the factory could make among importunate customers. Fasteners were wanted for fine purses and handbags; for the many pockets of golf bags; for the protective coverings of musical instruments; for vacuum cleaners bags; for coin containers; for rubberized one-piece suits, the work uniform of street cleaners; for hat bags; for raincoats. Quite definitely gone were the days when the representatives of Hookless knocked politely at the doors of potential customers only to be turned brusquely away. Now the customers lined up at Hookless' door, eager to get whatever supplies could be allowed them.

During the winter of 1922 Goodrich studied the performance of their new galosh with the Hookless fastener and were so pleased that they immediately prepared an advertising campaign to launch this new arctic under the name "Mystik Boot." The campaign was merchandised in advance to all Goodrich dealers in the United States and their reception to the idea was so enthusiastic that it was a sure bet that the boot would be an overwhelming success. But the salesmen still did not like the name. "Mystik Boot" sounded to them like something out of a fanciful tale for children, rather than a highly practical article intended to keep the foot on the ground secure against all threats of wetness and cold. They spoke the syllables *Mys-tik* so derisively that they began to sound like *mis-take*.

"What we need," President Bertram G. Work of Goodrich said one day at a sales conference, "is an action word . . . something that will dramatize the way the thing zips." Then, all in an instant, he realized that he himself had spoken the very word. "Why not call it the 'zipper'?"

A full, exultant satisfaction greeted this inspiration of the moment. The delighted salesmen realized that they had received something closely resembling an answer to prayer. Goodrich registered the word as a trade mark for the "Zipper Boot." But more had happened in that moment than the coining of a word. As zipper made its debut in the language, a new influence appeared in the American way of life. The verbal acceptance of the device advanced acceptance of its actual use.

Sir James M. Barrie once defined poetry as "the thing that tells you what you mean when you say so." Good advertising might, correspondingly, be called the poetry that tells you why you enjoy a thing when you use it. The very word zipper helped many people to enjoy the device. Within the next decade the perverse resistance to the slide fastener within the trade had disappeared entirely. Its attachment to scores of new articles made ways of doing certain things more adroit; certain tasks were accomplished with an ease that made effort unconscious. People could no longer imagine doing without the slide fastener.

The Goodrich galoshes offered the trade a revelation of how skillful design can turn something, the clumsiness of which had always been accepted as inevitable, into something neat and handsome. With the slide fastener attachment, this once-ugly gear became so trim as actually to flatter the foot, instead of transforming it into a heavy, shapeless burlesque of "the human form divine." The first good news about it came to Wallace Walker on January 25, 1923, with the word that the boot had won a blue ribbon at the Chicago Show for American Shoe Retailers. Akron had been able to deliver only four thousand cases of galoshes to the New York branch of the company, though its representatives were already demanding six thousand. Even the flappers began buying the Zipper Boot, and within the first year of the boot's existence Goodrich had increased its share of the rubber footwear business from 5 per cent to some 16 per cent.

Before the end of January, Goodrich announced that it had sold the entire number of arctics—480,000—fasteners for which had been covered by their original order. Lewis Walker, Jr., felt virtually "forced" to accept their additional order of 180,000 fasteners to be delivered before the end of 1923. He said:

> This . . . makes it absolutely impossible for us to take any additional orders for some time until we have carefully rechecked and gone over our possible capacity. In fact, I'm afraid that the two shifts we are planning for our factory will not be sufficient. We may have to go into a third.

The shape of things to come was already evident: expansion was to follow expansion, as the unique position of the company —sole manufacturer in the United States of a product for which there was increasing demand—gave it a broad dominance. Colonel Walker, who had been unobtrusively right for thirty years about the future of the fastener, now had the future firmly in his grasp. The device which during that time had been disciplined into so many adaptations, and which had even learned to turn a corner, as in the automobile curtain application, had also turned the corner in the metaphorical sense. The zipper had truly arrived and, under the trade name of "Talon" which was adopted in 1928, its popularity was to grow and grow until it would become a part of the American way of life. So spectacular were the sales of the Talon zipper that even through the Depression of 1929 the factory was humming at top speed and new workers were being hired every day. Many of these workers, desperate for employment, traveled hundreds of miles, having heard the rumor that there was a company in Meadville that actually was hiring people to make a "new kind of zipper thing." In fact Meadville was described in Robert Ripley's newspaper feature, "Believe It or Not," as "the town that never knew there was a depression."

During the period from 1930 to 1940 the Talon company continued to prosper and the zipper became the standard closure for men's trousers, women's ready-to-wear jackets, corsets, swim wear and just about everything that had need for a fastening device. Today Talon has annual sales of over fifty-four million dollars and has sales offices and factories throughout the country.

It is now fifty years and some seven billion Talon zippers since the first Talon zipper made its debut in 1913. What's ahead for the Talon zipper? Well, for one thing, it will probably be one of the first of America's products to reach the moon, because there are about thirteen Talon zippers on an Astronaut's space suit.

P. W. PERDRIAU

B. F. Goodrich

P. W. PERDRIAU, corporate vice-president of The B. F. Goodrich Company and president of B. F. Goodrich Tire Company, a division, joined the company in 1934 immediately after his graduation from Harvard University with a B.S. degree in engineering and industrial chemistry. During World War II he served as production manager in Akron and in Los Angeles. In 1945 Mr. Perdriau was named manager of the company's Los Angeles tire manufacturing plant. Two years later he returned to Akron as superintendent of the tire division, being appointed director of employee relations for the tire company in 1954. He was named general manager of B. F. Goodrich Aviation Products Division in 1956, and President of B. F. Goodrich Industrial Products Company, also a division, in 1960.

Slow-Outs Instead of Blowouts

The Development of the Tubeless Tire

BY

P. W. PERDRIAU

When inner tubes started blowing out on the early horseless carriages, tire engineers agreed that there had to be a better way of retaining air. The inner tube was inefficient, they reasoned, and contrary to sound engineering principles.

The ideal tire, they figured, would be one that could hold its own air without an inner tube—a tubeless tire.

So for about fifty years various ways of developing a tubeless tire were explored. Whenever an approach looked promising, tire companies put their top development men on it. Some professional inventors painstakingly set about to produce tubeless tires. Others dreamed about them in attics and experimented on them in cellars.

But the tubeless tire eluded them all. After a while, the concept of a tubeless tire became somewhat like the theory of perpetual motion: fascinating to contemplate and just about as practical.

Every now and then a new idea or a new material would be

discovered and tubeless tire development activity would flurry. From 1903 to 1948 no less than sixty-six patent applications were filed on tire constructions that "would eliminate the objectionable inner tube" because it: "deteriorates during use"; "is fragile"; "causes too much vibration for vehicles"; "causes the constant chafing that takes place between the tube and the casing"; "is expensive"; "sometimes becomes pinched in replacing the burst or punctured inner tube"; "creates the constant danger of breakage or puncture."

The patent literature defined the problem well, but none of the proposed tires worked. Most of the ideas involved complex devices and schemes for clamping the tire to the rim and somehow sealing off the interior of the tire so it would hold air.

The B. F. Goodrich Company followed this approach, going a little further than others. In 1942 the company announced development of a heavy-vehicle tubeless tire that had a "specially designed locking member which retains the air in the casing." This was a complicated flap arrangement held in place by the weight of the tire against the wheel. The product worked, but only under ideal circumstances, and eventually this approach too was abandoned.

B. F. Goodrich engineers believed in 1942 that they had gone in search of tubeless tires as far as anybody could. Their development work on the heavy-vehicle tubeless tire had been inspired by the hope of saving precious rubber during wartime. As it turned out, their designs resulted in only a negligible savings in rubber. Officially, the technical people put the tubeless tire on the shelf.

However, the idea still intrigued a few people at B. F. Goodrich. Unofficially, tubeless tire development work was kept alive.

One of the company's engineers, Frank Herzegh, conceived an idea for a passenger car tubeless tire while engaged in development of a military truck tire that couldn't be stopped by bullets or shell fragments. Tires for this special purpose were made with tough rubber linings which provided the necessary support even without air.

For a passenger car tubeless tire, Herzegh thought, why not

use a thin rubber lining extending all around the inside of the casing—as it did on the combat tire—to keep air from seeping through the tire's fabric reinforcement? Then, instead of trying to develop a flap to keep air from escaping at the rim, the wheel itself could be used as part of the air-containing "envelope."

He developed a method of sealing the tire to the rim and it was tested in March of 1942. Four months later, the idea was tossed out as impracticable. Again, conditions had to be perfect in order for it to perform satisfactorily. Herzegh was given another assignment. But he could not forget about the tubeless tire.

Herzegh made tubeless tires and put them on his own car in 1942, and for more than a year and a half he worked on his own to improve his tubeless tire by experimenting with various liner treatments.

Progress was slow. Finally he went to his boss and requested that he be allowed to work on passenger car tubeless tire development. As I recall it, Herzegh got permission, but not very much encouragement.

It should be pointed out that Herzegh was just one of many tire engineers at B. F. Goodrich in the forties, all of whom were working on various projects or parts of projects closely allied to the war effort. While attention was being paid to passenger car tires at that time, emphasis was on conserving rubber, improving combat tires and making aircraft tires as efficient as possible.

The company's tire development heads had been up and down the tubeless tire road so many times that they just couldn't get excited over Herzegh's new "wrinkle."

Word usually filters down through a company. This time it worked its way up. And it took time. It was February, 1947, nearly five years after Herzegh made his first tubeless tire breakthrough, before the word got to John L. Collyer, then president of The B. F. Goodrich Company.

When he heard about the tubeless tire development, the story goes, Collyer got up from his desk and strode nearly a half mile down halls and over ramps connecting the various BFG Akron buildings to the office of Earl Gulick, superintendent of tire manufacturing. He walked in unannounced and said:

"I understand about half our tire technical people are riding around on tubeless tires. Does it have a future?"

"Yes, sir, I think it does," Gulick said, "if we have the guts to stick with it."

"All right," Collyer said. "We'll see."

He turned and headed back to his own office, having committed The B. F. Goodrich Company—in that brief conversation —to the introduction of the passenger car tubeless tire.

There were tests to be made, data to be confirmed, capital expenditures to be allocated, equipment to be designed and built, people to be trained in manufacturing, sales, service and marketing strategies to be devised, and hundreds of decisions to be made along the way. (How do you dispose of several million dollars' worth of perfectly good inner-tube-making equipment?)

There would be many reasons yet to come for forgetting about the whole thing. To put the tubeless tire on the road, B. F. Goodrich would spend $50 million. It would end up suing its leading competitors over tubeless tire patents. It would encounter production problems that no one could have imagined. It would find that the tire industry wasn't ready for the tubeless tire, and neither was the American public.

Still, the feeling throughout the company was that Collyer and his management would not turn back. Actually, the decision to go with the tubeless tire was not the snap judgment it appeared to be. By the end of 1946, B. F. Goodrich people had tested hundreds of tubeless tires on their own cars.

Collyer had every reason to have faith in his company and in his people. He was proud of B. F. Goodrich and its fine record of accomplishment during World War II. This was felt throughout the company. The company's leadership in synthetic rubber development had been unquestionably established, and its research and development team enjoyed the highest reputation in the industry. Collyer had served as special director of rubber programs on the War Production Board, and had received from President Truman the nation's highest civilian award, the Medal of Merit, for "foresight, ability and energy in the development and execution of a program to provide the armed forces and the country with the rubber products needed in the war effort."

B. F. Goodrich had been cited for its outstanding wartime performance. At the presentation ceremony a high government official told employees the development and production of synthetic rubber contributed more to winning the war than did the atomic bomb.

The company was looking around for a new challenge. What could be better than the tubeless tire, goal of the tire industry for half a century?

Tubeless tire development had moved slowly, cautiously and quietly deep within B. F. Goodrich for five years. When Collyer walked out of his tire division superintendent's office on that February day in 1947, the tubeless tire became the company's number one project.

Within a few weeks, tubeless tires were put on test in taxicab fleets in the company's Cincinnati sales district. Information was collected on the performance of hundreds of tires on cars owned by BFG employees. The Cincinnati taxi tests were evaluated. Production schedules were worked out. On May 12, 1947, The B. F. Goodrich Company announced that it had developed and perfected a tubeless tire for passenger cars.

The economic facts of life also supported Collyer's decision to challenge competition and win public acceptance for the new product. Sales forecasts for 1947 were optimistic. The automotive industry was moving into high gear and the war-depleted pipelines were beginning to fill.

B. F. Goodrich was moving in several directions to capitalize on the postwar boom. It was building a modern tire plant in Tuscaloosa, Alabama, an aircraft wheel and brake plant at Troy, Ohio, a plastics products plant at Marietta, Ohio. A synthetic rubber plant in Louisville was being converted to plastics, and a 6-million-dollar research center was being built at Brecksville, Ohio.

B. F. Goodrich, a 145-million-dollar tire company in 1940, was on its way to becoming a 410-million-dollar industrial complex in 1947. A good, aggressive run with the tubeless tire was likely to win further prestige for BFG, and assure the company a larger share of the tire business.

One other factor, perhaps the most important one, influenced Collyer's decision to go ahead with the tubeless tire. This was the passionate desire to be first.

For many years, B. F. Goodrich had held leadership in rubber industry research and development, initiating many of the truly significant developments in rubber chemistry. When Collyer joined the company in 1939, he set out to capitalize on that early leadership and inspire a resurgence of the competitive spirit within the company. He changed the company's slogan to "First in Rubber." Lists of "Famous Firsts" were compiled and widely publicized.

New developments which followed under Collyer's prodding were announced as "Firsts." The desire to be first spread throughout the company. In this atmosphere, the opportunity to lead with the "First successful tubeless tire" was too much to resist.

As it turned out, Collyer could have delayed his decision for many years and B. F. Goodrich might still have been first with the tubeless tire. If B. F. Goodrich had not introduced the tubeless tire in 1947, and—as Collyer was told—had "the guts to stick with it," nearly seventy million automobiles and fourteen million trucks and buses would probably still be riding on tires with inner tubes today.

The American motorist wasn't ready for a revolutionary tire innovation in 1948. He was still buying tires to replace the ones he had used through the war. As long as they were round and made of rubber, he'd buy them just as fast as the industry could make them.

It wasn't until the mid-fifties that the major tire companies really needed to come up with product innovations to hold onto their share of tire sales.

Through this period, B. F. Goodrich stood alone with the tubeless tire. For five years it seemed that none of the other companies were the least bit concerned about the tubeless tire. The tubeless tire was not an innovation, these companies told their dealers and customers. It was a publicity stunt, a sales gimmick. And they assured their dealers and the public that the tubeless tire was just a passing fancy.

The tubeless tire created some prodigious production problems. Standard tire-building machines had to be modified and the manufacturing steps carefully worked out so the new tire could be made efficiently.

The most serious bottleneck was caused by the types of rubber used in the tire. One of the secrets of the tubeless tire was an inner lining made of butyl rubber, a new synthetic that held air about ten times better than natural rubber. Butyl wouldn't stick to anything, and special adhesives had to be developed to make it an integral part of the tire.

Meanwhile, questions were being raised by the sales department. How do you sell a tubeless tire? The motoring public had learned to live with the inner tube, and to take it away suddenly might cause some anxieties.

What were the strong selling points of a tubeless tire? Herzegh, the inventor, proudly answered: "It doesn't have an inner tube. It weighs less than a tire and tube. It runs cooler and, therefore, longer. It permits better balancing than tires with inner tubes by eliminating one element, and better balance permits increased speed with greater safety and comfort."

The sales department was not impressed. Joe Hoban, the sales manager, recalls: "It looked the same as a regular tire and it was difficult to determine what the benefits to the consumer would be. We told the development people that we must have a product we could demonstrate—one with advantages that the consumer could see and actually feel."

After a series of meetings, someone suggested adding a puncture sealant to the tubeless tire. This, it was thought, could give the salesman a positive safety story: "The tubeless tire that automatically seals its own punctures."

The engineering department and Herzegh resisted the sealant idea. They argued that adding the sealant would add weight and therefore cancel out some of the engineering advantages of tubeless construction. Besides, BFG had been making self-sealing inner tubes for years. Putting it in a tire was a relatively minor engineering feat. But sales won, and the famous spikeboard test was conceived to prove the unique characteristics of the new product. Herzegh admits today that it was the sealant, more than anything else, that sold the tubeless tire to the American public.

But even with the sealant, the tubeless tire somehow seemed to offer something less than the American motorist was accustomed to using. The sales people were worried because something—a tube—was being subtracted from the package. How would tire buyers react?

There was too much at stake to leave consumer reaction to chance. Important facts had to be established before the company committed millions of dollars to the marketing of tubeless tires from coast to coast. Localized test marketing offered the logical approach.

In those days, test marketing was a radical departure for a tire company. The practice had been to maintain as much secrecy as possible during the development of a new tire and then to spring it on the public—and the competition—all at once.

In June 1947 the sales department asked the business research department to develop a test market program for early 1948. The program was established not only to determine customer reaction, but to discover any performance defects that might show up when the tire was placed in service by a wide cross section of drivers.

By limiting introduction of its new product, the company reasoned that it would be in a position to correct product difficulties uncovered in the test market before national introduction of the tire. The program was also designed to obtain bench marks for national sales forecasts and to evaluate advertising appeals. Valuable experience could be gained at the local level also, in developing effective training programs for BFG dealers and store personnel throughout the nation.

The Cincinnati district was selected as the testing ground for the following reasons: it was two hundred miles from BFG's home base, Akron, close enough for service and maintenance to cover, but far enough away to be out of the company's sphere of influence; it covered half of Ohio, most of West Virginia, the state of Kentucky, and a part of Indiana; it had city streets, hills, mountains, winding roads, rough roads—practically every type of driving that could be expected to be encountered anywhere in the nation.

The first tubeless tire was offered for sale in Cincinnati on February 2, 1948. Demonstrations of the tire were held for the press, with police chief Eugene Weatherly and other local officials participating. The *Enquirer* reported:

> The new product looks like any other tire, but has no tube and seals itself both when punctured and when the puncturing object is withdrawn. This phase was demonstrated graphically during a test held after the luncheon when Frank Herzegh, inventor of the tire, drove his heavy car equipped with the tires over a board from which 3-inch spikes projected.

Our attitude surveys produced some valuable data that allayed the fears of our sales people and justified management's confidence in the development of the tubeless tire.

The overall impression we got from carefully analyzing the verbatim comments of the people we interviewed was that young people were somewhat enthusiastic about the idea of a tubeless tire; older people had some hesitancy about accepting it.

The surveys showed that people wanted to know how the tire held air, how it could be held on a rim or wheel, whether it was as safe or safer than a tire and a tube.

We found that tire dealers were hesitant because they thought problems of servicing the tubeless tire would differ from those connected with the conventional tire.

It seemed that our job was one of communicating. The problems were not insurmountable. The tubeless tire was off and running!

The Cincinnati test market uncovered a few bugs in the tubeless tire. These were quickly corrected.

Sales experience during the test indicated that this tire would increase B. F. Goodrich volume in the replacement tire market;

its volume was not obtained primarily at the expense of existing products in the line. Sales experience also gave us an idea of the appropriate price level for the tubeless tire, indicated the probable national demand, forming the basis for the planning of future production requirements.

At the dealer level, the Cincinnati experience revealed the type of training program required for instruction in the proper servicing of tubeless tires.

The period of market testing firmed up the most significant selling features of the tire and the nature of the buying reaction, providing a guide to the direction we should take in formulating advertising and sales policy.

The Cincinnati introduction was so successful from the standpoint of publicity and sales, that it was decided to "repeat the act" in other sales districts.

Thus began a series of city-by-city introductions of the tubeless tire, based on the Cincinnati demonstrations, that stretched over three years and twenty-five cities. The spikeboard test was repeated again and again before cameras, and a photo of this—certainly the most famous of all tire publicity shots—became the symbol of the tubeless tire.

One of the most important safety features of the tubeless tire was discovered by accident. The tubeless tire had been sold to the public for about two years before it was discovered from service department reports that the tire resisted blowouts. After a careful study in the field, the sales people conceived the "slowout instead of the blowout" story. Tests by BFG and independent firms confirmed that the tubeless tire liner would—under "blowout conditions"—develop small holes that allowed the air to seep out slowly. An inner tube, on the contrary, bursts suddenly when the casing is ruptured.

B. F. Goodrich had sold more than one million tubeless tires by the time its competitors decided to get into the picture. In 1951 Firestone announced a tubeless tire. This, like BFG's puncture-sealing tubeless, was a premium tire, priced higher than the tires produced by the companies for original equipment on new automobiles. U. S. Rubber's announcement came in May of 1954, and

Goodyear's in August of that year. Both of these were original equipment tires designed for use on new cars. They followed BFG and Firestone announcements of original equipment tubeless tires earlier in 1954.

In February of 1953 B. F. Goodrich brought suit against Firestone over its tubeless tire patents. In June of 1954 it filed a similar suit against U. S. Rubber. *Business Week* magazine commented at the time:

> No matter what the other companies say about earlier developments and Goodrich patents, it was B. F. Goodrich that introduced the tubeless tire to the civilian market. The others have followed and they have taken their own sweet time about it.

The court dockets were crowded. It was not until the summer of 1956 that the tubeless tire patent case was heard. The decision, which came as a great disappointment to practically everyone in B. F. Goodrich, was that the patents were so broad that they did not apply to the company's competitors. The tubeless tire was in the public domain.

On the last day of that year, John L. Collyer told BFG employees: "Our past expenditures in the development of the tubeless tire and the costs involved in attempting to protect our patents are the price of leadership."

Whatever the outcome of the legal squabbles, the tire industry definitely went tubeless. All the new cars since 1955 have been equipped with tubeless tires, and, as the competing company dealers learned how to sell and service the tubeless tire, the new development gradually took over the replacement tire market.

The real winner is the American motoring public. The tubeless tire has lived up to the engineers' dreams. It is a better, more efficient, safer tire—a milestone in the history of automotive progress.

JOHN R. KIMBERLY

Kimberly-Clark Corporation

JOHN R. KIMBERLY, chairman of the board and chief executive officer of Kimberly-Clark Corporation, has been associated with the company since 1924. In the early years, he worked in various operating divisions of the paper and cellulose products manufacturing firm. His next positions in the company were in the marketing area. In 1942, he became sales vice-president. He was elected president in 1953 and president and board chairman in 1955. Mr. Kimberly is a trustee of the Rockefeller Foundation and Alumni Term Member of Massachusetts Institute of Technology.

Better to Use, Cheap Enough to Throw Away

The Disposable Paper Product

BY

JOHN R. KIMBERLY

The room had an Edwardian elegance—high ceiling, oak-paneled walls, a fireplace, a sense of destiny and decision. Through the high, narrow windows, across a narrow channel filled with choppy green water, the yellow brick walls of an old paper mill were visible. In that building some seven years earlier, Kimberly-Clark Corporation had first produced a paper product which was to alter the pace and prosperity of an industry and was to change basic living habits for an entire nation by opening up a whole new field of disposable paper products.

This new product, absorbent wadding, was brand-named Cellucotton and during World War I it was a vital substitute for cotton in treating the wounded. Now, with that view across the water as a reminder of the past and the present, the chief executive officers of Kimberly-Clark Corporation were gathering to review the melancholy record of the peacetime product developed out of

Cellucotton—a product as necessary as blinking, yet as difficult to sell as yesterday's newspaper—and to decide whether to go on trying to market it.

The time was 1921. The nation was slipping swiftly into a postwar recession. Our company had invested heavily in absorbent wadding and in the first consumer product we'd ever produced. But sales were discouragingly low—and it is easy to see why. The product, sanitary napkins, was brand-named Kotex, and it was the target of taboos that bordered on the mystical.

For hundreds, even thousands, of years an almost spectral dread hung over discussing feminine hygiene. Menstruation was viewed not with the grandeur expected of a key element in the cycle of reproduction, but as something that was to be shuttled conversationally into the darkest corners of life. Mothers were loath even to discuss it with their daughters. As a result, many young girls experiencing their first "period" thought, in their ignorance, that they were hemorrhaging internally and that they were about to die. Even as recently as the 1920's, women were haunted by a number of myths and fears about their periods. "The loss of menstrual blood weakens you," was one myth. "If a dentist fills a tooth during menstruation, it won't stay in," was another. "A pain between periods means that something is wrong," was yet a third.

All these fears were arrayed against Kimberly-Clark when it first tried to market Kotex. Women wouldn't talk about the product. Magazines wouldn't accept advertising for it. And many retailers refused to stock it. (Those that did frequently tucked it out of sight in a back room.) So on this day in 1921, the company found itself in a highly-implausable market position: it was trying to change consumer habits with a product that many people wouldn't stock, wouldn't sell, and wouldn't even talk about.

The men who gathered around the polished-oak table in the conference room to discuss the problem were men of the times, oriented to manufacturing, finance and to sound business management generally. They were accustomed to twelve-hour days; they knew their plants well; they knew their employees well, and they knew all customers personally. They represented, in short, an old-line company that was a respected leader and they were not about to jeopardize any of this. But neither were they attracted by a policy of standing pat: the rewards of growth had become apparent during a prosperous half-century, but so had the problems. The issues before them were clear—and more complex than any they had faced before.

On the one hand, the company was marketing a totally unprecedented product and sales were poor. It was engaged in a field of marketing consumer products, a field entirely alien to previous experience. And finally, it was pioneering in a field of paper manufacturing still new to the entire industry—that of disposable paper products.

On the other hand, there was an obvious need for the product. Indeed, it is difficult now to understand how women survived some four thousand years of recorded history without something like it. Also, Kimberly-Clark had a big investment in absorbent wadding; after the war it was able to market some Cellucotton to hospitals as a substitute for cotton, but that market failed by far to approach what management thought to be the enormous potential for the product.

In the discussion that followed, the issues were explored thoroughly by an experienced executive team that could examine complex issues impersonally and skillfully. It was not cowed by unfavorable economic conditions: the company was born just before one depression and achieved some of its greatest growth in risks taken just before another. Indeed, there was among this group a magnetic attraction in certain risks—as long as there was confidence in the ability to surmount them. That confidence was reflected in—and the decision shaped by—a comment made at the time: "We knew this wasn't a penny-ante game when we got into it. The pot is big and we've got to put more into it. I say, let's not drop out."

Kimberly-Clark decided to stay in the game—the boldness of the move hedged slightly by the formation of a separate company to promote and sell the new product without involving the established company name. The old and new companies traveled separate though related paths for twenty-nine years before they

again converged and became one. However, success in creating
a demand among American women for the first disposable sanitary product was soon apparent. It was apparent to others, too,
and within six short years there were scores of similar products
on the market.

That decision was to be profoundly meaningful not only to the
company but to the paper industry as a whole and, indeed, even
to the way Americans expected to lead their lives. For it was one
of the earliest in a long series of disposable paper products that
were to give new comfort, convenience and economy to our lives.
Consider for the moment the everyday paper products that were,
by and large, almost unknown a generation or so ago: paper
plates, cups, facial tissues, towels, napkins, place mats, aprons,
even throwaway paper diapers. The housewife of today, deprived
of these paper products, would find her weekly laundry pile increased, on the average, by thirty linen napkins, by thirty-five
handkerchiefs, by several dozen kitchen and bathroom towels.
By using paper products, she saves an estimated forty loads of
wash a year. Moreover, there is more progress expected in the
future. Already corporate laboratories have developed a cloth-like
material of paper which is used for disposable pillow cases and
sheets, utility clothing, and graduation gowns, and which shows
promise as a low-cost fabric for a complete disposable wardrobe
in the years ahead. In short, paper not only offered new dignity
to the American woman—in helping her conquer the problems
of feminine hygiene—but liberated her from the washboard and
scrub basin. And it is opening vast new horizons of convenience
and savings for the family of the future.

At the same time, the move into the consumer products field
helped the entire paper industry embark on a new era of product
development, prosperity and expansion. One hundred years ago,
in 1864, each person in the United States used, on the average,
six pounds of paper a year. In those days, paper was used mainly
as a means of communication—in newspapers, books and as stationery (though paper bags were just beginning to appear as replacements for the market basket). In 1920, at the time Kimberly-Clark Corporation began marketing disposable paper prod-

ucts, the per capita consumption of paper was 145 pounds. In the last forty-three years or so, that figure has tripled; today consumption of more than ten thousand paper products is so great that it averages out to 453 pounds per person.

This basic change—in which the wastebasket largely displaced the laundry basket—took a considerable amount of doing. It required not only technical and engineering skills, but tremendous capital outlays. It demanded also some solutions to difficult marketing problems, solutions which may not all have been so knotty as how to build a demand for feminine napkins and a market for another great disposable product that came along almost at the same time. For Kimberly-Clark, the decision to continue with Kotex feminine napkins gave great impetus to company growth. It led to a generation of constant expansion, a growth so compulsive that—with the development of another disposable paper product, Kleenex tissues—the company's work force actually expanded during the Depression. And since that time, it has grown five times over.

The decision that led to all this did not, of course, spring spontaneously from one meeting in which a group of men felt peculiarly audacious. It was, rather, the result of a half-century of decision-making in which the habits and hopes that shaped Kimberly-Clark—and its growth—had been tested. When the company was formed in 1872, it was largely in response to a regional need for printing paper. The nation was expanding to the West —the Union Pacific and the Santa Fe railroads were just building their lines—but the paper industry was still largely locked in the East. The nearest important source of good newsprint for newspapers in the Midwest was some three hundred miles to the east of Wisconsin and freight rates to the Midwest for such papers were abnormally high. So the market was in the Midwest—then "the West"—and so was the raw material.

In the days before the Civil War, Neenah was a flour-milling center located near the mouth of the Fox River where its waters flow from Lake Winnebago. It was then—and still is, for that matter—a smallish city of one- and two-story buildings along the main street and comfortable homes on the shores of the river and lake. But behind its quiet façade was a resource that was to prove enormously important in a society rapidly becoming industrial: power. In a stretch of forty miles, the Fox River drops about as far as the height of Niagara Falls, and the tumult of the plunging waters—as well as the constancy of their flow—offered the power vital to any mill operation. So the founders of Kimberly-Clark chose to remain in their home town, Neenah, when they set up the firm in a mill that could produce two tons of paper a day.

Their minds, however, ranged far beyond the home town. In response to business demands, they diversified into different types of papermaking. They opened more mills. By the end of the nineteenth century, they had begun to put together an industrial complex. And they were on the brink of a great venture that would bring even swifter expansion.

Behind all these changes was the swift development of papermaking. As late as 1860, about 90 per cent of all paper was still made from rags. Yet there had always been a shortage of this raw material. Even in the time of George Washington, fancy bags graced every parlor for the collection of cloth scraps. It was against the law to be buried in anything but wool (which could not be used for making paper). One Massachusetts papermaker imported mummies and used the cloth for papermaking—a grotesque situation that gave point to a sardonic saying: "Rags make paper, paper makes money, money makes banks, banks make loans, loans make beggars, beggars make rags."

All over the world, researchers were trying to find some raw material for papermaking other than rags. They tried, among other things, moss, tulip leaves, dandelion roots, and even potatoes. About the middle of the nineteenth century, a way was discovered to grind the long fibers off the side of a log in such a way that they could subsequently be bonded together into paper. This was called the groundwood process and it swiftly made wood the primary raw material for paper. It also made paper more plentiful: in 1870, newsprint was fourteen cents a pound; by 1897, it was down to two cents a pound.

The wood-grinding process is essentially a *mechanical* process, one that is still used to make certain types of paper. But even as it came quickly into use, research was being undertaken on how to treat wood *chemically* for papermaking. Kimberly-Clark got into the chemical processing of wood as early as the 1880's, but it was not until 1913 that it firmly concluded that chemical processing offered the greatest opportunities for the future and thus started shaping plans along these lines.

That in itself demanded a decision of almost visceral intensity. For papermaking had long been an art of the individual. Craftsmen in Kimberly-Clark mills could judge the quality of paper by rubbing it with their thumbs or sniffing it as it went through the papermaking process. They used their sight to gauge its color and double-checked all their decisions by crumbling a sheet in a fist to see how it felt, crinkling it close to an ear to see how it rattled, spitting on it to test its sizing, or poking a finger through it to test its strength. These men were, in a real sense, artisans of the highest order; the company was fortunate to find so many men with the proper combination of skill and temperament who could raise a craft to the level of an art.

But as the graphic arts progressed and higher-speed and more precise printing presses were developed, better and better paper had to be developed to accommodate them. And so papermaking became less an art than a science. The metamorphosis, however gradual, demanded a profound change in attitude for management—which had grown up in close association with, and admiration for, the artisans—as well as for the working force. For it was apparent that science was here to stay and that expansion of the plants, and of the labor force, could be achieved only by adjusting to the shift, indeed only by exploiting it.

In the years before World War I, the European paper industry had progressed farther than the American industry in developing the science of papermaking. They had problems of material supply and product demands in Europe which did not exist in the United States, and they adjusted to those problems scientifically. In fact, European papermakers had opened a technical institute at Darmstadt, Germany, to conduct research into papermaking and to train scientific personnel. In 1914 the Kimberly-Clark Company sent two executives to Europe to learn what they could from the advanced techniques on the Continent.

The outbreak of the war cut their trip short. But when they returned, they were filled with new ideas which eventually developed into two important processes that insured future growth for Kimberly-Clark and, to a certain extent, for the entire paper industry. One was for making bleached paper out of the wood-grinding process that was ideal for reproducing photographs in newspapers, magazines and mail order catalogues. It gave our company, for many years, a premier process in turning out paper for rotogravure sections, a process that eventually made possible today's high quality, coated printing papers.

The other was for developing a cellulose product that was as fluffy as cotton and even more absorbent. Kimberly-Clark called the product Cellucotton absorbent wadding and found a ready —though tragic—market for it: the armies at war. The violence and horror of World War I were to give new dimensions to the human experience. For almost half of the men who entered all the armies in that war were killed or wounded. (By comparison, one out of every eight men in World War II—except the Russians —was killed or wounded.) In the very first month of the war, an estimated 300,000 Frenchmen—some 10,000 a day—were killed or wounded. In one subsequent battle, the Battle of Verdun, more than one-and-a-half million men were killed or wounded. Whole nations were virtually bled white. In a very small way, the company hoped that Cellucotton would be useful in saving some lives—by being used in bandages—and in mitigating the suffering in others.

When the war ended, so did the principal need for the product. Somewhere there had to be found a new and big market for wadding.

But what market?

It was obvious that it could be used by hospitals—and it was. But that failed by far to absorb the capacity for producing the material. Kimberly-Clark had heard that during World War I some nurses had packed Cellucotton in gauze and used the combination as sanitary napkins during their menstrual periods. Even in makeshift use, Cellucotton was much more comfortable, secure, and effective than other methods then in use. The potential market was obviously a large one but it was hardly beckoning. No product in history was likely to encounter such taboos as one aimed at open discussion of feminine hygiene. Yet our executive team elected to devote more than a year of research into exploring and evaluating the sanitary methods then in use and how Cellucotton could improve on them.

In 1920 the company began to sell Kotex napkins made from Cellucotton and almost immediately it began encountering difficulties. The frustrations led to the meeting in 1921—and the decision to stay in the game. This required that ways be devised to meet the marketing difficulties.

Public attitude of the time dictated that the new product was one you couldn't talk about and it did not take a genius to realize that such obstacles to the sale of Kotex must be eliminated. Not only did women have to be informed of its use in a tasteful manner which would inspire great confidence, but dealers had to be found who would sell it.

To persuade dealers to stock the product, the new sales force had to offer them twenty-two free packages for every twelve dozen they ordered. To encourage them to bring the product out from under the counter, advertisements headlined "Kotex, Don't Hide It" were placed in trade publications, prizes were offered for the best window displays and the company paid for each photograph received of a window display. In an effort to gain new users, free samples were offered through magazine and newspaper advertisements and later directly from retailers. Nurses also were offered samples of the product and encouraged to recommend it to patients and friends. Modesty prevented many women from buying this new helpful necessity in public. To make it easier for them to buy it without mentioning the product, the company sold some Kotex through vending machines. Early advertisements also pointed out the convenience of ordering sanitary napkins by telephone, for the stores that sold Kotex all had delivery service.

In 1924 the sales force introduced an even more effective means of making Kotex easy to buy through retail outlets without embarrassment. We persuaded dealers to make it available —already wrapped in plain paper—on counters where women could simply pick it up without asking for it. Dealers were told in trade paper advertising that "the ready-wrapped package makes Kotex as easy to buy as soap. It removes the only obstacle to sales—that of asking a man clerk for it, especially within hearing of other customers." While today the product can be purchased in attractive, clearly labeled packages like any other commodity item sold off the shelves of grocery, drug or department stores, this wrapped package idea was important in the buying evolution of all feminine hygiene products.

The company also launched a massive educational program to take feminine hygiene out of the Dark Ages and bring it into open study. Over the years, this proved to be one of the most gratifying and successful aspects of the whole program. For it had something of the nature of a public service and it helped change the attitudes, as well as the buying habits, of a generation of women. At first, it was built largely around an advertising campaign designed to enlighten women as well as to persuade them to buy the product. Early ads told how the first napkins were discovered by nurses and how this discovery would benefit women by ending the uncertainty of old ways. They emphasized that the new product was the most satisfactory of all sanitary protection; that it provided protection against many common ills traced to unsanitary, makeshift methods; and that it was a product everyone could afford, cheap enough to throw away. It was found that by designing the ads around the advice of a nurse, magazines could be persuaded to accept them. In fact, some of them soon were running articles, as well as ads, on the problems of feminine hygiene.

Then a booklet was published telling how a mother might explain feminine hygiene to her daughter. It was called "Marjorie May's Twelfth Birthday" and it was distributed to millions of families. That was followed by another booklet advising young girls what to do on their "difficult" days. It was called "As One

Girl To Another" and had a circulation of more than two million. Eventually, the company went on to produce two other booklets, "Very Personally Yours" and "Now You Are Ten," not only in English but also in Braille and in foreign languages. The education program even included a ten-minute color film, made by Walt Disney, on "The Story of Menstruation"; it has been seen by close to fifty million persons, largely through the good services of schools.

This educational program, started early and persistently carried out through the years as a service to mothers, young women and girls, helped develop an early and unusually strong brand loyalty for Kotex. And coupled with constant product improvement and wise and tasteful advertising, it accounts in large part for more than forty years of overwhelming leadership by Kimberly-Clark in a field where confidence is a matter of extreme importance.

Even as the Kotex campaign was developing, company people were immersed in creating yet another disposable product— Kleenex tissues. It, too, had its origin in World War I when Kimberly-Clark came up with a way in which to process cellulose into a very thin and soft tissue—one which could be used as a filter in certain types of gas masks. After the war, the company began exploring ways of using it in the consumer market.

As it happens, that was a period in which—more than ever before—the American woman began using cosmetics and cold cream to heighten her beauty. To remove the cold cream, she used a towel which was frequently hung on the inside of the bathroom door. The "cold cream towel"—soggy and dirty— quickly became a familiar part of a bathroom's adornment. Now, in the early 1920's, Kimberly-Clark began adapting the new tissue to serve as an economical "cold cream towel" that could be thrown away after every use. In 1924, the tissue went on the market as Kleenex. It was identified as a "sanitary cold cream remover" and later simply as a "cleansing tissue." Though sales were encouraging, they were by no means sensational. Yet the company went purposefully about improving the product. The tissues were made softer and stronger. The most important improvement in packaging was the "pop-up" box—still associated with Kleenex—that allowed one tissue always to be pulled to fingertip availability as the preceding one was taken from the box.

All this time, the company was getting a certain "playback" from the public which helped to re-direct its advertising and marketing efforts: Kleenex tissues were being used by many as a handkerchief as well as a cleansing tissue. If this were so, men as well as women would be brought into the market as potential users of Kleenex. So in 1930, a test of consumer reaction was set up in Peoria, Illinois, in which users of Kleenex were asked whether they thought of the tissue as a cold-cream remover or as a handkerchief. Of those tested, 61 per cent thought of Kleenex as a handkerchief, 39 per cent thought of it as a cleansing tissue.

That greatly altered management's way of looking at Kleenex— and its way of marketing it. Again the company found itself with the task of changing a deeply-ingrained habit—in this case, shifting from the use of cloth to tissue as a handkerchief. So a whole new advertising campaign was designed to sell Kleenex as a handkerchief. (You may remember one of the slogans: "Don't put a cold in your pocket.") In the next year, sales more than doubled. The surge generated enough strength to keep a healthy employment situation even during the heart of the Depression and enough confidence so that the company spent nearly double its net income for new equipment and improvements during a period when three million dollars was hard to come by. This confidence was well founded, for today the sanitary napkin and facial tissue markets, prime markets which did not exist in the 1920's when Kimberly-Clark created them, total more than $350 million in the United States alone. These two products and other disposable household paper products that followed have been responsible for much of the industry growth, as well as for the growth of the corporation. For these products helped to provide a broader base for Kimberly-Clark to diversify into such fields as cigarette and fine papers, business and writing papers, specialty and converting papers and non-woven fabrics. The latter, and newest, field of corporate product development already is providing a whole new family of disposable paper products which will keep Kimberly-Clark in the business of changing habits for years to come.

Many responsibilities and rewards are products of the initiative shown in 1921. We learned more than how to be successful with a few established products: we perceived the promise of diversification at a time when the word had little meaning in the industry.

DANIEL F. GERBER

Gerber Products Company

DANIEL F. GERBER, a man whose name has become synonymous with baby foods, entered the food field in 1912 when he was fourteen years old, working during the packing season with the Fremont Canning Company, the predecessor of the company that today bears his name. After World War I he rejoined the Fremont Canning Company and rose to the presidency through a succession of jobs, succeeding his father as president in 1945, when the elder Mr. Gerber became chairman of the board.

Babies Are Our Business

The Story of Commercially Prepared Baby Foods

BY

DANIEL F. GERBER

It all started on a summer evening in 1927. I had dressed for an evening with friends and was beginning to fidget at my wife's delay in getting ready to go. Dorothy was in the kitchen of our Fremont, Michigan, home preparing supper for our two daughters, seven-month-old Sally and three-year-old Scotti.

Scotti was in her high chair and doing very well on her own. Supper for Sally, on this occasion some strained peas, was another matter. A tedious session with a kitchen strainer, a table fork, and a strong elbow action had to come first. I said something about speeding things up a bit and Mrs. Gerber responded with a knowing smile and a suggestion that I could expedite things by taking over the pea-straining chore. I didn't know it at the time but, to borrow from a later-day expression, I'd been "had."

The following twenty minutes shouldn't happen to any man. While Mrs. Gerber dressed, I launched the battle of the strainer. Rolling my sleeves high, I armed myself with a serving spoon and went about the business of demonstrating man's superiority over woman. I pushed and squashed valiantly, and the peas soon were everywhere but in the strainer. The splatterings on the sink and floor became evidence of defeat. The meager amount remaining for Sally left me frustrated and with a feeling that there must be an easier way to feed a baby.

Mrs. Gerber, dressed and ready for the evening ahead, returned to the kitchen with the look of a woman who had a scheme afoot. She didn't know a piece of canning machinery from a colander, but a stranger would not have realized this from her remark. "Why can't we end all of this nonsense? You can purée tomatoes at the plant, why not vegetables for Sally?" The plant was about a mile from home. My father, Frank Gerber, and I operated the Fremont Canning Company and packed a general line of fruits and vegetables for adult consumption. It was a modest but thriving midwestern business.

I promised Dorothy to see about it. Somehow I just couldn't believe my experience of the previous evening. Then, too, maybe something more effective than a tablespoon—perhaps an instrument on the order of a potato masher, only rounded to fit the oval-shaped strainer—would make the job easier. Not until years later did I confide what went on in the office the next day. Working with a can of extremely tender peas which we had packed, a strainer purchased at a Fremont hardware store, and a number of tools ranging from a fork to a soup ladle, I absorbed myself in "research." The peas resisted as firmly in the office as they had at home, although the mess in our cutting room was somewhat less than that made in the kitchen the previous evening. I abandoned this first effort, but one idea stuck—the realization that thousands of American mothers struggled with this job every day.

While thousands of mothers were adding endless hours of cooking and straining foods for babies to their already overburdened schedule, there were even more who were not. This was a period when most infants still were confined to a liquid diet for most of their first year. However, a number of medical men were engaged in research projects in the field of infant nutrition, and these far-sighted gentlemen were beginning to introduce some rather startling ideas on the subject of infant feeding. Mrs. Gerber and I, like most of the more fortunate parents of the day, had been exposed to this revolutionary thinking. A Grand Rapids specialist in pediatrics had become our regular doctor for both children, and, like many of his colleagues, he advocated a basic change in traditional baby feeding—solid foods for Sally in her fifth month. This introduced the tiresome practice of straining various foods for Sally.

During the next few days, I kept thinking about my wife and those many mothers who were straining foods for each meal. Finally, I asked my father the question that was nagging me: Wouldn't it be reasonable to assume that mothers would welcome modestly-priced, commercially-prepared foods for babies? It wouldn't be quite true to say that Dad jumped through the hoop with joy at this suggestion. On the other hand, he said he couldn't think of any good reason why mothers wouldn't like the idea and suggested that I go ahead with the project. I have often been asked why my father, head of a company already working at peak processing capacity, would grant permission to "toy" with what could perhaps be called a son's whim. My answer always has been the same. Years earlier, my father's family changed a successful tanning business into a successful wholesale grocery business and later into an even more successful canning company as the last forests which surrounded Fremont gave way to farming. My father was as alert to change as they had been, and his permission did not surprise me.

Our production men were called together and told about the idea. The first batches were to be an experiment, of course, and Sally was to be the first tester. Some of our people had babies of their own and the idea of prepared baby foods was received enthusiastically by them. Would we be straining enough for them to take some home to their babies? We would, and the first batches of strained fruits and vegetables were produced. Mrs. Gerber sampled them and found them to her liking. She even admitted that they were better than her home-prepared variety. We were able to get much fresher produce than was available on the market, and were able to exclude much of the air during the straining process to minimize vitamin destruction and conserve mineral values. Baby Sally seconded her mother's reactions by taking to the new foods. Similar scenes took place in the homes of some of our production people. Mothers set aside their strainers and spoon-fed their little ones a variety of strained foods. It was natural that word of this event spread through our town of two thousand inhabitants and we soon were deluged with requests for samples from mothers throughout Fremont. Their acceptance of our experiment strengthened our belief that mothers would welcome outside help in preparing baby foods and, bolstered by such encouragement, we began to give serious thought to adding baby foods to our line. Many questions arose, however. Would the medical profession recommend commercially prepared baby foods? Would a grocer, who had never been asked for baby foods, agree to stock them? Would a cautious mother, who knew nothing about our company, buy this strange product? While seeking answers to these questions, many months were spent improving processing techniques and determining how the product could be refined and produced at a reasonable cost.

When in the late summer of 1928 I showed the line, ready for the market, to our pediatrician in Grand Rapids, he told me that in spite of my enthusiasm I was still underestimating the real potentials. How right he was had to be proved later. For me this was a tremendous moment. We had received our first professional blessing.

More family conferences were followed by countless consultations with nutritionists and home economists and by months of research and testing. Nutritionists and home economists, all familiar with a baby's need for the nutrition that could come only from strained foods, were even more enthusiastic than we were with the great possibility that lay ahead. As we delved further into the project, company enthusiasm mounted. Even the more dubious members of management began to believe that a good adjunct to the company's line of adult foods might be in the making.

Not everyone saw it that way. Some brokers and business friends quietly advised that we shelve the idea. "You've got a good thing going for you in adult foods," they said. "Why take a chance? A failure in this venture could break the company."

Dad and I thought about it in what I later referred to as our "Amos and Andy" meetings. We really had nothing to go on. No evidence of what was sold last year, no way of knowing what to forecast for the coming year, no way of knowing what crop volume to plan on. Most of the products were seasonal and had to be produced when the crop matured. And our guesses had to be fairly accurate, or we would either be completely out of stock before the following season or have an overstock. But we had a way of adding 50 per cent here, subtracting 25 per cent there, and, somehow, coming pretty close to the answer. We weighed the advice of our business friends, all of them sound men with wide experience in the food industry. We considered the encouragement given us by nutritionists and home economists and the more forward-looking pediatricians. But most of all, I recalled the time Mrs. Gerber exposed me to the exhausting chore of straining peas. That made the decision easier. The Gerber family would launch baby foods in a big way, aiming for national markets and not just local neighborhoods.

Obviously, national distribution did not have the same meaning in 1928 that it does today. We simply could not dream that much. Our goal was to have our baby foods available, at least in a few stores, in every area of the country. For 1928, this was quite a goal, especially for a small company operating out of a single plant. Our fledgling business was under way. We were moving into uncharted waters and, to learn something of the new market, we conducted a national survey to determine the buying habits of young mothers. National surveys were quite rare for small concerns, but we believed such a move had to be a first step in setting up our marketing strategy. The survey told us that mothers would be receptive to the idea of prepared baby foods, providing they were reasonably priced and could be purchased in grocery stores along with regular family staples.

Right then and there Gerber established its policy of producing top-quality baby foods at sensible prices. It may seem strange today that, with no volume in hand, our initial prices were set at

15 and 25 cents a can. Our first line was to consist of five basic strained varieties: peas, prunes, carrots, and spinach (each packed in 4½-ounce cans at 15 cents), and vegetable soup with beef (in a 10½-ounce can for a quarter). The prices were established, not for what we thought the traffic would bear, but because we believed that it would be foolhardy to price baby foods as luxury items if national distribution ever was to be achieved.

Our approach to marketing baby foods was based on three fundamentals. First, since the Fremont Canning Company already had established contacts with the wholesale grocery trade, this was the obvious outlet for the new baby food line. Next, since the new products were food (although a special kind), the logical place to sell them was through food markets. And finally, since food wholesalers and retailers were able to operate at comparatively low profit margins because of the volume and nature of their business, baby foods could be retailed at lower prices. We had learned by now that strained foods for babies weren't an entirely new idea, but the idea of selling them on a national basis through grocery outlets was. Strained foods were being offered through a few eastern drugstores at 35 cents a container. Firms which later became successful in the baby foods industry followed Gerber's philosophy of marketing through grocers.

Since the Fremont Canning Company always had marketed through food brokers, we counted on them to take over the selling of Gerber baby foods to wholesale grocers and grocery chains within their market areas. At the outset, however, we found that many of our regular brokers were cautious about taking on an untried line, particularly when the prices, though considerably below the drugstore variety, were high by comparison with canned foods for adult consumption. While brokers realized strained foods would have to be priced higher than adult foods due to the special machinery and techniques required for production, they questioned whether mothers would pay 15 cents for a 4½-ounce can of strained peas when an 18-ounce can of regular peas cost only 10 cents. Not all brokers were pessimistic. Many, in fact, were enthusiastic. I recall one predicting: "This could be a great idea. Someday, you ought to sell a million cases a year." That forecast came true sooner than anyone could have imagined. Just thirty-five years after we began, more than sixty million cases were sold in a single year.

But that is getting ahead of the story. To help offset the reluctance of hesitant brokers, we decided to employ as sales manager for baby foods a broker who believed in their tremendous sales potential. Who could better convince other brokers, we reasoned, than one of their own who firmly believed in the mass marketing of commercially prepared baby foods? The idea was sound and soon even some of the dubious brokers agreed to introduce the nation's grocers to Gerber baby foods. We saw no reason for grocers to get very excited about what we had to offer without some indication that something was being done to acquaint new mothers with the products we had to offer. Concurrently with the start of the broker's work, we launched a national advertising campaign, with literally no distribution. We gambled $40,000 on a three-month advertising program, starting in the fall of 1928. This was a very large sum of money for our company at that time—although budgets of $2 million a year were not uncommon for some food companies of the day. We believed that the outcome of our modest campaign probably would determine whether we would rise or fall in our baby food venture.

Because our advertisements would be small we saw the need for an illustration that would help attract mothers' attention. A number of conferences with our advertising agency led us to the conclusion that the illustration should be a healthy, happy baby. No other single tool has done more to establish the Gerber image in the market place than has the Gerber Baby. Perhaps fate smiled on us in its selection, for today the Gerber Baby is, without question, the world's most familiar baby. It now appears on labels of more than a billion containers a year, is seen in all Gerber advertising and is readily recognized by mothers in a score of nations.

But we are getting ahead of the story again. In 1928, a number of elaborate oil paintings of babies were submitted for review. The Gerber Baby was to be chosen from these. As judging time neared, one of the artists submitted a small, unfinished charcoal sketch of a baby's head. The artist asked if the drawing was about the right age and size baby we wanted. If so, she said, she would be happy to finish the sketch. The drawing was hung among the far more lavish paintings. As you have surmised, the sketch was never finished. The judges chose the small charcoal sketch without question, for it had a freedom of line and an expression of freshness that would only have been spoiled by additional work.

The advertisements featured our newly adopted Gerber Baby and a coupon offering mothers an introductory assortment of six cans of "Gerber's Strained Vegetables," as our products were then known, for the return of the coupon and one dollar. Mothers were asked to fill in the coupon with their names and addresses and the names of their local grocers. Within days after advertisements appeared in such publications as *The Journal of the American Medical Association, Good Housekeeping* and *Parent's Magazine* (then called *Children*), along with several baby publications of the day, mothers responded and the dollar bills literally flowed into Fremont.

Just as startling as the success of this first campaign was the immediate reaction to the Gerber Baby. Mothers by the score began writing for reprints of the picture. Then, as through the years, thousands commented: "Our baby looks just like the Gerber Baby." The illustration's appeal to parents later prompted us to establish the Gerber Baby as an official trademark.

The coupons provided the key to our next step. We had the names of thousands of mothers, all of whom had purchased our product through an advertisement, and most of whom had given us the names of their grocers. Backed by such a show of interest, brokers were able to approach wholesale grocers with a really convincing sales message. Attitudes changed when they saw coupons listing their retail customers and the names of women who shopped at their stores. Many immediately placed orders. Brokers kept busy talking and selling and, some sixty days after the first advertisements appeared, we could report spotty national distribution. Within six months, Gerber baby foods were on grocery shelves in most major areas throughout the nation. Sales for the first twelve months were far greater than anticipated and our gross reached $345,000 the first year. This was October, 1929, and the outlook was good, so we expanded the advertising program to step up the demand, planned for additional crops to meet anticipated needs, and made ready production schedules for the year ahead. Then suddenly, without warning, an era ended in the great stock market crash. With it "Coolidge prosperity" came to a close.

In some manner, however, our new baby foods at this very anxious stage of growth escaped the fury of those bitter days. Baby foods had been considered a good supplement to our regular business. As the nation entered the Depression, baby foods began to carry the load. The Fremont Canning Company faced a major decision—whether to ride with the times, or to expand its sales and advertising efforts. We gambled again, and baby food sales continued to climb. Ignoring the Depression, we enlarged our staff, installed an experimental kitchen and set up a fully-equipped research laboratory. It goes without saying that mass production of a special type of product requires a specialized staff as well as individual methods of meeting the problems peculiar to each particular product. A home economist with a doctor's degree in chemistry joined the growing Gerber family. A chemist, fresh from the University of Minnesota, moved in and the foundation was laid for what was to become the Gerber Research Division.

Baby food sales kept our heads above water as the effects of the crash continued to spread, and in the midst of it a carefully planned agriculture program was instituted. Technicians trained in the science of agriculture were engaged to work closely with growers, experimental stations and agricultural colleges. Our objectives were to improve the crops from which Gerber baby foods were to be produced and add to the variety of the line. By 1932, the original five varieties had been expanded to a line of nine with the addition of tomatoes, green beans, beets and canned cereal.

During the early thirties, aggressive competitors began to appear. It was lucky for us that we did have good, aggressive competition. Our idea was to sell baby foods to consumers everywhere and, to accomplish this, we had to educate them about the convenience and nutritional advantages of commercially prepared baby foods. Our competitors helped to carry a part of that responsibility. Today our share of the baby foods industry is far greater in volume than we could have attained had we been operating alone.

By the middle thirties, we were well established in the market and were learning there were other approaches to sales than salesman to grocer. To maintain leadership against the food giants then entering the field, we had to be expert about babies as well as baby foods. It was obvious the best way to keep abreast of new ideas in infant care and nutrition was to establish a closer liaison with the medical and dietetic profession. It was imperative that we have the blessings of these groups if we were to gain and hold mothers' confidence.

We originated a unique educational program designed to aid these professions in helping young mothers with infant feeding problems. Our first nutritionist wrote a number of non-commercial booklets designed to be easily understood by young mothers. These booklets, revised through the years, conform to the highest standards of the medical, nursing, home economics, and nutritional professions and provide information most pediatricians and other doctors want mothers to have. The decision to pioneer in the distribution of this kind of educational material did much to cement relations with the medical and allied professions. These infant care booklets have been placed in the hands of millions of mothers through doctor's offices, hospitals and well-baby clinics.

Personal contact also was established with physicians, nurses, and dietitians during the thirties, but the task lay with the salesmen who spent much of their time calling on grocers. As the years passed, this method proved inadequate, and we began to see the need for a special department which could relieve the salesmen of professional contact. As a consequence, we established our Professional Services Department, headed by a manager experienced in working with doctors. He built the staff of contact men who call on professional groups concerned with the welfare of infants.

In the field of education, we published classroom guides for both teacher and student. These publications were directed toward dietetic and home economics students in high schools and colleges, and like our consumer booklets, were non-commercial in tone. They were among the very first school aids of their kind to be accepted by teachers.

Just as we recognized the need for maintaining a liaison with the educational, medical and allied professions, we realized an even more direct line to the consumer was vital if Gerber was to grow in usefulness to mothers and babies. We established this line by providing free educational material through physicians, by conducting product research tests in which mothers and babies participate in a nation-wide panel program, and by giving special consideration to all communications from mothers.

More than 100,000 babies have participated in our panel program. The Marketing Research Department, experienced in the scientific aspects of product preference tests, public opinion surveys, and market and sales analyses, determines the number of mothers and babies to participate in a particular test, the age of the babies, and the method of selection and geographical area. Each mother invited to participate receives samples of two or more products and a questionnaire on which she reports her baby's reaction to flavor and texture of the product. Tests may compare a jar of strained peaches made with New York State fruit against one made from Michigan peaches. Another might involve comparison of various shapes of teething biscuits or testing two orange puddings, comparing one made with Florida orange juice, the other with California orange juice! Whether it is the selection of a new product or improvement of an established one, mothers enter into these tests with considerable zeal. More important, they respond promptly, honestly and understandingly. Through the years they have provided us with the kind of compliments, criticisms and advice that have helped us produce top-quality foods for babies.

One anecdote illustrates the willingness of mothers to participate in our baby panels. A few years ago a small town postmaster wrote us in desperation. A test jar sent to a panel member failed to arrive and she held the postmaster responsible for the loss. His pleading note, which included return postage, read: "Please send me another jar of #65 so I can have peace at my post office again!"

From the very first, mothers were encouraged to write the company. Fan letters, letters seeking advice, special requests, pleas from servicemen's wives or just proud-parent letters pour into Fremont at the rate of some 20,000 a month. The letters are friendly and reflect a sincere desire on the part of the writers to be good parents. Most letters are personal messages to Mrs. Gerber, who many feel is almost an intimate friend—someone to talk things over with. Mrs. Gerber, a mother who has a sensitive understanding of other mothers' problems, personally answered these letters for the first few years. Then, with the volume increasing steadily, the Consumer Service Department was established to help Mrs. Gerber handle mothers' correspondence.

One never knows what the morning mail will bring. There may be a greeting card for Mrs. Gerber. She is asked for reproductions of the Gerber Baby for framing, for a baby picture seen in an advertisement, for baby shower suggestions, and for advice sought by young baby sitters. Mothers in doubt write for all kinds of advice and pose countless questions like these: "How can milk stains be removed from a baby's bib?" "What toys would you suggest for a four-month-old baby?" "What can I do to cure a balky napper?" "Which varieties do you generally recommend for babies just beginning?" "I have heard that you have a baby milk called Modilac. Can you tell me a little more about it and does it have to be prescribed by a doctor?" "I have heard people say you are not supposed to give orange juice to the baby because it has too much acid in it. Does this mean Gerber too, or is your orange juice acid-free?"

And thank-you notes by the thousand pour in from parents who have received Mrs. Gerber's suggestions. This correspondence has remained a personal relationship between Mrs. Gerber and the mothers through the years. The company has never used these mother letters in any form of advertising.

Mrs. Gerber recently sent this letter to an Ohio mother in the hospital following the birth of a daughter. The mother's answer is one we will prize for years to come. Here is Mrs. Gerber's letter to the mother:

. . . I am sure that you, like all mothers, have made wonderful plans for your sweet new baby, and I hope that every one will come true. Having cared for five children of my own and now helping with twelve grandchildren, I know how many dreams are held in each tiny hand.

Perhaps there have been Gerber babies in your family already and I don't need to introduce myself. A short while ago I received a letter from a mother who wrote, "You needn't introduce yourself to me, Mrs. Gerber. I met your baby foods three babies ago." Anyway, some years ago, as I cared for my own babies, I became convinced that mothers would welcome cereals, vegetables, fruits and meats which had been cooked and strained, and were ready to serve to their babies.

Right now you're probably impatient to get home and start caring for baby yourself. The literature enclosed has been prepared by specialists with long experience in the baby field and, we think you'll agree, contains many helpful, practical suggestions. After you have finished reading these booklets, probably your husband would like to read them, too.

Naturally, you realize that good health is the most precious gift you can give your child, and you intend to do all you can to help your baby get a good start in life. Your doctor will tell you how essential good food is to good health, and will advise you carefully about feeding schedules.

For a while, your baby will be on an exclusive liquid diet, but soon your doctor will tell you to start serving solid foods, and then you can try Gerber strained foods and meats, by presenting the enclosed coupons at your favorite store.

Happy homecoming—and warmest wishes for a happy, healthy baby.

Cordially,
Mrs. Dan Gerber

A few days later, this warm reply was received:

. . . You probably will be surprised to hear that I had planned to write you—not three babies ago, as mentioned in your letter—but six babies ago! Our first five—three darling girls and, shall I say, two healthy, happy boys—all were Gerber babies. And now our sixth, another sweet baby girl, will become, please be sure, another Gerber baby.

But I didn't intend to write just to say that I was sold on your product. I always thought you might like to know that I, too, was a Gerber baby and, since I soon will be 35 years old, about the same age as your baby foods, I might even be considered an "original." Dad has told me the story many times. He ran a grocery store for many years here and recalls the day a salesman walked in and tried to sell him some "strained vegetables" for babies. Dad thought he was some sort of a phoney and wouldn't buy any. But I guess he was a pretty capable salesman, because when Dad told him he had a baby girl at home doing okay on liquids, the salesman gave him six cans free to try out on me.

Well, to make a long story short, I guess I ate the food with relish and the next time the salesman called, Dad stocked up on Gerber and carried the line until he retired a few years ago.

I was a healthy, happy baby and Dad always said it was largely because of Gerber. After watching my first five follow in their mother's footsteps, you can be sure I'm not worried about how number six is going to turn out.

So, Mrs. Gerber, I may be 35 years late in telling you about this, but then, it is never too late to say thanks . . .

Although most mail comes from young mothers, Mrs. Gerber also hears from fathers, older brothers and sisters, expectant godmothers and doting grandparents. Letters come from children who say they are "Gerber graduates" and from tots who want samples to "play store." Snapshots of new babies by the score are sent to us and the parents proudly identify their infant as a "Gerber baby." Thousands of these baby pictures have passed over Mrs. Gerber's desk and mine since 1928 and this part of our "family" album actually fills several files in the company offices.

The acceptance of Gerber baby foods by the consumer and the medical profession and the rapid rise of supermarkets across the nation brought us to a major decision in 1938. Annual sales that year were near $10 million and cereals had been added to our growing line of products, to be joined the following year by chopped junior foods, a move that opened a whole new market for us.

In view of these factors and because it was becoming increasingly difficult to offer comprehensive merchandising assistance to wholesalers and retailers, we decided to change from the brokerage system to the setting up of our own sales force. The first Gerber district sales office was established in New York City in 1938 and, through the next three years, most brokers throughout the country were replaced by similar district sales offices.

We established a sales philosophy in 1938 that has been maintained ever since. Gerber salesmen do not sell for sales' sake alone. They are trained to sell only the amount which the wholesaler or retailer can profitably sell his customers without being overstocked or understocked. Orders are planned to assure adequate supplies at all times. Salesmen are taught to know exactly how to help their accounts take advantage of effective merchandising campaigns and to advise store managers on such things as rotation of stock, location of department, types of shelving and displays best suited to the individual market's needs. This technique has been developed to a point where most wholesalers and retailers now permit Gerber salesmen to write their own orders. It is a trust we value and make every effort to maintain.

Co-operation is a two-way street, and the assistance we have given store managers has been returned time and again. An excellent example of the co-operative spirit is shown in the wholehearted support they have given Baby Week since we first promoted this national observance to the grocery trade in 1932. Baby Week originally was introduced in department stores to encourage the formation of layette departments. We borrowed this phase of department store merchandising and spearheaded Baby Week as a promotional device to spur establishment of departments in grocery stores devoted exclusively to baby products.

The program's advantages soon were recognized by other baby products manufacturers and their participation, coupled with the efforts of promotion-minded store managers, did much to make the baby needs department a successful operation. Today, many supermarkets maintain special baby departments which feature a wide variety of baby foods along with such items as evaporated milk, special formulas, milk modifiers, baby toiletries, baby pants and other products for babies. Baby food still remains by far the most important element in these departments, however, just as it became our most important undertaking.

Gerber baby foods sales finally passed the volume of our canned foods for adults in 1941 and we elected to change the name of the Fremont Canning Company to the Gerber Products Company. As sales continued to soar the next two years, the problem of allotting sufficient produce for baby foods (grown mostly in the Fremont area at that time) while continuing to maintain our line of adult foods became more and more acute. Finally, there simply wasn't enough produce available for both lines and our plant capacity was being overextended.

We had seen the decision coming for some time but, because our long-established adult food line was well known in the Midwest, we had delayed taking action as long as we could. However, in 1943 our management gathered around a conference table and, after some considerable debate, voted a dramatic change in the make-up of our growing concern. We would discontinue packing adult food and devote our efforts and available produce exclusively to baby foods. Since then, we have been the only food manufacturer who can say, "Babies Are Our Business . . . Our Only Business." That slogan, which first appeared in advertising copy, later was to join the Gerber Baby on all advertising and labeling and was to further establish the Gerber name in the minds of the nation's mothers.

Even with the discontinuance of adult foods, the problems of raising enough produce in the area and producing enough baby foods to satisfy the appetites of the nation's babies were difficult. We had long since enlarged and improved the Fremont plant and the surrounding crop-producing areas for our mushrooming business, and, until 1943, we had been able to improve production methods and increase the volume so that our low unit price of baby food was maintained. In fact, despite increased labor, production, raw material and transportation costs, Gerber baby foods actually were selling for a lower price that year than in 1928. This is still true today. But the time had come when our Fremont facilities could not supply the nation's demand alone, so we took another significant step in 1943 by acquiring Elmhurst Packers, Inc., of Oakland, California, and thus adding a West Coast plant with its seasoned technicians and executives.

In 1945 I was named president of Gerber Products Company, succeeding my father, who became chairman of the board. My father continued to play an active role in management until his death in October, 1952. As the years passed, other foods given early in life were found to aid infant well-being. Our product line, which included 32 varieties in 1945, grew to more than 110 by 1962, and some 50 per cent of our annual sales that year were a result of varieties introduced since 1945. As an example, strained and junior meats for babies were added to the line in 1947 through a joint arrangement between Armour and Company and Gerber Products Company.

The need for new acreage, new production facilities, and improved distribution was with us at all times. In 1949 Gerber leased a canning plant from the Curtice Brothers Company in Rochester, New York, and, during the same year, joined forces with the Ogilvie Flour Mills Ltd. of Canada, forming a new subsidiary called Gerber-Ogilvie Baby Foods Ltd. A canning plant in Niagara Falls, Ontario, was purchased then and revamped to pack baby foods for the Canadian market. We purchased the Rochester plant outright in 1950 and building operations, specifically designed for processing baby foods, were begun in 1951.

The next dozen years were to see sales reach nearly $170 million a year, Gerber baby foods become a familiar name in forty-seven nations, plants arise in Asheville, North Carolina, Fort

Smith, Arkansas, and Mexico City, and licensees produce Gerber baby foods in Australia, Japan and Venezuela.

In 1962 we entered into an agreement with Corn Products Company, a leading American food producer with operations in twenty-four foreign countries, to produce Gerber baby foods in Europe. Twenty strained food varieties and two cereals were in distribution in France and West Germany by the spring of 1963.

As I signed the agreement that would bring Gerber baby foods to Europe, I couldn't help but smile as I compared the European situation in 1963 with the American picture of thirty-five years earlier. While baby foods had become a familiar product to the American mother by 1963, they still were relatively unusual on European mothers' shopping lists. Much of the pioneering effort which brought baby foods to their strong position in the United States still lay ahead in Europe.

But there were differences. Physically, four times as many varieties were being offered to European mothers as had been offered here in 1928. Even more important, Gerber went into Europe backed by thirty-five years of experience in baby foods and by the production and merchandising know-how of Corn Products, which has been on the European scene for an even longer span of time.

Looking back over those years, I think the thing that has helped Gerber grow so rapidly has been a kind of healthy dissatisfaction which our company has had with things static. Perhaps our greatest decisions are yet to be made, for our potential is as broad as the infant population of the world—and three are born every second. Our goal is to bring Gerber baby foods within reach of every one of them. Such a goal might be looked upon as wishful thinking but then, so was the idea that was born that evening many years ago when Mrs. Gerber proved to me that pushing peas through a sieve was a real challenge and a problem to be taken seriously.

PAUL S. GEROT

The Pillsbury Company

PAUL S. GEROT is president and a member of the board of directors of The Pillsbury Company. Born on a farm near Riverside, Iowa, he attended Iowa Wesleyan Academy and College, Mt. Pleasant, Iowa and Northwestern University. Mr. Gerot joined Pillsbury in 1926 as a salesman in the St. Louis Branch. He moved to Minneapolis in 1944 as assistant to the vice-president in charge of sales and advertising. He became executive vice-president of the company in 1951 and was elected president in June, 1952.

Convenience, Ease and Success from the Oven

The Story of Prepared Cake Mixes

BY

PAUL S. GEROT

When Oklahoma's Alfalfa Bill Murray was campaigning for governor during the Dust Bowl Days of the 1930's, he used to make a hit with the ladies when he'd declare: "Cooks could write as good a history any day as a sociologist and a militarist."

There is a good deal of truth in the statement. The story of cooking and baking has been closely related to a whole range of human activity from the movement of peoples and the exchange of ideas between different ethnic and trade groups to the improvements of transportation and communications, the casting and stamping of metals and all the developments and refinements in agriculture and marketing. The great events of history have all left a mark of one kind or another on the bread and board of the peoples involved.

During the past thirty-five years in America, we have traversed from concern for breadlines to worry over beltlines. We've moved through a major war and several smaller encounters. We've automated. Our living rooms are in contact with points of news and entertainment around the world. And all of these developments and many more play some part in the development of cake mix.

The Pillsbury side of that story might well begin on a warm August afternoon in 1947. A phone call that day from "Doc" Harrel, our research chief, brought some hopeful news on a project he had been assigned.

Following Harrel's call, a group of us from Pillsbury's grocery products division drove from our offices in downtown Minneapolis to the company's lab on the bank of the Mississippi. All we did at the lab that day was eat a piece of white cake, but it was the best idea for a white cake we'd ever come across and, most important, it tasted good.

That was the first day we were excited by the quality of cake our scientists could make from a mix. But it wasn't one of those classic laboratory scenes of revelation where the observers and the man in the white coat jubilantly pound each other on the back. That day in Doc Harrel's lab, in the shadow of Pillsbury's "A" Mill, had been planned and anticipated for some time. For just as the "A" Mill, largest in the world when it was built in 1877, had become a symbol of the early years of Pillsbury, the small, one-story research building had become the new sign of the times for the company following World War II.

The trip to the lab showed us that our scientists could produce in small quantity the kind of product we wanted. And we felt strongly that our ideas were timely according to our estimate of consumer demand. We also knew that between Doc Harrel's lab and millions of American kitchens lay an endless series of crucial decisions.

At that time there were other cake mixes already on the market. Although we had some prior experience in developing baking mixes, including government contract work during the war, we had not marketed a complete baking mix prior to 1946. Because of ingredient shortages, however, and the fact that no large and continuing campaign had been staged to promote baking mixes nationally, we felt that the potential market had not begun to be exploited. As we approached the postwar consumer market, therefore, we put together a series of requirements that we felt would not just get us into the race, but would get us out in front, hopefully, to stay.

Though all of these points weren't argued at the same time, and some of them were not to become firm, these were the three key approaches we decided on:

1. We would try to provide cake mixes that would approach home-baked quality. Convenience, we felt, would not be enough in the long run.

2. We would develop a specialty line of complete mixes covering the various popular cake flavors rather than produce an all-purpose base that the housewife could then doctor according to the flavor she desired. We became convinced that the future of cake mixes lay not in making them unique or special occasion products, but items that the homemaker would want to use regularly and in great volume. This would mean not merely intriguing her with a new way to make a cake occasionally, but giving her a total solution for her everyday baking routine.

3. We decided to provide complete convenience to the consumer, taking all the work out of cake preparation. This was the hottest controversy we had over the product in those days: whether to supply the complete mix, including the eggs, or to allow the housewife to add her own eggs. This point would be argued for years to come on many grounds.

As the weeks passed, the job to be done separated into three major fronts.

In research, there remained a great amount of work to be done to find out if the product produced in volume could keep the same standards we had reached in small quantity in the lab.

On a second front, our divisional management group began wrestling with problems of potential market, cost projections and profit expectations in order to sell the idea of cake mixes to the board of directors.

The program would require immense expenditures and at this time in the company's history, although we were under a mandate to expand vigorously in the area of new consumer products, the actual product category in which we would seek that growth was as yet unsettled. Pillsbury was essentially a flour miller facing a steady decline in the volume of all-purpose and cake flour sold to the homemaker due to equally steady increases in the amount of flour required by commercial bakers. The consumer franchise in Pillsbury's Best family flour was a mainstay of the company and we knew there would be serious questions concerning whether baking mixes would not cause further damage to the family flour volume.

On the third front, we faced the pay-off decisions of marketing. We were not only about to enter an area of the grocery store where products already existed, but we also knew that three or four other major companies were embarking on similar ventures. In those days we lacked much of the research intelligence and skills that have today become a part of the science of consumer marketing. Many of those services that we rely on today were created almost overnight as the need became apparent.

Leo Burnett's advertising agency had the grocery products account at that time and continues a vital part of our marketing effort. They were convinced of the latent power of the Pillsbury brand name, referring to the company's image as that of a "sleeping giant." Our major task, with the agency's help, was to awaken the "giant," mobilize all the elements we had working for us in the brand name and sell the concept of high quality, convenient baking mixes from Pillsbury on a national scale.

Pillsbury knew it was going to be in the race but there was never any guarantee that anybody was going to finish. Baking mixes, after all, were not new. And only in a few cases had they been successful.

The first "mix" might have been U. S. Patent No. 6418, assigned to Jay Fowler of Baltimore (in 1842), in which a balanced "self-rising flour" was prepared from an aged mixture of flour and tartaric acid. The product could be "manufactured into bread without the use of fermenting matter." This was quite a step forward in convenience. However, it would be another forty or fifty years before the product known as self-rising flour would move into broad channels. Ingredients had yet to be produced that could be blended with the flour and moved through the normal pattern of trade without loss of quality or performance in the hands of the consumer.

Many times in the early part of the century attempts were made to produce some kind of baking mix, but again the lack of quality, the need for special ingredients, or some other factor would stall its progress.

World War I created many shortages throughout the country. Two milling companies moved against the need evident in the commercial bakers' desire to remain in the sweet goods or cake business. They both manufactured what was described as a cake baking mix. Neither of the products reached a quality level high enough to become popular.

Successful cake mixes awaited the development of good dry egg whites, further developments in leavening and leavening combinations, and further developments in shortening and emulsifying agents which the industry had learned to incorporate into its shortening.

Two of the early baking mixes were produced by a Mr. Mc-Collum in New Brunswick, New Jersey, who marketed a corn muffin mix in 1920 and produced a pie crust mix in 1922. Mr. McCollum was a student of consumer research. He used church suppers and service club dinners for his research work. For example, he would place two corn muffins on a plate by each of his friends and ask them which one they preferred during the course of the meal.

With his pie crust mix, Mr. McCollum again turned into a student of the consumer as well as one of raw materials. He searched widely until he found the flour and the lard which gave him what he believed to be the best product and then, in the absence of specifications in the early days, he stuck with brand items.

In December of 1929, a molasses company in Pittsburgh, the Duff Company, was trying to find a way to keep molasses as a commodity in the homes of America. Their molasses sales were suffering quite badly as a household item, and they researched the manufacture and sale of a gingerbread mix. They succeeded in drying the molasses in a vacuum drying oven. The molasses formed a hard cake which they then milled into a fine flour or powder and blended with leavenings, eggs, spices and sugar.

The company then conducted a store consumer test by placing seventy-five packages of this mix on a counter in a store in Mount Lebanon, Pennsylvania. The consumers' acceptance of the product started them off to a real development. They used the same system of baking the dough when they introduced their white cake, spice cake and devils food cake mixes between 1930 and 1936.

The Dromedary Company of New Jersey followed closely on the heels of the Duff people and introduced a gingerbread on the Eastern seacoast. Both of these gingerbread products grew very rapidly and were accepted by the consumer prior to World War II.

Just before the war, the Army Quartermaster Corps had been called to evaluate several baking mixes which had been submitted by a number of manufacturers for Army daily rations. Most of the products were unsatisfactory. This result prompted the Quartermaster Corps Research Laboratories to start making studies of baking mixes. Committees were formed consisting of men from industry and from the Quartermaster. By 1943, baking mixes were well on their way into the armed services, but most of them had such rigorous specifications on shelf life that acceptability by the troops was limited. And again, produce improvements were needed in the areas of dry milk, eggs, yeast and an area that was assuming more importance, packaging.

One of the men who participated in the joint industry-government studies was Philip W. Pillsbury, then president and now chairman of the board of The Pillsbury Company.

In late 1939, Phil had been asked to participate in a series of talks on the nature and extent of research facilities in U.S. industry. He returned to Minneapolis from those talks with the view that our research wing should be built up. During the war years the new products area began enlarging, taking on programs in basic research, government projects on dry soup mixes, a dry cereal bar and cake mixes, among other assignments.

Other departments began to spring up in the company as a

result of some things we were learning about the consumer and also because there were some areas where we knew we only had a hunch. We established a commercial research department in 1944 and a year later followed it up with the Home Service Center, a department designed to receive and reflect the homemaker's viewpoint in our product planning sessions.

In 1944 we established our first commercial research department. In earlier years, commercial or market research had not carried a strong impact. We were basically a production-oriented organization—we sold what we could make—and that meant flour, pancake mix, cornmeal and a few other products. Perhaps because of our selling a commodity, we were slow in coming to the change that had been happening in the consumer market since the late 1920's. The purchase of family flour was already in a steady decline and at the same time commercial baking was increasing dramatically. In the family flour business, the era of the hundred-pound sack was drawing to a close and housewives were willing to pay a premium for a smaller package. The housewife, concurrent with the rise of consumer advertising, not only began to respond to new products that offered her convenience but she began to make demands on all manufacturers who provided her with household goods. The dominant voice of the consumer was beginning to be heard and it paid to stop and listen.

The introduction of baking mixes was pending as World War II broke out. And, although there were not many on the market, it was wartime that gave mixes a broad base of consumer acceptance. The living habits of Americans changed. In addition to the rationing of sugar and shortenings, there were more women beginning to work and there was generally less time for meal planning and preparation. This opened the door for time and labor saving foods. But if a shortage of baking ingredients was to discourage home baking and create an inroad for mixes, the manufacturer soon found himself a victim of the same shortages. And the area of baking mixes remained far short of potential expansion.

During these years, many companies had time to accumulate technical knowledge and develop the technical skills they would need when the field was once again ready to grow. And in these years, ingredient manufacturers advanced in the production of materials that would greatly assist in raising the quality of later baking mixes. Companies also had time to examine their marketing methods, improving consumer service areas against the day when they would require a close touch with the sensitivities of consumer trends.

Another step we took in this direction came about in setting up the Ann Pillsbury Home Service Center, a clearing house for recipe information, comments and requests. It was to be, and still is, a corner of the company that interprets and reflects the homemaker's viewpoint to the rest of the planning areas of the company.

Most of these areas were created by necessity as we filled in areas where we felt we needed more information or skill. And, at the same time, we continued on a determined course to the market place with a gradually clearing idea of what we wanted to be when we got there sometime in an indefinite future.

We arrived at the year 1946 with a rough semblance of a finished marketing team. And for the first time we had a close interplay of product research, commercial research, and production and marketing areas of the company. This interplay alone, with the promise of approaching some kind of a frontier, produced a pioneering enthusiasm.

Our first postwar introduction, as a direct result of this effort, was a pie crust mix. Then, from the spring of 1947, the race was on.

In his first sales meeting to introduce pie crust mix, H. R. Galbraith, then grocery sales manager and now head of our Canadian operations, said:

Five years from now, the food mix field will be dominated by only a few outstanding brands. Pillsbury intends to build a strong position in this field in the next five years and we are starting this campaign today. The program includes new manufacturing facilities, new equipment, additional manpower. The fact is that the sales projection figures on our new food mix line call for a greater total volume than the present total volume on our full line of package goods.

In the fall of 1947 Pillsbury introduced a hot roll mix, and the success of pie crust and this new introduction led us to cake mixes within a year.

We were going as fast as we could on cake mix formulation. Mary Kimball, a home economist who felt and radiated the enthusiasm we had, worked many unusual sides of the street in testing sample after sample.

One of the more bizarre problems that had to be tackled was the effect of altitude on the cake mixes. Because Miss Kimball was from Montana and was used to altitude's effect on baked goods, she recognized the fact that it might be a mix problem.

One summer she studied storage and baking problems on a 3,000-mile circle tour of Montana. In the trunk of her car were cartons of hot roll and pie crust mix, and one of a Lemon Gold Cake Mix we had formulated for the military. A recording thermometer told her the high and low temperatures for each twenty-four hours—the high for the trip was 110 degrees, the low, 46. For a time we used a different formula for mixes sold in areas where altitude could affect baking. Further altitude tests were later conducted at Rochester, Minnesota, where the U. S. Air Force no longer needed a pressure chamber. Today each mix has high altitude mixing direction on the package.

Going back to that first day in Doc Harrel's lab, there was never any guarantee that the product could be manufactured. We started testing a formulation by simply blending together home recipe ingredients in very small batches, say enough to make ten cakes. This formula had to be transferred from the very small batch to the pilot plant batch—anywhere from 100 to 500 pounds. This step was not crucial, since the pilot plant, like the lab, used a horizontal mixer method. But when the formula finally got to the mix plant—where they mix 1,000 to 2,000 pounds at a time—the mixing method changed. The fact that the results were sometimes different than those obtained in smaller mixing batches (perhaps the leavening and shortening would not be evenly distributed, for instance) was brought home to us with one particular chocolate cake formulation, highly satisfactory in smaller batches, but finally abandoned at the mix plant level.

We came out with a white cake mix in June of 1948, and followed with Chocolate Fudge Cake Mix a month later. At this point we rolled out all we had as fast as we had it—product and promotion. And, miraculously, the whole program came together at one time.

In analyzing our early experience in the cake mix market and the factors that have made Pillsbury a leader, we must point to the following as significant:

1. The decision to go the "complete mix" route.
2. The decision to enter the market with two flavors rather than one.
3. The decision to make these flavors definitive, that is, to call them what they are and to point out to the consumer exactly what she is getting—a white cake and a chocolate cake.
4. The decision to use the barrelhead, our corporate trademark, in package design.
5. The decision to place the Pillsbury name prominently, and in the same way, on each package.

Research contributed heavily to the first of these decisions. Early surveys revealed that while there was a slight quality preference for the "incomplete" mix, there was a slight "intention to buy" advantage for the "complete" (52 per cent to 47 per cent). We decided to go "complete" since:

1. All things being equal, as is roughly indicated by the above findings, we might as well go the route that gives the consumer more.
2. The women who would be initially attracted to cake mixes would be those urban consumers who had had poor results from their home recipe baking, who were not the experts, and to whom the *convenience* of "complete" mixes

would outweigh the slightly superior results of the "incomplete."

Research made some contribution toward the decision to make definitive flavors and to call these what they are. Some early interviews with women who used an all-purpose cake mix, with its underlying intention of straddling the cake flour and cake mix markets, revealed that women were not exactly sure what the new product would produce and for what purpose it was designed. We felt that there were distinct markets for both a white and a chocolate flavor and, in fact, that the impact of the one would benefit the sale of the other.

The package design decision, of course, was made very early in the game. Our thinking was borne out in the sales test conducted in a series of testing the barrelhead design against others that had been developed.

As we introduced a product market by market, we sustained these introductions with an intensive twice-weekly newspaper campaign. Then, as more and more markets came in, we went to four-color ads in Sunday supplements and then capped the campaign with four-color ads in national magazines.

We became associated with Arthur Godfrey both on radio and later on television, and Art Linkletter injected his own special salesmanship on the Pillsbury House Party.

Our introductory ads were news announcements, geared to dominate as much as possible the media we chose. A typical copy headline might read: "Pillsbury Announces a Revolutionary New Idea in Home Baking!" A secondary copy line that appeared on all the new ads was: "You and Ann Pillsbury can make a great team." This copy line was backed with: "Ann Pillsbury has developed this mix in her kitchen to save you time in your kitchen and give you perfect results every time."

In those mercurial days, selling and distribution were primitive compared with today. One man was often sent from Minneapolis to work with a local branch and introduce the cake mix. The product would be stockpiled in preparation for a market introduction.

We didn't know a great deal about consumer demand at that time. The tests we had made were not so much to determine the size of the market as to find out refinements we could make on our products.

As it turned out, demand exceeded our expectations and our production area was hard put to keep up with sales. Curiosity buying was self-generating. Thought leaders stimulated a great deal of back fence talk on the convenience factor of the new mixes. We sensed, however, that curiosity buying would be short-term and we leaned heavily on maintaining quality and advertising it right along with convenience.

By 1951 we entered the market with a yellow cake mix and then in May of 1952 introduced the first complete angel food cake mix. From then on the line of mixes which we had anticipated grew beyond the range we could ever have projected.

During the first six years of the explosive cake mix market, sales of prepared mixes soared. In 1947 sales of prepared mixes were estimated at about $79 million. Six years later that figure had jumped to over $165 million.

I wish we could say that we were all supremely confident and that we knew exactly what we were doing in making the required business decisions.

In retrospect, it now seems that we couldn't miss.

There were many reasons why those years after World War II were not only greatly stimulating for an enterprising company, but seemed to be ordained for those who could put together the right combination of product, people and program. Men were returning from the armed services with great ambition. The public had endured shortages and rationing and were ready to accept new products. The American food industry, which had just been exploring new frontiers of research at the outbreak of the war, was further captivated with the immense amount of knowledge that had been built up on food processing during the war, and was primed to translate that knowledge into a whole new generation of foods.

It is difficult to separate a viewpoint on the introduction of cake mixes and recollections of the briskness and color of the market place. But certainly here were products that contributed and became a helpful part of a new American mode of living. Ease of preparation, time saving, a good, high quality food, and all the other attributes that Americans have sought and demanded as part of an advanced way of life were part of the cake mix story. So were some hunches, some baling wire and a remarkable collection of colleagues and old-fashioned competitors.

KARSH-OTTAWA

JUDSON B. BRANCH

Allstate Insurance Companies

Judson B. Branch was elected president and chief executive officer of Allstate Insurance Companies in February, 1957. Mr. Branch, an alumnus of the University of Michigan, has been associated with Allstate since 1934. Except for Army service from 1943 to 1946 in the Pacific area, he progressed uninterruptedly from Allstate's investment department to treasurer to vice-president and finally to his present position as chief executive officer. As one of Allstate's first agents, he helped establish the company's revolutionary merchandising idea of selling insurance over the counter in Sears stores, which was the most recent development in Sears' "Counterrevolution in the Insurance World."

The Good Hands

The Counterrevolution in the Insurance World

B Y

JUDSON B. BRANCH

The Chicago Northwestern commuter train left Highland Park station at 7:28 on a frosty morning in 1930—destination: Chicago's Loop. On board, sleepy suburbanites dozed, read bankruptcy notices in the Depression news, or whiled away the time playing bridge.

Among the players on that particular morning were General Robert E. Wood, President of Sears, Roebuck and Company, and Carl L. Odell, an insurance broker. Odell held a winning hand—and an idea.

"Why don't you fellows over at Sears start an auto insurance company and sell by mail?" he asked General Wood.

So, like all good business adventure stories, this one began with an idea—a simple idea which at the time probably caused no more than a pause in the game, but that idea was destined to revolutionize the insurance industry, create an insurance group whose assets would one day exceed a billion dollars, and obtain nearly seven million policies in force with the pledge that "You're in good hands with Allstate."

To less visionary men, Odell's suggestion that a merchandising firm go into the insurance business might have been passed off as a completely impractical idea, for on this frosty morning in 1930, the times were anything but right for launching a new business venture. Only a few months before, the bottom had fallen out of the nation's economy, toppling long-established businesses into the depths of our greatest depression. The man on the street was chiefly concerned with closed factories, collapsing banks, and foreclosed mortgages. Automobile insurance was surely the furthest thing from his mind.

The story might have ended there.

But once General Wood recognized an opportunity to extend his company's services to the public he was not easily turned aside. The more he thought about Odell's suggestion, the more firmly convinced he became that even in those bad times there was a great need for low-cost auto insurance. Only then, he reasoned—when insurance protection was available to all— could development of the automobile continue.

In 1930 few men understood the important role the automobile was to play in reshaping the American economy. But General Wood realized that the increased mobility the auto provides would enable people to move from the shadow of the city smokestack into suburban areas. The farmer would soon drive beyond the nearest town's main street to buy his necessities. For these reasons, in the closing years of the 1920's, despite the skeptical reservations of many of his business associates, General Wood had established many new Sears retail stores around the perimeter of larger cities and in small towns, where they were to become the first outlying shopping centers, as we now know them.

So General Wood decided to "look into" the insurance business. He asked Carl Odell to prepare a memorandum outlining his suggestion. Experts were called in, and an exhaustive study of insurance problems was undertaken. Applying his own wide and varied background to the problem, General Wood saw that the whole business of selling and servicing insurance policies could be streamlined and simplified. He saw many similarities between the problems of insurance and the problems he faced and conquered in the field of retail merchandising. He knew that a modern insurance company would have to keep overhead costs down and sell quality services to the public at the lowest possible prices. Traditionally, the expense of getting new policyholders had contributed sizably to the cost of a policy. General Wood planned to save expenses by offering his insurance directly to the public.

"We'll keep the policyholder's interests well in mind," he said, "settle his claims rapidly and fairly and offer the best value in a policy, just as Sears offers in the merchandise field. Then our policyholders will renew year after year." The result would be substantial savings in the cost of getting policyholders, lower rates and better service. The General expected rates to average out at about 20 per cent less than those charged by most other companies.

These were the ideas which General Wood had on his mind in October of 1930 when he called a meeting of the Sears Officers' Board. The meeting was held in the General's office in Chicago. Odell's suggestion and a chain of supporting ideas were presented to the officers. All of the officers present were hard-headed merchandising men who were used to speaking their minds. Several challenged the wisdom of backing such a venture during the depths of the Depression. Others expressed considerable doubt as to the profit-making potential of the proposal. However, General Wood held firm and the meeting ended with the Officers' Board giving its approval.

General Wood put G. E. Humphrey, a Sears officer, in charge of the project. Humphrey prepared the following memorandum for submission to the Sears Board of Directors:

November 5, 1930

MEMORANDUM FOR BOARD OF DIRECTORS

It is proposed that Sears, Roebuck and Co. furnish the capital and organize an insurance company for the purpose of selling various kinds of insurance to their customers at reduced rates. While the company would be chartered to handle diversified lines, it would confine its activities at the outset to writing automobile insurance on selected classes of Sears' customers, in restricted areas, and would not advertise such insurance in the catalog until the organization had been perfected, experience as to loss ratios gained and reserves built up.

Sears, Roebuck and Co. is in a very favorable position to enter this field, due to its large mailing list, the sound character of its customer list and its facilities for reaching these customers at small expense. The cost of organization, the cost of producing business and the operating expense will be very moderate.

There is a large field for the expansion of automobile insurance, which is coming to be almost a necessity. In providing it at reduced rates to its customers, Sears will be performing a service for them which should result in increased good will.

The financial aspects of the proposal have been fully and carefully investigated and it is apparent that this business will not only furnish a substantial profit from underwriting operations but will also add greatly to the resources of Sears, Roebuck and Co.

The proposal has been fully presented to the Officers' Board and has its approval.

The Board of Directors will be asked at the next meeting to consider this question and approve or disapprove this investment.

G. E. HUMPHREY

What followed can best be described in General Wood's own words:

I took this memorandum and went out to New York and met the outside directors of Sears Roebuck in the Goldman, Sachs office. I can remember very well it was a dark day in Novem-

ber. The Depression was a year old and getting worse all
the time. And when I sprung this bombshell on them, though
they were all old friends and old associates, their reception
at the approaching was pretty frigid. However, I won them
over, and on November 17, when we had our regular meeting
in Chicago, this was the resolution that was passed:

"Resolved that this board generally approves the plan outlined by Colonel Humphrey with reference to the sale by
the company of automobile and accident insurance, and that
the president of the company be authorized at his discretion to adopt said plan and put the same into operation if
no additional objections are developed upon further investigation of said plan by the president [I then being president of Sears]."

On April 17, 1931, the Allstate Insurance Company commenced business.

However, a month before Allstate was officially incorporated,
leaders of the traditionally conservative insurance industry already were warily indicating their interest in the fledgling operation. On March 12, 1931, the *Wall Street Journal* carried the
following story:

Sears, Roebuck & Co. is preparing to sell insurance by
mail, as well as washing machines, harness, rubber boots and
other merchandise. . . .

Some insurance men asserted that, should the new venture
meet with success, it would result in substantial decreases in
insurance costs and have an adverse effect upon the present
agency system. Others contended that the nature of the insurance business presented unsurmountable obstacles to any
attempts to handle it through mail-order houses. All agreed,
however, that it was an interesting experiment and would
be closely watched by the insurance world.

Four days later, the *Wall Street Journal* carried a second story,
this one datelined Hartford, then the insurance capital of the
United States:

Sears Roebuck & Co.'s plan to organize the Allstate Insurance Co. to write automobile risks by mail will be watched closely. Insurance may be written without state license anywhere, but registrations and license are necessary to "do business" in a state. Sending an agent to solicit business or an adjuster to settle claims into a state constitutes doing business. Underwriting experience on business obtained without personal contact will be watched by insurance executives, who will also be interested in the experience in settling claims.

The experience of new companies engaging in business is that large sums are necessary to set up unearned premium reserves in proportion to the volume of business written. These reserves are proportionate according to one, two, three or more years of coverage. First year percentages are large. These reserves are drawn from surplus in newly organized companies, hence a large premium on the par value of stock is necessary.

A policyholder having a legal action against a company not licensed in the state where he lives has to go to the domicile of the company to get into court.

When Allstate commenced business April 17, 1931, it was the first time in the history of the insurance industry that a general merchandising firm had entered the field—a vital field already including hundreds of companies and steeped in long established traditions and procedures. The name "Allstate" was borrowed from Sears' line of auto tires.

While the rest of the country sang "Brother Can You Spare a Dime?" Sears financed the fledgling company with $700,000, of which $350,000 was set up as capital and $350,000 as surplus. All operations except claim settlements were to be by mail. The insurance was offered through the catalog with a clip-out mail coupon for those who were interested. Prospects who replied were mailed an insurance quotation and application form. If the form was returned with the premium, a policy then was mailed to the customer.

Lessing J. Rosenwald was the first chairman of the board of Allstate. G. E. Humphrey was appointed president. Odell, who acted as general manager, was listed as vice-president and secretary of the organization. W. N. Lowe, an experienced Sears methods man, was assigned to Allstate to make sure the mechanics of its operations conformed to Sears' principles and utilized fully the company's funds of experience in operating economies.

During the first year of operation, a total of twenty people handled the work in Allstate's "home office," which occupied 1,500 square feet in Room 124, a small, first-floor office in the Sears Administration Building in Chicago. Allstate, conceived as another merchandising department, was identified as Department 709. Allstate still bears this departmental designation within the Sears family.

During 1931, over a half million circulars were sent out, including a special mailing to Sears stockholders and employees. Ads telling of the new Sears-owned company, with prominent "Fill Out and Mail Now" coupons, followed suit in Sears catalogs and produced 40,000 inquiries.

William A. Lehnertz of Aurora, Illinois, received a circular in Allstate's initial mailing. He sent in the coupon, promptly received a rate quotation and mailed his premium back the same day to become Allstate's Policyholder No. 1. General Wood was the first member of the Sears employee family to purchase a policy. Shortly afterward the first claim was paid when an insured walked into our first floor office in the Sears Administration Building one noon hour with an automobile door handle in his hand. It had been broken off the policyholder's car in an attempted auto theft earlier that day. The entire twenty-man staff leaped into action—only to discover no one had arranged to have claim forms printed! Undaunted, the staff quickly ascertained the policyholder's loss and paid his claim.

Allstate's first precedent-shattering move, as noted above, was the sale of insurance by mail order, thus becoming one of the insurance industry's early "direct writers." * From that time for-

---

* Strictly speaking, a "direct writer" is an insurance company which sells by mail directly to the public without the use of agents or other sales personnel.

ward, any resemblance between Allstate and the traditional practices of the insurance industry as a whole was purely coincidental.

During the eight and a half months it operated during 1931, Allstate's mail-order operations brought in $118,000 in premiums, and 4,217 automobiles were insured. The company suffered a $70,000 operating loss. In addition, as the stock and bond market fell continuously during the year, there was an additional loss of $185,000 from that depreciation, making the company's total loss for 1931 $255,000. However, by the end of its second year of operation, Allstate's premiums amounted to $540,000 and it was operating at a profit, a phenomenal feat for any new company—especially as 1932 was the trough of the Depression!

The 356 per cent increase in premiums over 1931 was partly due to the company's becoming licensed in more and more states. Legally, Allstate Insurance Company could operate country-wide with only a license from its home state, Illinois. However, as the *Wall Street Journal* had pointed out, Allstate could not "do business" (that is, send in agents to solicit business or adjusters to settle claims) in any state in which it was not licensed.

Thus, although Allstate was able to sell insurance and settle claims efficiently by mail, it became obvious during the first year that the company's growth would be dependent upon becoming licensed in all states. However, as the company moved to become licensed in other states, a second roadblock appeared—many states forbade a casualty insurance company to write any form of *fire* insurance, even on an automobile. To meet this new situation, the Allstate Fire Insurance Company was incorporated on December 30, 1931, with a capital of $200,000 and surplus of $75,000.

Although its charter permitted it to write the standard lines of fire insurance on dwellings, the Allstate Fire Insurance Company at first limited its writing to physical loss or damage to automobiles. It also absorbed similar insurance already written on automobiles in states which demanded a separation of the two types of protection.

The two companies' combined premium volumes, all written

by mail, reached $673,000 in 1933. Nevertheless, the limitations of selling insurance solely by mail, which were apparent to Allstate's management from the very first, became even more pressing now.

During the first months following Allstate's organization in 1931, Odell and Lowe had discussed the possibility of hiring salesmen and placing them in Sears store locations where they could sell Allstate insurance and make telephone contacts with prospects in the area who had written and inquired about auto insurance. As an alternative, Odell and the Allstate management team had placed metal Allstate Insurance signs, with small boxes holding auto insurance pamphlets, in Sears retail stores in Chicago.

In January of 1933, Odell received a report from Sears based on a limited survey of store managers. The report indicated that the small stores were receiving more inquiries about Allstate Insurance than were the large stores. This was due to the fact that Allstate advertising had been concentrated mainly in the catalog and in mail sent to catalog customers. The percentage of customers familiar with the catalog was greater in small towns than in the cities. This study made one thing apparent: Allstate had not yet tapped the greatest field for selling auto insurance—the metropolitan centers. The report recommended the possibility of hiring insurance agents to work in Sears stores and to call on prospects in their homes.

A few months later, Odell received another report, this one from his own staff, which indicated that Allstate was not securing its share of new business because it was operating exclusively by mail and was, in fact, losing a few renewals because it had no local agents to develop and maintain personal contacts with the public. This report also recommended that agents be established in Sears stores.

Later in the year, by way of an experiment, Allstate opened its first sales office—in the Sears display in the Transportation Building at the Chicago "Century of Progress." On the Fair's Midway, the first Allstate agent made his debut—a young man named Richard E. Roskam, who today is our Pacific Coast sales manager. The success of this sales experiment, plus continued requests from Sears store managers for "someone to answer insurance queries from customers," led to a decision to open sales offices in Sears retail stores. The following year, the first permanent over-the-counter sales-service office was opened in a Sears store in Chicago, at 63rd and Halsted Streets. I am proud to say that I had the privilege of being one of the first Allstate salesmen pioneering in that store. This was the nucleus from which grew our outstanding agency force, that has done so much in helping us achieve our phenomenal growth.

Shortly after we opened this first sales office in 1934, sales offices were opened in eight additional Sears stores and Allstate moved from its initial phase of being a direct writer to its present stage of being an "exclusive agency" company. In order to explain these terms and their significance, we must first consider the state of the insurance industry when we entered the field.

Today, there is intense competition in the casualty insurance business, but it was another story when we began. When we began in 1931, the field was staid and had been dominated for years by companies which operated under the so-called American agency or independent agency system. These companies marketed their insurance through a system composed of agents who sell the policies of several companies at the same time.

Besides operating under this system of distribution, most of these companies belonged to a "bureau" or organization which compiled statistics and established the rates they would charge in the various states. By agreement, all member companies charged the same rates.

Since rates and forms generally were the same, the companies sought favor with the agents rather than with the public. Thus, under this system, most competition by the companies in those years was for the business of the agents through payment of higher commissions and special allowances.

At the same time, a small share of the total fire and casualty business was written by certain insurance companies (mostly mutuals) which used a different system to sell their insurance. They were called exclusive agency companies. (In the life insur-

ance field, most companies operate as exclusive agency companies.) The essential characteristic of the exclusive agency system
is that the agent sells the policies of only one insurance company or group and does not sell insurance for any other organization. (In addition, Allstate's agents are considered employees so
as to be eligible for our liberal employee benefit program, including the right to participate in the famous Sears Profit Sharing
Plan.) A few exclusive agency companies also were distinguisha-
ble from the independent agency and bureau companies in that
they offered their policyholders lower net rates—either through
a dividend at the end of the year or in rare cases through a lower
rate structure. Their volume was relatively small and their competitive impact slight.

When Allstate began selling by mail in 1931, it caused considerable stir among the conservative elements in the insurance business, not only because it was then operating as a direct writer
but was deviating from the standard bureau rates, thereby forcing price competition for the public's favor. In fact some of our
earliest ads were built around the price theme. An early ad read:

Pay Yourself

A 20% Commission

Every Year on Your

Auto Insurance

Under the Allstate auto insurance plan,

because you sell yourself, you get this

protection . . . any or all coverages offered by

any standard stock insurance company . . . at 20% lower cost.

So long as we operated as a direct writer, our old-line competitors were fairly certain our growth would be so slow that we
would not be able to challenge their domination of the field.
However, imagine their alarm when that small group of us were
hired as agents and Allstate thus became an exclusive agency
company. The reactions were extreme, sometimes bitter, and occasionally humorous.

For example, the magazine called *The Insurance Broker* published one letter from an insurance broker that began, "The re-

cently adopted Sears, Roebuck & Co. plan of selling insurance over the counter and by mail order is hardly complimentary to the veteran insurance man who always believed that his occupation was a profession with advisory relations carrying beyond the realm of a mail-order transaction." It ended with the following paragraph:

"In the name of humanity and common sense, we, the insurance people of Chicago, believing that our system is still worth saving and can be saved, and invoking the co-operation of insurance and other thinking people throughout the land, call a halt to the encroachment of these destroyers who by the accident of their existence at this time and place see in it only the opportunity to rush in and grab to the exclusion and deprivation of those who are not proud to be named their fellow sojourners."

Another broker sent a copy of the letter from the magazine to General Wood. In his cover memo, this broker wrote that the letter "is respectfully referred to you as expressing the views of many engaged in the profession of insurance as a salesman, if you please. As insurance brokers licensed by the State to engage in that profession as are doctors, lawyers and other professions, we believe that the buyer of insurance can best be served by personal contact with a person properly fitted to engage in the profession by long experience if necessary or intensive schooling of shorter duration and I for one am 'fighting it out' along that line." General Wood dryly referred the correspondence to Carl Odell with a simple "Please note."

What these detractors failed to point out, or to admit, was that Odell, who acted as general manager of Allstate, had been an experienced and highly successful broker himself, and that Allstate was pursuing the policy of giving its agents intensive training before they applied for and received state licensing.

What was the basis of this antagonism? Why were the "independent agency" advocates so vociferous in their attack on our fledgling company? Apart from the dislike many feel for having the ranks of their competing companies increased by one, much of the concern was over the fact that we were in a position to bring about real competition between the companies, which could ultimately benefit only the public under the American free enterprise system.

The reason Allstate was in a position to set competition was not only because it was using the revolutionary marketing technique of selling through retail stores, but also because it, a stock company, had chosen the exclusive agency method of selling.

Under the independent agency system there had developed intense competition among the insurance companies for the favor and business of the independent brokers. Often this resulted in higher commissions and most always a lenient attitude toward the acceptance of questionable and sometimes obviously undesirable business. As part of his ownership of and control over the ultimate policyholder, the independent agent traditionally prepared the actual policies, collected all the premiums, and generally handled much of the detailed clerical work. The decentralization of routine operations to this degree was less efficient —in dollar terms, at least—than having the work done in large central offices.

On the other hand, under the exclusive agency system, the agent is truly a salesman, since selling and counseling are his primary function. These agents are usually trained by the company and then must be licensed by the state in which they sell, just as are the independent agents. But, unlike the independent agents, they are not overburdened with clerical work. Instead, they forward the signed applications and any premium monies collected to the company office, where underwriting review, policy issuance, billing and related clerical detail are handled.

With clerical expense as well as office and advertising costs paid by the company, the Allstate agent receives lower compensation per unit sale than most independent agents. But because he is free to devote full time to building a large sales volume, our experienced agents traditionally have been among the best paid in the business.

A natural result of the exclusive agency system is that the agent is dealing with the policy forms, rating plans and manuals of a single company or group of companies. This saves considerable time and effort, compared with the independent agent's attempts to keep current on the forms, rates and manuals of a number of different companies. Thus, the exclusive agent has that much more time to devote to selling and servicing his customer instead of shuffling papers. Dealing with a single set of underwriting guides is also timesaving and promotes better agent underwriting.

As a result of these characteristics, Allstate, as an exclusive agency company, was able to offer lower net premiums because of expense savings due to more efficient mass handling of routine clerical work. The lower rates, in turn, have attracted a large number of better-than-average drivers, bringing further loss savings.

However, in our early years our detractors sought innumerable roadblocks to put in our way. In some states, for example, we were not allowed to offer our auto insurance at lower rates than those charged by the bureau companies, even though we demonstrated the soundness of our lower rate structure and the obvious public benefit it represented.

I am happy to say that most of the distractions were temporary and did not prevent us from growing. Our expansion continued at a rapid pace. Each year the company became licensed in additional states. New sales and claim offices opened all over the country.

In its fifth year of operation Allstate's premium volume passed the first million. This impressive rate of growth continued until World War II, when gas rationing and the halt in auto production naturally slowed progress, but failed to stop it.

The staff of twenty people with which Allstate had started in one room of the Sears Administration Building had expanded rapidly. Allstate's dazzling success and prospects attracted ambitious and aggressive people to its employee family.

One of their first accomplishments was the establishment in 1939 of a rating plan that would differentiate between various types of risks. The "father" of this plan, known as the tailored rating plan, was Clarence B. Kenney, who had answered Allstate's "underwriter wanted" ad in 1931 and had taken charge of Allstate's underwriting problems from the beginning. Annual mileage, use of car, driver's age and other factors are taken into consideration in determining rates under Allstate's tailored rating plan. This method, further refined by Allstate several times since, proved to be so successful that most other companies eventually adopted similar rating plans.

The man primarily responsible for our growth during the war and postwar years was Calvin Fentress, Jr., who joined Allstate in 1932 as head of our newly created investment department, rose to executive vice-president and then to president in 1941.

During the forties, state after state passed financial responsibility laws, making it both practical and wise for automobile owners to carry property damage and bodily injury liability insurance. Because we were known to be easily accessible to the public, by virtue of our convenient locations in Sears stores, and because of our aggressive advertising program during this period, a great portion of the motoring public in these states turned to us for their auto insurance. In fact, the demand was so great in one large Eastern city that on the night before the financial responsibility law was to go into effect, long lines were still forming at the Allstate location when it was time to close the Sears store. The store stayed open a couple of hours longer, but finally had to close. So as not to disappoint the people who had been waiting so patiently, the Allstate agents moved card tables to the sidewalk in front of the store and prepared insurance applications until every last customer in the line was served.

One of the reasons Allstate was in a position to handle the public's demand for insurance at this time was partly the result of a decision made during the early days of World War II to hire women to replace the agents who were called into service. The man partially responsible for this decision was Davis W. Ellis, who joined Allstate in 1942 as educational director. To him fell the job of recruiting outstanding saleswomen and training them in the insurance field. These women took the assignments "for the duration," understanding that they would be replaced by the men when they returned from service. It was largely as a result of the women's efforts that Allstate even managed to grow during the war years and was able to meet the public's sharp demand in states where the financial responsibility laws were enacted. A third result of the decision to use a female sales force was that Allstate was in a position to begin its expansion immediately after World War II was over and did not have to wait to build up a new sales force. We were able to launch our postwar sales plans without a hitch, while the returning veterans gradually replaced the women on the sales force.

Since many of us still think of the end of World War II as the relatively recent past, it is revealing to note the size of our operation at year-end 1945. Policyholders had reached 327,000 and premium volume, $12,030,000, and while this represented a significant attainment, the years ahead obviously were to bring far more rapid growth. By 1963, the policyholder family had increased to almost 7,000,000 and premiums from the fire and casualty operation alone exceeded $631,000,000.

The intervening years, under Mr. Fentress' leadership, were marked by one product improvement after another. For example, to help the policyholder understand exactly what coverage he had or had not bought with his policy, Allstate, in 1947, introduced the tradition-shattering Illustrator policy. Unlike the usual standard forms, it contained illustrations to call attention to important sections of the policy, and was written in fewer words and simplified language. With this change began years of research on the part of Allstate which has further simplified its later insurance policies' terminology and design. Newer contracts also have afforded increased coverages. The Allstate Crusader auto policy introduced in 1956 then offered the broadest coverage in one policy in the history of auto insurance. The policy contained more than twenty improvements and several new coverages never before offered in an auto insurance policy.

With the new Crusader policy, in many states Allstate offered voluntary protection against losses caused by uninsured motorists. This has proven to be one of the most important developments in the automobile insurance industry and now is widely offered by most companies as a more effective answer to the problem of uninsured motorists than can be provided by any form of compulsory insurance.

To speed adjustment of claims and provide greater convenience to customers, Allstate, in 1952, opened the first of its more than 350 drive-in claim offices. While pioneering and popularizing this service, the company has developed the largest full-time salaried claim staff (almost 6,000 people) in the automobile insurance business. No other company has exerted such tremendous influence in making insurance understandable and convenient to the public.

The establishment and smooth operation of our drive-ins and hundreds of other local sales-service offices would not have been possible except for a major decision to begin an extensive program of decentralization after World War II. Since the company was organized in 1931, the home office in Chicago had kept a heavy hand on the controls. But in 1947, I was assigned the responsibility of making the decentralization idea a reality. During the next few years, an increasing number of zone and regional offices and local service offices were established to carry on the day-to-day insurance business directly with the customer.

In decentralization, there are three organization levels. Home office establishes policy and is responsible for basic planning, research, and product development. Zone offices (we have four) interpret home office policy and give guidance to the regional offices. At the twenty-nine regional offices, the plans are translated into action.

Regional management, working within the framework of these plans, helps establish sales and income goals for its area and is then held accountable for their achievement. The regional offices administer a total of 1,600 local sales-service locations. This philosophy of decentralization has strengthened Allstate because service can be given and problems ironed out immediately at the local level without delay or inconvenience in referring the policyholder to the home office. Freedom of regional management to experiment invariably leads to improved methods—a factor which has contributed greatly to Allstate's tremendous growth during the fifties and early sixties.

While Allstate had sold auto insurance by mail order or from sales offices in Sears stores in the thirties and forties, we were well aware that a large segment of the insurable public did not go shopping for insurance. To reach this market, a new sales program was inaugurated in 1950. Agents formerly spending full time in Sears stores now make appointment calls to the homes and businesses of prospects. Also, other agents were assigned to local sales offices or insurance centers separate and apart from Sears stores.

It was during this same period that our famous slogan, "You're in Good Hands with Allstate," was born. The Allstate slogan had its beginning in a crisis involving the family of one of our officers, Davis W. Ellis. In the spring of 1951, when he was our general sales manager, Mr. Ellis's youngest daughter was stricken with hepatitis a few days before she was to graduate from high school.

Late that summer, Dave Ellis, our advertising manager Robert Gorman, and advertising agency representatives were planning Allstate's first big national advertising campaign for the coming year. The group felt the need for a basic theme, an idea which would symbolize Allstate's unique position in serving its policyholder family. As the day wore into evening, suggestion after suggestion was discarded. When the group was about to give up for the day, Dave remembered a talk he had with his wife shortly after their daughter fell ill. Upon arriving home after the girl had been admitted to the hospital, his anxiety was relieved considerably when his wife met him at the door and said: "The hospital says not to worry. We're in good hands with Dr. ————."

Then and there the slogan was born. Dave's subsequent suggestion that it be illustrated by a drawing of a pair of hands cradling a car also was accepted. Drawings of a house and of people were added later as Allstate entered the homeowners and life insurance fields. The slogan has become one of the best-known in insurance.

Allstate management concentrated not only on physical expansion, but also on the number of products it could offer the public and the quality of protection promised in each policy. For example: auto insurance, which had been Allstate's sole product for two decades, was joined in the fifties by a full line of insurance products. Comprehensive personal liability, residential fire,

theft, homeowners, health, and boatowners insurance, plus Allstate life insurance, provided a full circle of protection for the
Allstate policyholder.

As had been the case in the automobile line, very little price
competition existed when we entered the residential property
and, later, the commercial insurance lines, despite the fact that
hundreds of companies had preceded us into each of these fields.
However, our marketing philosophy and policyholder service
methods soon helped establish a new competitive climate which
we believe has been to the ultimate benefit of the public.

In 1957, when I was elected president of Allstate and Mr. Fentress became chairman of the board, a new Allstate philosophy
was taking shape—the philosophy that an agent has not filled
the insurance needs of the individual until he has offered what
we call a Full Circle of Protection for income, car, home and
business. Allstate's alert response to public need was illustrated
in the late fifties when compact cars caught the public's fancy. In
October, 1959, Allstate's liability and collision insurance was
offered at a 10 per cent discount on compact domestic and foreign cars. Allstate was the first major insurance company to offer
premium discounts specifically to owners of the increasingly popular small automobiles.

In May of 1960, Allstate came up with one of the most significant innovations in automobile insurance history. Until that time
automobile liability insurance could be canceled by companies
at any time for any reason upon only ten days' notice. Then Allstate introduced its revolutionary Pledge Against Cancellation
Plan—a plan never before offered by any other company. As I
indicated earlier, this plan promises policyholders in writing that
cancellation of auto liability insurance cannot be initiated because of accidents for periods up to five years once the insurance
has been in force sixty days. This plan is offered in most states
and covers more than four million policyholders.

In 1960 a distinctive Allstate Good Driver Plan was introduced
in many states offering good drivers the lowest rate for their
particular driver classification, while persons with chargeable accidents pay higher rates. This Good Driver Plan, coupled with

the Pledge Against Cancellation program, placed Allstate in a class by itself. No other auto insurance company had ever before offered such an attractive product. It also was in keeping with Allstate's determination to always make competition, not just meet it. As is the case in most advances under our free enterprise system, this move was in the best interest of the public, and many other auto insurance companies have followed suit in a limited way, but with most their pledges apply only to the balance of the one-year or six-month term of their policies.

In business insurance Allstate expanded its products during the fifties to include commercial fire and commercial liability. In 1958 Allstate began offering group life insurance and group health insurance through its Special Accounts Division. Allstate also has become one of the world's largest insurers of truck and automobile fleets, insuring the vehicles of almost three thousand companies. The Special Accounts Division services these accounts and many other risks whose exposures extend beyond the territory of any one regional office.

Allstate has serviced the accounts of some of the largest companies in the world—names like Ford, Westinghouse, Glidden, U. S. Gypsum, International Shoe Company, Kimberly-Clark, American Oil, Sears, A. O. Smith, and H. J. Heinz, to name but a few.

Paralleling Allstate's growth in products during the fifties was its expansion into markets outside the United States. It began in Canada in 1953 with the opening of a regional office in Toronto and a second in Vancouver a short time later. Within three years Allstate was one of the largest auto insurers in Canada and it now writes the full circle of insurance coverages there. Allstate expanded into Alaska in 1955 and Hawaii in 1956, anticipating the growth of our country to fifty United States. In 1959 the organization of Allstate International S.A., and a subsidiary, Altstadt Versicherungs, AG., both headquartered in Zurich, Switzerland, marked Allstate's entry into the international market. In 1960 Allstate further extended its foreign insurance operations by becoming affiliated with a Mexican company.

Another important service which has been created to serve the

Allstate policyholder family and members of the interested public is the Allstate Motor Club, a division of Allstate Enterprises, Inc. Organized in 1961, the motor club offers the first truly national service of its kind in the United States. Memberships are offered through Allstate insurance agents, who also are representatives of Allstate Enterprises.

Allstate Enterprises, which also is a Sears subsidiary, offers auto financing services in many states, operates two savings and loan associations in California, and provides other non-insurance services as companion products to Allstate insurance.

Thus, when Allstate Insurance Company's thirty-third anniversary rolled around in 1964, the foresight and initial decision of General Wood can be said to have resulted in one of the largest multiple line insurance groups in the world, with international offices in Europe, Mexico and Canada, 29 regional offices, 219 district service offices, more than 1,600 sales-service centers, assets exceeding $1 billion, more than 6.8 million policies in force, and more than 5,000 professionally trained, state-licensed agents backed up by an additional staff of some 14,000 service personnel.

In telling our story, we have necessarily had to limit our account to selected aspects of our development. Left untold is the story of our Allstate Life Insurance Company, which surpassed in 1963 the historic one billion dollar level of individual policyholder's insurance in force in the record-breaking time of six years. The Allstate Life Insurance Company is wholly owned by Allstate Insurance Company and will contribute significantly to our future growth and income.

Looking at our past, four ten-year bench marks in terms of premium volume give a good idea of how our fire and casualty operation has grown.

NET PREMIUMS WRITTEN, ALLSTATE INSURANCE COMPANY

1933	1943	1953	1963
$673,000	$7,348,000	$173,613,000	$631,285,000 (est.)

How was this growth of nearly 1,000 per cent achieved? By price alone? Actually, it was achieved largely and primarily through the high quality of our people—our agents, claims personnel, service people, planners and all of the other men and women who have been attracted to our company over the years and have made our philosophy of a good insurance product, fairly priced and made conveniently available to the public, a reality.

These figures are, of course, one measure of the success of our company. No less a measure are the innumerable community service contributions Allstate and its employee family have made during the thirty-three years of the organization's existence. These public service contributions also are in accord with the philosophy of Allstate's founder, General Wood, who has said, "Business must account for its stewardship not only on the balance sheet, but also in matters of social responsibility."

The fact that the "Good Hands" of Allstate grew from a few hands of bridge on a commuter train also is in accord with the American dream, where the free enterprise system has made it possible to bring the greatest good to the greatest number, whether in insurance, material products or economic opportunities.

WARREN LEE PIERSON

Great Western Financial Corporation

WARREN LEE PIERSON has been chairman of the board of Great Western Financial Corporation since it was organized in 1955. Mr. Pierson graduated from Harvard Law School in 1922. After practicing law in California, he became special counsel for the Reconstruction Finance Corporation in 1933 and served as president and general counsel of the Export-Import Bank from 1936 through 1944. He is also a past president of the International Air Transport Association and of the International Chamber of Commerce. In 1951 he was U.S. delegate to the Tripartite Commission on German Debts with the rank of ambassador.

The Savings Accounts That Build America's Homes

The Growth of the S & L's

BY

WARREN LEE PIERSON

One day in the summer of 1955, I received a phone call from Paul Manheim, a partner of the distinguished New York investment banking firm of Lehman Brothers.

"Warren, we've just become interested in a little company in California we'd like you to head up if you have the time," Manheim said. "It's in the savings and loan field and although there's not much money involved, we think the company has good prospects."

Because a number of the companies of which I was then a director were clients of Lehman and I had come to respect that firm's judgment, I agreed, although I didn't think of the company Manheim described as much more than "just another mortgage company." The major function of a savings and loan association is, of course, to use its savers' funds to make real estate loans, primarily on homes.

Certainly, little did I realize at the time that the company that was to become known as the Great Western Financial Corporation would eventually grow to be a billion dollar financial giant and become the largest publicly-held company of its kind in the world. Nor that it would play an important role in changing the character and accelerating the growth of the nation's now-$100 billion savings and loan industry which today serves as custodian of the savings of more than 35.5 million Americans and provides the financing for nearly half of America's new homes.

All this is particularly surprising in view of the casual, almost accidental, chain of circumstances which, as I soon learned, led to the beginnings of Great Western, to say nothing of the obstacles that threatened its very formation and growth. An added element of drama in the Great Western billion dollar success story also lies in the fact that the two key persons most responsible for it started out in life as poor boys who had learned to make their own way in the world.

One was Morris Natelson, another of the House of Lehman's partners, who, several months before my conversation with Manheim, had made a trip to Southern California in connection with the public financing of an insurance company in Los Angeles. Though a native New Yorker, Natelson had always been a great believer in the future of California. As a knowledgeable investment banker, he also sensed the great growth that lay ahead for both population and housing in the state. While in Los Angeles on this particular trip, Natelson asked the people in the Lehman Brothers' office there to investigate the home financing business in California and send him a report on it.

Several weeks later, Natelson, back in New York, found the report on his desk. It painted a glowing picture of California and contained numerous figures attesting to its rapid growth. During the preceding ten-year period, population in the Los Angeles area alone had increased from 3,510,000 to 5,265,000—or by 50 per cent. New residents were now flocking in at the rate of five hundred a day—one every three minutes. This population explosion spawned many new, expanding industries—aerospace, rubber, auto assembly, to name only a few. However, the report noted that none had posted the growth statisticians had recorded for the relatively old savings and loan business, which had become synonymous with home financing in California. To meet fast-growing Los Angeles' housing needs, some 700,000 family dwelling units had been built since 1945. And in 1955 savings and loan associations were already financing more than a third (37 per cent) of the homes in the area—were, in fact, the largest institutional home lenders there. On a statewide basis, the figures were equally as impressive. The report concluded with a summary of the development and tremendous growth of the savings and loan business not only in California but in the nation as a whole.

Natelson read the report with great interest. With it, to his surprise, was a letter from his Los Angeles office indicating that a local company known as the Great Western Savings and Loan Association might be for sale. The association's president, the other key person in our story, was a man named Adolph Slechta, whose life in many ways is the personification of the American dream.

Born in 1904 to poor Czech immigrants, young, hard-working and astute Slechta was brought up in St. Louis but, like many others of his generation, moved to California in the early 1930's to broaden his opportunities in a place where, according to legend, money grew on trees and the streets were paved with gold. Though handicapped by the lack of a college education, Slechta became a public accountant, a calling which he had studied largely by correspondence and in night school. One day in 1943 he was hired to unravel the tangled financial affairs of a Los Angeles escrow company. (Escrow companies, which are peculiar to Southern California, perform, for a small fee, the vast majority of the real estate closing services that are connected with real estate title transfers. This function is more customarily filled elsewhere by title companies and attorneys, and by the escrow departments of banks and other lenders.) Soon after, one of the two partners in the escrow company decided to retire and Slechta took advantage of his offer to buy a half interest in the business. Three years later, Slechta had built this into a chain of eight escrow companies and bought out the other partner.

Ambitious to expand still further, Slechta saw a perfect tie-up between his escrow business and the savings and loan business. "I saw that with a good lending source I could expand the volume of my escrow business. I knew that we could produce loan volume through our escrow connections. Brokers who brought us escrow business were also seeking loans for their clients and quite often would ask us to recommend lending sources."

Inquiring around as to how to get into the savings and loan business, Slechta learned of a family-owned association that was for sale. It had been started in a room on the ninth floor of a downtown Los Angeles office building as the Great Western Building and Loan Association back in 1925. Its object, according to the association's bylaws, was "to encourage industry, frugality and the accumulation of savings among its shareholders, members and others for the purpose of aiding them in acquiring and improving real estate . . ."

Building and loan associations (which are also known elsewhere by such names as homestead associations and co-operative banks) were not new in 1925. Primitive forms existed in China about 200 B.C., and the real forerunner of the modern association can be traced back to a "building society" which was organized in Birmingham, England in 1781. The first association in this country was formed as the Oxford Provident Building Association in Frankford (now a part of Philadelphia), Pennsylvania in 1831. Each member contributed a certain sum monthly. When a fund of $375—enough to build a house—had been accumulated, the members bid against each other for the privilege of borrowing it. As the treasury was replenished, every member had the opportunity to obtain a similar loan.

By 1840 there were six associations in the United States and by the turn of the century, almost 5,000, with assets totaling over $550 million and about 1.5 million savers. In comparatively young California alone, there were 146 such firms. One of the reasons for the formation and proliferation of the associations was that banks would generally lend only to the fairly wealthy.

From a more positive point of view, there were good reasons to start Great Western Savings in 1925. There were no mutual savings banks at all in California, as there are none even today. The movie industry had begun to bring millions of dollars into the state, and other industries followed. The state, particularly because of its climate, was attracting a huge influx of tourists and permanent settlers. Business volume was at the highest peak in the nation's history by the end of 1924, and 1925 was showing signs of being even a better year.

Nevertheless, the fledgling firm did not get off to a very auspicious start. Its four officers, who also comprised its entire staff, spent their early days feverishly sending out letters to friends and neighbors soliciting their support of the infant organization. The firm took whatever business it could get. One of the first transactions recorded involved a female customer who volunteered to deposit $7,500 on condition that Great Western pay her 7 per cent interest (as against the 6 per cent then customarily paid on savings accounts). The officers agreed, but on condition that the woman leave her deposit untouched for a period of three years. (Needless to say, such dickering is no longer possible today.)

By the end of its first year, the firm's savings accounts amounted to only $40,119, its assets totaled $82,869, and it had made only fourteen loans. And its growth during the next two decades could not be called sensational. The books which closed the year 1928 showed assets of $351,644, but a profit of only $1,574! Because it remembered the words "moderation and conservative management," the firm somehow did manage to survive the 1929 crash and weather the Depression years when—as one of the early officers put it—"so many other financial houses and associations cracked on their foundations and tumbled into ruins." And not once did it default on its quoted interest payment. By 1946, the company was still relatively small, with assets of only $3 million after twenty-one years of struggle. The owner, a Dr. Felix Janovsky, was ready to sell out. Janovsky was also of Czech origin and the fact that the two men were able to converse in the same language was influential in inducing him to sell to Slechta.

When Slechta took over the company, it had only six regular employees and one who worked part-time in a small office which

Slechta has since described as a "hole in the wall." Within a short time, he remodeled and modernized the office, raised the interest rate to 3 per cent, and launched a new advertising campaign.

"People have to promote savings and loans just like you promote any other business," Slechta said. "The company had just not been doing much about promoting its business. And so I started to advertise more heavily and more vigorously. At the time not everybody advertised interest rate—in the minds of some people, to do so was undignified, although now everybody does it. But I could see no reason why, if we paid a certain rate, we shouldn't tell the public about it. I couldn't see why there should be one rule as to the way to conduct a banking or savings and loan business, and another for the conduct of other businesses."

Under Slechta's leadership, Great Western (whose name had been changed from "Building and Loan" to "Savings and Loan" in 1943) grew from $2.8 million in assets on August 1, 1947, to $8 million on December 31, 1948, or an increase of 186 per cent in just eighteen months. By the end of 1949, which marked the beginning of its Silver Jubilee Year, Great Western had 34 employees, 7,500 savers, 4,000 borrowers, and total resources of $12.9 million. Four years later, it was the second largest state-chartered savings and loan association in California, with assets of $63 million, and by 1955, these had about doubled.

To keep up with the financial expansion of the firm, Slechta opened a branch office in the rapidly-growing Crenshaw district of Los Angeles, and another in the adjacent city of Gardena. By 1955, the expansion-minded Slechta also had twenty-two companies in his independently-operated escrow chain. Together, the escrow companies and Great Western were grossing nearly $6 million a year at the time of Natelson's visit to California.

A few days after Natelson's visit, a young man named Robert Rhodes dropped in at the Crenshaw office of Great Western and asked to see its president, Adolph Slechta. Employed in Lehman Brothers' Los Angeles office, Rhodes at the moment was out soliciting mortgage insurance for a company he had helped to establish in Texas.

When asked to state his business by the receptionist, Rhodes jocularly said, "Tell Mr. Slechta I want to buy his business." The message was conveyed to Slechta, who was having coffee in his office while conversing with a couple of his assistants.

"Tell him I'm not interested," said Slechta. Other people, Slechta thought, had from time to time sounded him out about buying his business, but nothing had ever resulted from these overtures. He then went on with his conversation while idly glancing at the engraved card his secretary had handed him. It read: "Robert Rhodes, Lehman Brothers, Investment Bankers, New York."

On an impulse, Slechta buzzed his secretary and said, "Well, maybe you had better have Mr. Rhodes wait. I suppose I might as well talk to him, too."

To Slechta's bewilderment, Rhodes immediately plunged into the sales talk describing the insurance program he was launching. When he had finished, Slechta said, "Well, I don't know if I want you in the insurance business. I happen to own some insurance agencies myself. Nevertheless, thanks for coming in to see me."

Although Rhodes had been facetious when he told the receptionist he wanted to buy Slechta's business, he suddenly recalled Natelson's visit. "Would you consider selling your business?"

"I don't know," said Slechta. "But just for curiosity's sake, what do you think a company like Lehman Brothers would be willing to pay for my business?"

"I can't tell you for sure," said Rhodes, who, while waiting in the reception room, had picked up and studied a statement of the company. "But I may be able to get you about ten million dollars."

"Let me talk it over with my wife," said Slechta, "and I will give you my answer tomorrow."

That evening during dinner, Slechta told his wife, "Well, honey, there was a man in the office today, and he wants to buy the business. I think this one really means it. He said that for the savings and loan business and the escrow companies he might get us about ten million dollars."

Without hesitation, Mrs. Slechta said, "Well, take a million less if you have to, but sell." She had long been concerned with how hard her husband had been working all his life, and was worried about his health. Although Slechta was only fifty-one years old, she had long been after him to retire.

The next morning, Slechta called Rhodes and said, "I think we can make a deal if you can get me ten million dollars."

"I will contact my New York office and let you know shortly," Rhodes said.

For several weeks, both Rhodes' letter about Great Western and the accompanying industry report sat on Natelson's desk in New York. "I looked at them off and on, but had no idea what to do—if anything," he now recalls. "I knew nothing about the industry except that it seemed to be attractive, even though highly competitive—in the Los Angeles area, there were ninety-one other savings and loan associations, to say nothing of banks, insurance companies, and other institutional and private lenders in direct competition with Great Western."

Something about Great Western intrigued Natelson. He was impressed by the growth prospects of Southern California and with the potential for the home financing industry there. In the spring of 1955 he flew to Los Angeles in connection with another matter, and while there he went to see Slechta. The two men were of almost exactly the same age. Like Slechta, Natelson had also sprung from relatively humble beginnings. A native New Yorker, he had earned a business degree from the College of the City of New York and then worked for two years as office manager of a leather goods company before joining Lehman Brothers in 1927. Twenty-three years later he was named a partner. Since 1940 he had also been a director of a realty company and so had more than a casual familiarity with mortgages and the other intricacies of real estate financing. He and Slechta soon agreed on the general basis on which they could complete the transaction. The sales price arrived at was remarkably close to that estimated by Rhodes: the exact figure finally decided on, after weeks of negotiation, was $10,473,628 for the association and the escrow companies.

Not that Natelson as yet had any clear idea as to what to do with the company. His work as a Lehman Brothers partner involved him in many of the traditional functions of investment banking: the raising of venture capital, the syndication of stock issues, the management of an underwriting or selling group, the creation of new financing business, and the arrangement of private placements.

Natelson's first thought was to act as a broker and find a buyer for Great Western, thus earning Lehman a commission on the transaction. Accordingly, he offered Great Western to a number of individuals and companies with large cash holdings. "Their immediate reaction to a savings and loan association was one of either amusement or horror," recalls Natelson. "In some cases, when I tried to describe what the business was, I couldn't get past the first sentence. People were not only completely uninterested, but they wouldn't even listen. To them, the mere mention of the phrase 'savings and loan association' conjured up the image of an establishment not quite as sound as the kind with three gold balls over the door."

In part, this reaction was due to prejudice, probably stemming from recollections of some of the uninsured associations which had been active and failed in the late twenties and thirties. In part, it was due to ignorance as to just what a savings and loan association was. "People had the idea that a savings and loan association took people's money and invested it in real estate mortgages on a highly speculative basis, and it was therefore considered the least desirable field in the loan business," says Natelson.

Unable to find a purchaser for Great Western, Natelson one day was struck with an idea: Why not have Lehman Brothers buy it?

When Natelson first broached the subject at a staff meeting, he encountered a remarkable lack of enthusiasm for the proposal.

"Look," argued Natelson, "here is a situation that can be bought for about $10.5 million that has savings of about $90 million, and is earning at this point at the rate of $2.7 million a year, or 3 per cent net on its savings. The growth in savings and earnings has been remarkable. During the past ten years, this firm has multiplied its assets forty times and in the next three years will probably double its earnings."

Its growth had been little short of phenomenal, for the assets of the savings and loan industry itself had, during the same period, jumped more than fourfold—from $8.7 billion in 1945 to $37.5 billion in 1955.

There were still some doubts as to the feasibility of the proposal. Lehman had from time to time bought a number of companies privately and then eventually resold them or offered their stock to the public. But never before had investment bankers done anything with a company in the savings and loan industry.

One of the principal objections voiced was that the industry, in spite of its rapid growth, was still relatively unknown to savers and almost completely unknown to members of the financial community and the stock-buying public. In fact, the stock of a savings and loan association had never before been offered to the public nationally, much less listed on a stock exchange.

"Why risk sponsoring an underwriting that could fail?" was the big question asked by several of the partners. "If we can induce brokerage firms to handle the initial offering of stock—and we're not sure that we can—the public may never go for it."

There was a formidable combination of resistances to overcome. Certainly, in the minds of most people—brokers and laymen alike—savings and loan associations at that time did not have the standing and reputation of commercial or savings banks, or even finance companies. For one thing, as a hangover from the experience of the dark Depression years, the savings and loans were not regarded as safe: a bank was where you traditionally put your money for safe-keeping. Contributing to the aura of safety and stability of banks were the solid museum-like structures in which they were invariably housed. By contrast, many savings and loan branch offices were located in small, unpretentious quarters, often in the upstairs floor of a building or above a store front.

That this popular view as to the difference in safety between savings and loan associations and banks had no basis in fact is completely beside the point—people believed it. No less widespread was the equally mistaken notion that it was generally more difficult to withdraw savings from a savings and loan association than from a bank.

Yet, these prejudices would somehow have to be overcome— first by Natelson, to win the support of all his partners; then, in turn, by the partners, to win support from the financial community. Then would come the much more difficult job of the newly-acquired company gaining the acceptance of the investing public.

At a series of meetings that followed during the next few weeks, Natelson mustered arguments to secure approval of the idea. "It took a great deal of selling on my part," Natelson recalls.

"Few people remember that 12,837 commercial banks—compared to only 1,606 savings and loan associations—failed between 1930 and 1940," Natelson said at one meeting. "Up to 1934 alone, over 9,000 banks failed. And their failure was far more harmful to the economy—as well as to individuals and families —than the failure of the much smaller number of savings and loan associations."

He also summarized the crucial legislation enacted to strengthen the solvent savings and loan associations to the point where most were virtually as safe as the strongest banks. One law, passed in 1932, established the Federal Home Loan Bank (FHLB) System, which provided reserve funds savings and loan associations could draw on, giving them help similar to that received by banks from the Federal Reserve System. Another, creating the Federal Savings and Loan Insurance Corporation (FSLIC) in 1934 (with important amendments in 1950) provided federal insurance for savings and loan accounts comparable to that furnished by the Federal Deposit Insurance Corporation (FDIC) for bank savings.

"Gentlemen, although I have had no previous contact with the savings and loan field," said Natelson at another meeting, "I am convinced that mortgage lending on real estate is a perfectly legitimate and responsible business. I don't see it as any less sound than the personal loan field. Why should a personal loan company that is engaged in making loans on no security to speak of have any greater respect in the financial community than the association which makes loans secured not only by the credit of an individual but also by his most valuable property— his home?"

From the beginning, several senior partners had felt that there might be some merit in Natelson's proposal. With their support and his own powers of persuasion, the firm decided unanimously to buy Great Western if financing could be obtained to raise the $10,473,628 necessary to make the purchase. A pension fund agreed to provide the funds needed to complete the acquisition. Its decision was motivated by its confidence in Lehman's ability to sell the entire stock issue. However, there was a proviso that Lehman Brothers would take a risk in the transaction of at least $1 million.

The original plan was to purchase the stock of the association and reoffer this to the public, but then legal complications clouded the picture: restrictions as to the par value of a savings and loan association stock meant that the price of each share would run into many hundreds of dollars, also there would not be enough shares to create a market for the stock. Both were conditions that would make impossible the wide public sale contemplated.

The decision was therefore made to use the corporate device known as the holding company, although this had never before been done in the savings and loan business. Through this device, a corporation—now known as the Great Western Financial Corporation—would be formed which would buy all the stock in Slechta's association and twenty-two escrow companies. Then, a large stock issue in the newly-formed corporation would be offered to the public at a relatively low price.

Enough stock was to be offered the public to repay the $10,473,628 borrowed from the pension fund. (Actually, the fund guaranteed a bank loan made by the holding company for that amount.) Lehman's risk in the transaction was one million dollars—a liability it faced if the public offering planned was not made within a year.

For a while, it looked as if the firm would suffer such a liability. Some of the important underwriters with whom it had worked in the past refused to participate in the new stock offering. "Despite our missionary work, they just didn't understand the savings and loan business," recalls Natelson. "They thought it would be impossible to sell the stock."

Their forebodings seemed justified when the 500,000 share issue was offered to the public at $23.50 in late August, 1955. The public, also doubtful of the savings and loan business, in addition did not see much romance in the business of lending on homes. The stock sold down to as little as $21.00, and did not get back to its offering price for six or seven months. Then suddenly the stock started to climb at a rapid pace. (Stock purchased for $1,000 in 1955 was worth about $9,000 in September, 1963.)

There was good reason for the turn-about in the fortunes of the stock in early 1956. Great Western Financial Corporation's first public statement showed the new holding company's assets to have climbed to a record $131 million during 1955, 41 per cent above the total chalked up by the association and twenty-two escrow companies the year before; earnings had increased 48.5 per cent to $2.9 million! The phrase "savings and loan holding company" was on its way to becoming a new, popular term among brokers and investors.

True, contributing to Great Western's growth were a number of independent factors—the same factors responsible for the surge of the savings and loan industry since the end of World War II. Setting the stage for this surge were the beneficial laws of the 1930's establishing the Federal Home Loan Bank and Federal Savings and Loan Insurance Corporation which, by strengthening many of the nation's savings and loan associations, also instilled the beginnings of public confidence in them.

What sent the savings and loan industry skyrocketing, however, was the big postwar housing boom, a product of the nation's ever-expanding population, the new families of the returning GI's, rising personal incomes and standards of living—all coupled with the long pent-up demand and need for homes created by war-halted construction.

Other key factors behind the savings and loan surge were the adoption of the now generally used long-term monthly amortized real estate loan, the Federal Housing Administration's mortgage insurance program, and the GI Home Loan Program under which the Veterans' Administration guaranteed lenders against losses on loans made to GI's. Savings and loan associations actually pioneered the latter program, making 80 per cent of all GI loans during the first six months of its existence.

Yet, the emergence of savings and loans as a dominant force in the home loan field was achieved virtually by default. For they were filling a need that other financial institutions were either unable or uninterested in filling. In addition to offering the saver a higher return on his money than commercial banks, the associations were the only financial institutions specializing in home loans, usually repayable over long-term periods of up to thirty years.

On the other hand, commercial banks then regarded savings accounts as a nuisance and offered a variety of services, concentrating on short-term (one- to five-year) loans, generally of a business or personal nature (such as for the purchase of an auto). Mutual savings banks, although investing most of their savings in real estate loans, operated largely in the relatively slow-growing Northeast. Insurance companies were mainly interested in the fifteen-to-twenty-year loan market and preferred to lend on homes higher-priced than those generally financed by savings and loan associations.

To attract savings—which, of course, provides us with the basis for our business of making real estate loans—a lot also had to be done to overcome many of the false notions held by the largely uninformed public regarding savings and loan associations. As early as May, 1956, we discussed at a board meeting the importance of using informative, responsible and dignified advertising in both local and national mass media to tell the truth about our industry. Prior to this, very little advertising had been done by associations except at the local level. (Today, the typical appearance of as many as fifty different savings and loan association ads in a single issue of the nationally distributed *Wall Street Journal* may be said to be a consequence of Great Western's early pioneering efforts.)

Our predominant advertising theme was naturally our higher rate which has ranged as high as 4.85 per cent per year in the majority of our associations. Savings and loan associations in California can offer a higher interest rate consistent with maximum safety because a larger percentage of our money is invested in real estate loans, which generally pay a higher return than the overall loans made by banks (or by savings and loan associations in the Eastern states).

To overcome the fears people mistakenly had regarding the safety of savings and loan associations, our advertising also displayed the emblem of the Federal Savings and Loan Insurance Corporation, which now insures accounts up to $10,000 in 4,200 of the nation's 6,300 associations, including almost all those in California. We also pointed out in our advertising and brochures that no one had ever lost a penny in an account protected by FSLIC insurance. (None of the Maryland associations which failed several years ago was insured by FSLIC.)

As for the notion persistent in some quarters that FSLIC Insurance is not as safe as that offered to the banks by the Federal Deposit Insurance Corporation, let me dispel this through no less an authority than John A. O'Brien, assistant general manager of the FSLIC. In a recent speech, Mr. O'Brien quoted a banker, Gaylord Freeman, president of the First National Bank of Chicago, as frankly admitting before the Illinois Bankers Association: "Many bankers have sought to point out the difference between the insurance offered by the FDIC on one hand and that offered by the FSLIC on the other. This effort is almost totally without merit, for there is virtually no difference between the two types of insurance . . ."

As mentioned earlier, some people have also had the mistaken notion that it is more difficult to withdraw money from a savings and loan association than from a bank. Actually, the withdrawal rules of both are similar, as a comparison of passbooks will indicate: either institution is legally permitted to require a limited notice of intention to withdraw from its savings accounts. However, this option is rarely ever exercised, and Great Western's now seven associations have a perfect record in honoring all withdrawals. Yet, to help assuage this fear, our advertising has also displayed the emblem signifying our membership in the Federal Home Loan Banking System from which we can, if necessary, borrow funds to meet any unusual or heavy demands on the part of our savers as well as borrowers.

In other advertising, Great Western undertook to clear up the popular misconception that it was safe to keep only up to $10,000 in a savings account. Apart from citing the fact that thousands of savings accounts in our seven associations exceed $10,000 (some are over $1 million), it showed how a family of, say, three can through a combination of individual, joint, and trustee accounts, have up to $140,000 in fully insured savings in any one of Great Western's seven associations, or almost one million dollars in all seven.

Insurance of accounts is only one of the safeguards afforded our thousands of savers. Our management policies and tremendous resources are obviously our greatest safeguards. In addition, however, the savings and loan holding company is probably subject to more government controls than the companies of any other industry. Since our associations are members of the FSLIC and FHLB, we operate under both state and federal supervision. As a publicly held and listed corporation, we are also subject to the regulation of the Securities and Exchange Commission and the New York Stock Exchange.

Actually, apart from the need to solve the problem of finding a ready market for the stock, there were other reasons behind the idea of forming a holding company.

Significant economies could be effected by a statewide group of associations exchanging information and ideas. Funds could be more effectively used in all areas of the state, depending upon loan demand, by associations sharing a common management objective and a mutual interest in the future of California.

It would be easier for a group of associations to provide more efficient management through this constant exchange of data. We would have a greater opportunity to train and utilize our personnel through the various challenging assignments afforded by the affiliated associations.

We could also improve efficiency in our acquisition of savings. By advertising as a group, our seven associations have been able to offer investors throughout the world the convenience of writing just one check for the placement of funds in savings accounts at each association. This advertising has also helped to tell the story of the savings and loan industry and of our company to many people, particularly those in the business and financial community.

Our holding company's first property, Great Western Savings and Loan, whose current assets of $630 million now rank it as the third largest association in the country, operates in the Los Angeles area. The choice of the others acquired involved many crucial management decisions involving the future of our company. The next two acquired, Bakersfield Savings and Loan and Santa Ana Savings and Loan, both purchased in 1956, extended our operations to Kern and Orange Counties; and our fourth, West Coast Savings and Loan, purchased early in 1957, gave us an operating base in Sacramento. Our three other associations are Guaranty Savings and Loan of San Jose and First Savings and Loan of Oakland, both in the San Francisco Bay area; and Central Savings and Loan in San Luis Obispo.

Federal legislation enacted in September, 1959, now prevents savings and loan holding companies from acquiring any additional associations, but expansion is still possible through the opening of new branch offices. Through thirty-three conveniently located offices, Great Western's group of seven associations are now able to serve 99 per cent of California's population. (Typically, associations confine their lending to a hundred-mile radius; savings, however, can be accepted from people anywhere.)

What was also instrumental in inspiring public confidence in savings and loan associations was their move to modern, larger, more attractive quarters. Today, the most imposing structures in many cities are occupied by savings and loan associations. Great Western's Gardena office building, for example, was designed by the world-famous architectural firm of Skidmore, Owings & Merrill. The new head office of Bakersfield Savings is a beautiful seven-story structure, the tallest building in Kern County.

To attract savings from those who preferred the convenience of saving by mail, we started a Save-by-Mail Program now used by thousands of savers not only in California, but in all fifty of the United States and in seventy foreign countries. Ten per cent of our funds now come from outside of California, in some cases from places halfway around the world. One of our recent ads featured the headline, "This man in Bagdad has a Great Western Savings account," and showed a mustachioed Arab holding our passbook. Indicating our inroads in other meccas of international finance, today we receive funds from such symbols of safety and stability as Swiss and German banks! And from English, French and Dutch banks as well.

However, in keeping with their role as essentially local institutions, our associations have also been active in community affairs. Great Western Savings' Gardena branch has a community room available gratis for everything from Boy Scout and Kiwanis meetings to charity drives and polio shots.

And to meet the especially intense competition of recent years, we stepped up our advertising and other promotional efforts, increasing our expenditures for this five-fold between 1959 and 1962. Part of these were to sponsor community services and public-interest TV programs ranging from one on NORAD (a documentary dealing with a simulated air attack on the United States) to a telecast of Easter Sunrise Services from the Hollywood Bowl.

The results of all these pioneering efforts, duplicated by many other savings and loan organizations, are reflected in the status of the savings and loan industry today: since 1945, savings accounts in savings and loan associations have grown from $7.4 billion to some $86.5 billion, or almost twelve-fold. Comparable deposits in the nation's 13,500 commercial banks (more than double the number of savings and loans) have not quite quadrupled—increasing from $29.9 billion to $105 billion. Another set of figures may also be illuminating: during the same period, the share of America's savings held by savings and loans has increased from about 7 to 28 per cent; while that of commerical banks has remained at about 31 per cent.

Today the gap is fast narrowing as Americans are now putting more of their savings—a record $9.5 billion in 1962—into savings and loan associations. With these funds to work with, savings and loans have also now become the nation's leading home lenders (with banks and life insurance companies running far behind), and, in fact, finance more homes in the under-$20,000 category than all other lending institutions put together. Total assets of the savings and loan industry crossed the $100 billion mark in 1963, twelve times what they were in 1945!

Over the years, public confidence, along with financial faith in the industry, has grown. And whether or not people still think of associations as just another kind of bank, they now at least think of them to be at least as safe and stable as banks. Characteristics of typical association borrowers and savers have changed, too: according to a recent survey, they have higher than average incomes and are also relatively high on the educational ladder, compared to the average American.

To a large extent responsible for the growth of public confidence—and in recent years, the growth of the industry itself— was the very fact that Great Western Financial Corporation was formed. The unprecedented public offering of the new holding company's stock and its subsequent listing on the American Stock Exchange (in December, 1957) and, later, the New York Stock Exchange (January, 1960) brought widespread attention to the savings and loan industry. People, in watching the stock being traded every day, got some idea as to its market value and growth potential. The subsequent success of the new company built prestige for the industry as a whole, and led to the formation of twenty-five other publicly-held savings and loan holding companies in California (and several in other states).

At first, even Paul Manheim, who heads Lehman's Investment Advisory Service, hesitated to recommend Great Western to his select accounts (minimum size accepted: $500,000). Today, however, twelve of the seventy leading investment trusts maintain holdings of over one million shares of the stock, or about 12 per cent of all that outstanding.

The reason can be seen in Great Western's growth. In November, 1961, one of our ads was able to proclaim an important "first" in our industry—"We're now a billion dollars big!" (Since then, only three other savings and loan organizations have entered the exalted billion-dollar circle). Assets had climbed to this mark from $131 million only six years before. Earnings had correspondingly increased from $2.9 million to $14.8 million. And the firm now numbers over a thousand employees.

This was quite a growth record for a company that very nearly wasn't formed in the first place. Morris Natelson has said that when he gave Slechta the check in payment for his business the latter said, "Morris, I hope you are not sorry now that we have closed this deal. This company will continue to make more money than you have ever dreamed it would."

What about Adolph Slechta? He never did retire completely, as he had planned. In spite of his early suspicion of us Easterners, he agreed to serve as president of the new corporation for several years and then to continue in an advisory capacity. Like Natelson, he is also a member of our present board of directors. In 1959 Slechta finally retired and was succeeded as president by John F. Marten, who had held top management posts in the savings and loan industry before becoming Great Western Savings' executive vice-president. Marten is a past president of the California Savings and Loan League.

In terms of the future, the growth of Great Western, influential as it has been in the national scene, is, of course, primarily linked with the growth of California—and the state's housing needs. Savings and loan associations, among institutional lenders, are now financing 71.6 per cent of the state's homes—advancing $4.024 billion for home loans of $20,000 or less in 1962. This is almost triple the $1.497 billion advanced in 1955, the year Great Western was formed. And every reliable forecast projects a doubling of the state's population from about fifteen million in 1960 to about thirty million in 1980. By then—in sixteen years—California must build more than five million additional dwelling units, more than the number of homes built during the first one hundred years of California's existence as a state.

To what extent Great Western will participate in this growth, I won't even venture to guess. Certainly, when I was asked to head up what I thought of as just another mortgage company back in 1955, I never dreamed the company would grow as it has continued to do.

WALTER L. MORGAN

Wellington Fund

WALTER L. MORGAN was born in Wilkes-Barre, Pennsylvania, on July 23, 1898. He received an A.B. degree from Princeton University in 1920, and became a certified public accountant shortly thereafter. Subsequent to serving with two nationally known accounting firms, he formed his own firm (Morgan & Company) in 1925 and founded Wellington Fund in 1928. Mr. Morgan is one of the pioneers of the mutual fund industry, and is the "dean" of the industry in that he has served as a mutual fund chief executive longer than any man now active. He also founded Wellington Management Company, which (with its subsidiaries) is investment manager, sponsor, and national distributor for Wellington Fund and Windsor Fund, a sister fund formed in 1958. Combined resources of the two funds approximate $1.7 billion, owned by more than 385,000 shareholders.

Main Street Comes to Wall Street

A New Investment Concept Is Born

BY

WALTER L. MORGAN

The growth of a financial institution—although it may appear cold, statistical, or impersonal—is in many respects as interesting and vital as the growth of a child. Both must be conceived, born, and nurtured. Both must gain experience as they grow, through the difficult and sometimes painful process of trial and error. Both must develop a set of basic standards upon which they will operate—a philosophy of life, if you will. Then, if they are healthy, if they have a sound purpose, if they put service before self and—most important of all—if the warm sun of good fortune shines upon them, they will be successful.

This is the story of how one such new financial institution, one special mutual fund, was born. This is not, as such, its success story, for Wellington Fund's success is attested by the facts and figures of today: more than $1.6 billion of resources, 350,000 shareholders (among the world's seven largest corporations in this respect); an uninterrupted string of 136 dividend distributions, paid in varying amounts every three months, with income dividends totaling $335 million and capital gains distributions exceeding $330 million. These facts and figures, however important, are the less colorful side of the story. Of interest now is how the Fund was born, and the influences that came to bear on its formative years. For these events were the foundation that gave Wellington Fund the stamp of character that accounts for its success and that remains a basic part of the Fund today.

December 27, 1928, was the day the Fund was born. Not an important date, really, but simply the date on which were filed, in the State of Delaware, the variety of drab legal documents that breathe life into a corporation. At that point in time, then, an idea became a business in being. Small, humble, and insignificant, to be sure, but with the potential of success in its future—a future that in many respects had been determined by what went before.

The idea that kept coming into my mind in the early days was, like most good ideas, the essence of simplicity: to combine a group of individual investment accounts into a single large fund, which could be diversified broadly over perhaps a hundred or more securities, and managed efficiently by trained investment experts. To develop such a "mutual fund," of course, would require promotional, analytical and managerial abilities that were to come in part from my heredity and my training, and in even greater part from my good fortune in surrounding myself with people who knew more than I did.

The earliest evidence I can remember of the promotional instincts that were threaded through my family background was a rather extravagant prospectus for the Rival Promoting Company, written in 1907 by my maternal grandfather, James L. Lovett. In his flowery words: "Extraordinary is the promise of this new company as a profit maker . . . the only small thing about it is the present price of its shares. Within a few weeks that won't be small either. When the high character of the management and the exceptional merit of the property (a gold mine) is considered, it is safe to predict absolute security and enormous profits and dividends to every purchaser at, or near, present prices."

My grandfather also had a wonderful humanitarian instinct, a most appropriate companion to his long Santa-Claus white beard, and the Rival prospectus pointed out that he was raising the money not only to recoup rewards from the gold, but also "to make the mine safe for man or beast." His claims for the mine (probably less extravagant by the standards of the turn of the century than they would be judged today) proved overzealous, and the Rival Promoting Company did not fulfill its promise. There was gold in the mine (doubtless it is still there), but it cost too much to get it out of the ground. His other investments—generally of a radical and speculative flavor—also worked out badly, and the nest egg he had accumulated for his retirement was entirely lost by the time he reached the age of seventy. I can recall no other financial event in my lifetime that made such an indelible impression on me, demonstrating as it did the need for careful and conservative financial management.

Nevertheless, there was still a great deal I had to learn from my own experience. I was confident I could be a successful investor, and was impressed by the fact that my grandfather Lovett made a vigorous financial comeback and accumulated over $100,000 after he was seventy (no mean achievement in terms of the buying power of the dollar at the start of the twentieth century). My father and my uncle were also fairly active investors—albeit with mixed success—and I intended to be the same. My first venture took the form of putting several hundred dollars in a wild-cat oil scheme on the advice of a friend in my Princeton class of 1920. Almost before I could calculate my hoped-for profits, however, the venture failed, and I had learned a lesson far more valuable than the small amount it had cost me.

Even this lesson was not enough for a bold and optimistic youth, however, and I continued in a small way to "play the market" actively after graduating from Princeton. On balance, helped by a strong upward tide in the general level of stock prices, I made profits, which by 1926 amounted to a figure which might have been regarded as "considerable" for a young man just trying to get himself established in the world. It was then that I thought I had a chance to "get rich quick." I learned that Philadelphia Electric Company was about to merge with United Gas Improvement Company, and felt that here was a real chance for a sure profit. I put up all my money as a 10 per cent margin to buy Philadelphia Electric, borrowing the remaining 90 per cent. The merger fell through, and the price of Philadelphia Electric stock dropped almost in half in a few days. Only a family loan kept me from insolvency. Once more I learned first-hand what was meant by "investment risk," and I have never borrowed since.

But I am getting a bit ahead of the story. As I was accumulating actual investment experience, I was also building a personal foundation of statistical, analytical and research experience. (If I was at first remiss in failing to apply this knowledge to my own personal financial affairs, I had only myself to blame.) After Princeton, I took a series of accounting courses, and became a certified public accountant, one of the youngest C.P.A.'s in the state of Pennsylvania. I did this in order to understand better the financial figures that went into a company's profit-and-loss statement. I knew I had to develop talents in the area of statistics and research, and I wanted to use these talents constructively to help others. More than ever, my accounting training made me conscious of the help that financial professionals could give to people who needed management for their business and their money.

My first job was with the firm of Peat, Marwick and Mitchell, certified public accountants. I was ambitious (perhaps even brash); and although I hated the routine detail, it was good discipline. After a year's time, I asked the firm if my abilities and efforts merited an increase in my salary (then $125 a month). I was told in no uncertain terms that, as far as wages were concerned, I was overpaid. As to the quality of my work, my boss said, "We are not particularly smitten with it!" Showing the "lion-in-a-cage" impatience which seems to be characteristic of me, I went with Haskins and Sells, another fine C.P.A. firm, and negotiated a $50 monthly increase in the bargain.

While my accounting background was in many respects essential to what was soon to become my life career, five years of working for large accounting firms convinced me that I wanted something more. I wanted to do much more than the routine dollars-and-cents, debit-and-credit and balance sheet auditing in the public accounting field. I was much more interested in the application of what I found—how it could be used profitably; how to help companies earn more profits; how to help people keep their money and make it grow by investing in stocks and bonds. At the same time, I discovered that the feeling of security that came from working for a large firm was not enough for me. I wanted to start my own firm, to be my own boss. When I expressed these views to my superior at Haskins and Sells, his reaction was clear and simple: "Morgan, you'll never amount to anything!" I was just obstinate enough to do everything in my power to prove him wrong.

My own accounting firm, Morgan and Company, opened its doors for business in 1925. One of the series of lucky breaks that seemed to occur at important points in my career was not long in coming. I went out to solicit new accounts, and—through an old Princeton friend—made an appointment to meet with representatives of the Ludington family, one of the most prominent families in Philadelphia, with extensive financial interests. The day before I met them, they had received what they considered to be an exorbitant bill for accounting services from a large national firm. They wanted a new accounting firm and—as a result of the cold canvass I had providentially made—they said, "Let's give the job to Morgan." My newly-organized firm had won its first major account. Little did I know that, in a few short years, the Ludingtons would be among my best clients, would encourage me to add tax and investment counseling to my accounting service, and ultimately would put up a major portion of Wellington Fund's initial capitalization of $100,000.

It was not long before investment advice and tax counseling became the dominant part of my business. In these areas, I was able to mix whatever imagination and venturesomeness I had with the analytical experience and accounting training I had gained. One of Philadelphia's large banks (now the First Pennsylvania Banking and Trust Company) proved to be a valuable source of contacts for me, when the bank hired me "part-time" as a tax expert to advise their clients on the proper filing of federal income tax returns. Long lines of people quite literally formed at my temporary desk in the Pennsylvania Company as the March fifteenth tax deadline approached each year. And these were all people of substantial means; they had to be, in order to have tax problems, for a married couple with $10,000 of income in 1929 paid a tax of only $52. (The tax liability of a married couple with $25,000 of income was $838 in 1929; today, by way of contrast, it is $6,268.) In looking over their tax returns, I naturally asked about their investments: "Why don't you sell that stock and buy this one?"

As a result of my interest, many of the fine contacts I made in tax work for the bank soon were calling at my office for more help and advice. I was of course glad to advise these people, not only on their tax affairs, but also on the handling of their investments, because this was my first love and still is. At the same time, a recurrent theme kept repeating itself over and over in my mind: There must be a better way to handle investment management than to advise a large number of individual accounts. There must be a better way to diversify investments than the purchase of only a few securities. There must be a better way to handle the problems of safekeeping a large number of securities, clipping hundreds of bond interest coupons, recording multiple purchases and sales and dividends. There *must* be a better way.

The solution to the problem was obvious: if substantially the same investment problems were shared by all of these individual accounts, why not consolidate them into a single fund?

Banding together for strength, entrusting specialized tasks to specially trained persons for efficiency, and spreading risks over a number of different ventures for safety: these principles are nearly as old as civilization. I had no monopoly on them. Indeed, applying them to the investment field was not even a "new" idea, dating back to at least 1822, when King William I of the Netherlands formed the earliest known investment company. The thrifty Scots further developed the idea in the mid-nineteenth century, and as early as 1875, an English barrister named Arthur Scratchley (in his "Treatise of Associations for Provident Investment") wrote as good a definition of a mutual fund as has ever been written:

> Whether a man has a large or small sum to invest, he runs the risk of making a mistake in his individual purchase from not understanding the peculiarities of the stock; whereas, if he subscribe to a general fund, which (assisted by the advice of persons of experience in such matters) would divide its purchases carefully among a selected variety of investments —each member would derive greater benefit with much security from loss by the distribution of the risk over a large average.

In the mid-1920's, the unique American promotional genius began to apply itself to the investment company field. Whereas up to 1926, perhaps 20 investment companies were formed each year, the late twenties saw a veritable explosion of the so-called investment trusts: in 1927, 140 were organized; in 1928, 186; and at the climax in 1929, 265 such trusts came into being. (Of the 591 trusts organized in this three-year period, however, only 222 were still active at the end of 1936.) This was the era when the sky was the limit, when stocks soared to the highest prices they were to reach for another quarter-century, when speculative fever made people see only the possible profit, not the potential risk, created by the dangerous leverage of a 10 per cent margin.

The investment trusts of those days were known as the "closed-end" type. That is, they would float a large issue of securities to the public at one time, and then "close up" and invest the proceeds of the underwriting. In many respects, these trusts were promotional ventures, and their sales literature (while not quite as exuberant as Grandfather Lovett's) was enough to make us blush by today's standards: "the uncertainty of selecting the profitable companies of the future has been overcome," "an investment protected by 400 seasoned securities," "a proved method of profiting with safety in the constantly increasing growth of the United States."

Stimulated by such catch phrases and the hope to "get rich quick," investors flocked to the closed-end trusts. Many people in the financial field were amazed at the eager public reception accorded these trusts, which was epitomized by the phenomenal success of The Goldman Sachs Trading Corporation. This trust, organized by one of Wall Street's largest and best-regarded investment banking firms, raised capital of $330,000,000 between December, 1928 and the summer of 1929. Even today, this still stands as the largest such offering ever to take place. Its shares, originally offered at $100 each, soared upward to $222 in February, 1929, despite the fact that the underlying investments were worth only half that much. And here was the basic weakness of the closed-end company: the price of its shares was not "pegged" to the market value of its investments; shares might trade at twice what they were worth (as in early 1929) or half that value (as was the case before 1929 drew to a close).

For this reason, I felt that another type of investment company —the so-called open-end type—was more to my liking. Such companies (and only three or four had been formed by 1929) had an "open" capitalization: they were constantly issuing new shares (at the current asset value of the underlying investments, plus a sales commission) and stood ready to redeem shares from existing investors (also at the current asset value). Perhaps even more important, these companies had a more conservative capitalization than their closed-end cousins. By avoiding borrowed capital, the open-end companies were not saddled with the high leverage that was to prove so perilous in late 1929. I had had long discussions with W. Wallace Alexander, who in 1907 formed perhaps the first predecessor of this type of fund—the Alexander Fund. He pointed out that the open-capital feature virtually required investment in good quality, readily marketable securities, since the list had to be valued daily, and since securities might have to be sold to meet redemptions at any time. He encouraged me to put my ideas to work.

The open-end fund (today known as the mutual fund) also afforded me another necessary advantage: it could be developed over a period of time and therefore didn't require a large initial underwriting. I recognized that Morgan was not Goldman Sachs (J. P. Morgan may have been, but Walter Morgan wasn't). I therefore realized we could not create a ground swell of public demand for a mutual fund in a short time. We would have to do it the "pick-and-shovel" way: starting with capital from clients who knew what we could do and had confidence in our idea; using what training and abilities we could put together to manage the fund and build a good record of investment accomplishment; and using our promotional aptitudes to attract new investors to join the venture. At first the group would be primarily family and friends, but we were hopeful other investors too would recognize the merit of the mutual fund idea.

I was not brash enough to think that I could do it all myself: no one could. I knew that I had to surround myself with experts —people who knew more than I, and I set out to do this. My first job was to get a securities broker with a good background in security analysis and statistics, and—quite by accident—I found the man I sought right down the hall from my office on the thirteenth floor of Philadelphia's Packard Building. A. Moyer Kulp was an executive in the Philadelphia office of a New York Stock Exchange investment banking firm. He was a thorough student of company financial figures, no easy accomplishment in 1929. For this was the era when corporate facts and figures were available on only a limited basis (usually in a company's annual report) and such basic figures as sales revenues, for example, were considered vital and secret information. Kulp, however, had proved good at selecting stocks for profit, and he also had a remarkable knack for sensing market trends, and timing purchases and sales accordingly.

The Kulp-Morgan team was not well-known (if it was known at all) and I decided we needed a "name" in our group. Without hesitancy, I asked C. Stevenson Newhall, then executive vice-president and later president of the Pennsylvania Company, to join our initial investment committee. Not surprisingly, he declined. But he thought enough of the idea to say that he would permit a man he considered the bank's most competent investment management officer to serve on our committee. And so Brandon Barringer, a truly remarkable student of stocks and bonds and business trends, joined our small original Wellington team. His range of knowledge, his breadth of view, and his intimate familiarity with the nation's business and credit structure—all of these were to prove invaluable in the difficult months ahead.

The phenomenon known in Wall Street as a "bull market" had been with us through most of the 1920's. From a low of 65 in 1921, the Dow-Jones Industrial Average of stock prices had risen to 300 —a five-fold increase—by the end of 1928. Not only had stock prices risen, but the trading in stocks reached a level of frantic activity that was never seen before, nor again. Nineteen-twenty-nine was the only year in our history when more than 1.1 billion shares of stock changed hands. What a contrast with today! In the course of a typical recent year (in the 1950-1963 period), one share was traded for every eight shares of stock outstanding. In 1929, by comparison, *nine* shares were traded for every eight outstanding. The public (with the help of enormous margin accounts) was in the market and eager for profit.

Confidence begets confidence. As stock prices soared, the profits that investors were making—on paper—encouraged them to buy more stocks, and to push prices even further upward. People borrowed increasingly large amounts, in order to pyramid their gains on thin margins. Speculation was rampant early in 1929, and the few words of caution that were uttered fell upon deaf ears. Nevertheless, Abe Kulp, Brandon Barringer and I all felt that our proposed fund should be managed conservatively. To a man, we felt that stock prices had outstripped any reasonable appraisal of future prospects. Many stocks were selling at fifty to a hundred times earnings, and the wild market was approaching the edge of unreality. As the Fund commenced operations, therefore, we came to a conservative and common sense conclusion in an era of speculation: that the prices stocks commanded were just "not in the wood"; hence we should not invest the Fund's resources merely in stocks as the other investment trusts had done. Rather, we should have "an anchor to windward" in the form of a large position in fixed-income securities such as bonds and preferred stocks. By this conservative investment decision, what came to be known as the "balanced fund" concept was born. This "balance" was what proved to differentiate the Fund from its major competitors for thirty-five years, and made Wellington Fund unique.

Wellington Fund, however, was not the original name of the Fund. We initially felt that we needed a name that would fit the times, a name that called forth the imagery of American industry, one that would give investors a picture of the power of our growing economy, one that would promise investors what they wanted. And so the Fund was first named: Industrial and Power Securities Company.

Raising the initial capital of the Fund proved—by reason of my good fortune in having a fair number of investment counsel clients—to be less of a problem than I expected. I was able to put up $25,000, mainly in the form of securities I had received in payment for several major auditing and consulting jobs. The Ludingtons subscribed $25,000 initially, and the remainder of the $100,000 starting capital came from three other investors with whom I had close family, business or client relationships. These people placed their trust and confidence in our small management team, they believed we were doing something that was worthwhile and should prove profitable. They gave the initial impetus to the new financial institution that was to prove durable and successful beyond our wildest dreams.

On July 1, 1929, Industrial and Power had slightly over $100,-000 of assets and began operations. It is interesting to review the Fund's first journal, which I personally wrote in longhand. (This was long before the automatic computing equipment we use today.) It shows that most of the early investors contributed securities rather than cash to the Fund. These securities were generally sold rather promptly, and at prices that were soon to look exceptionally high. Curtis Publishing, for example, was accepted by the Fund at a value of $123 per share and sold at $124. Within five years, it traded at $5 per share. We sold U. S. Steel at $258, only to see it drop to $24 in 1932. Guaranty Trust was sold at $679; it was later to fall 500 points.

Early in the summer of 1929, about 75 per cent of the Fund's modest resources were invested in common stocks. Although this "balance" was extremely conservative in the light of the standards of those ebullient and effervescent days, our group still felt uneasy; after all, we were dealing with money that many of our clients could not afford to lose. So, as stocks continued to surge hysterically upward, we continued to sell them, and in September, 1929, as the Dow-Jones stock average reached a record peak of 381, we had cut back to about a 40 per cent common stock position. In other words, at the peak of common stock prices, some 60 per cent of our resources were invested in fixed-income securities. Then came the crash.

It was first gradual, then electrically sudden. By mid-October, the stock price average had eased away from the early September peaks, to about the 350 level. In the following week, it dropped another 25 points, but the daily volume of shares traded stayed at the usual three-to-four-million level. The next week saw another 25 point decline, and rising volume hinted that storm clouds might soon appear. On the first day of the following week (October 28) the storm really hit us. In a single day, the Dow-Jones Average dropped precipitously 40 points amidst the turmoil of nine million shares traded, and panic spread throughout Wall Street and the nation, as millions of Americans watched in horror as the ticker tape reported lower and lower market quotations. And the worst was yet to come. The next day, Black Tuesday, October 29, 1929, saw sixteen million shares change hands, a record that exists to this day. In the panic, the Dow-Jones Average dropped another 45 points to 212—down almost 40 per cent from two weeks earlier. Although the average recovered slightly by the day's end, the "new era" philosophy was dead. The concepts that the stock market was a one-way street, and that America's growth insured corporate profits were "out the window," as a result of the sweeping financial crisis of October, 1929. The bubble had burst.

In retrospect, we had chosen the worst time in the financial history of the United States to launch a new investment vehicle. Yet in another way, what good fortune we had to launch a conservative fund just a few brief months before the merits of conservative investing were to be so amply demonstrated. And how fortunate we were that the perception, the ability, and of course

the good luck of our management team in selling stocks in a substantial way before the crash were vindicated by the events of
that tragic October.

As a result of our conservative philosophy and our management moves, the Fund's asset value demonstrated a resistance to
decline, a relative stability of value, unmatched by virtually any
other investment trust or mutual fund in the last half of 1929.
New capital had started to flow little by little into the Fund and
as our first year ended, total assets were $195,000. We were on
our way!

The old adage that "the first year is the hardest" gave us confidence in what lay ahead as 1930 began. The nation's confidence,
however, had been too severely shaken for a rapid return to nor-
malcy. This lack of confidence on the part of businessmen, investors, and the public proceeded to make itself felt in the early
1930's, and the stage was set for the worst economic depression
in America's history.

The economic and market conditions of 1930-1933 were disas-
trous. The economy went further and further down into the
depths. Total U.S. national income dropped by more than half—
from $88 billion in 1929 to $40 billion in 1933. Unemployment
soared from one-and-a-half million people in 1929 to almost
thirteen million in 1933—one out of every four in America's labor
force was out of work. Responding to these events, the stock market continued its decline. As 1930 began, the Dow-Jones Average
was at 250; at the end of 1930, 165; at the end of 1931, 78; and at
mid-1932, 41—a 90 per cent decline from the 1929 high. The decline was steady and unremitting, with few upward surges to
break the monotony. I can recall talking to Abe Kulp on the telephone after the market opened each day and asking, "How's the
market?" And each day (or so it seemed) the answer came back
with all of its discouraging sameness: "It's down again."

Although more economic adversity was still to come, by mid-
1932 the worst was over for the market. Even the Roosevelt bank
holiday—which dried up billions of dollars in the nation's money
supply—followed by the United States reducing the gold value of
the dollar, was not enough to drive stocks below the earlier bot-

tom. Stocks rallied late in 1932, and moved upward in 1933 and—after a consolidating phase in 1934—again in 1935.

Our management group—like most other investors, institution and individual alike—did not foresee the full extent of the Depression. But we did better than most, and, despite the decline in the Fund's asset value, our dividends held constant during the three-year market drop. Substantial cash reserves had been put back in the market after the 1929 break, and it was not until mid-1931 that we had learned our lesson. We re-accumulated substantial cash reserves late in that year, and were rewarded by a relatively favorable showing in 1932. The conscious need for changing our common stock position in anticipation of possible business and market changes, however, was to stay with the Fund all through the years. We were determined that "balance" would not mean a static investment position. Rather, balance would be dynamic. We would aim to provide more protection (through larger cash and bond reserves) if markets appeared high; we would attempt to build up profits (through a larger common stock position) if stocks appeared undervalued. We knew that the future was too unpredictable, the markets too sensitive, to bat 1.000 in our efforts. However, we believed that as experienced professionals, we could turn in a better batting average (or performance record) than the average investor could earn for himself.

Investment management problems were not the only hurdles we faced in the early 1930's. The key area of distribution was also a daily challenge. Our initial aim had been to build a record for the Fund, and thereby attract new investors to purchase its shares. We had in fact built the record, a record of conservative management which preserved share values relatively well in the light of the extraordinary economic decline we encountered. Now there was the problem of selling this record to the public.

It is a substantial understatement to say that there were fewer people who wanted to make an investment—even a relatively conservative one—in the early thirties than there were in the late twenties. It was all too close to the truth to say, as many said, that "you can't even *give* an investment trust away." Yet I called on stockbrokers all over Philadelphia trying to spread the gospel of the balanced fund. It wasn't easy. In some firms, we couldn't even get in to tell our story. In others, our story fell on deaf ears. On occasion, I was politely asked to leave or given a mighty cold shoulder. But we continued our efforts because of the firm conviction that the Fund could grow to substantial size only through the efforts of independent securities firms, whose representatives would recommend it to their clients. We had to win their respect, confidence and good will.

We even considered the possibility of building sales on our own. In 1931 we formed a retail selling organization (W. L. Morgan and Company) in addition to the management company (Wellington Corporation) we had formed two years earlier. Just as the management company provided both the Fund and our individual clients with administrative and investment advisory service, so the sales company handled both the distribution—at wholesale as well as retail—of the Fund's shares, and a general brokerage business. We recognized that a fund does not grow by itself, but only by years of management and sales effort on the part of the separate sponsoring company.

The early distribution efforts were mostly a "one-man" job, however, and my hands were so full with the whole complex of my activities—accounting, investment counseling, tax work, and sales —that the efforts were not crowned with notable success. Nevertheless, sales did come along gradually, as the Fund's record and our management reputation began to gain recognition. Each year, investors subscribed to some 20,000 new shares, and by the beginning of 1934, Fund assets had crossed $500,000. That year, furthermore, marked a major forward step for us. An able Philadelphia stockbroker named Wallace M. McCurdy became interested in the Fund, and was impressed with its record. His firm, Thayer, Baker & Company, began to recommend the Fund to its clients, and the first crack opened in the stone wall that had been confronting our distribution efforts.

During the next year (1935), two events occurred that would leave their impression indelibly on the Fund, and launch it on its way to the heights ahead—heights that were by no means visible at that time. The first was the Fund's name. I mentioned earlier that the name "Industrial and Power Securities Company" was chosen because it was in tune with the twenties. For the thirties, however, it was rather off-key. The trials and tribulations of the closed-end trusts, many of which had gone completely and forever underwater in the cataclysm that shook the economy, had given the over-used "industrials" a bad connotation. "Power" in particular was bad news, as a result of collapse of the utility holding companies. Perhaps even more important, no one could remember our name, and more and more people began to refer to Industrial and Power Securities as "a Wellington fund"; that is, one of the accounts under Wellington Corporation management.

I had chosen the name Wellington for the management company for a variety of reasons. I had been a student and admirer of the life of Wellington—"the Iron Duke"—for years, and was fascinated with the history of his military campaigns. On trips to Europe in 1926 and 1928, I had visited Apsley House, his London home, and had tramped over many of his battlefields, most notably Waterloo. My admiration for the Iron Duke carried over to many things English, especially antique silver and furniture. The Wellington name, furthermore, had not been used by other American financial institutions, which was not the case with the well-known United States heroes—Washington, Jefferson, Hamilton, Lincoln, and others. Most important of all, Wellington was a name easy to remember; it was distinctive; it had a magical ring to it, a sort of indefinable air of quality about it that made it almost perfect as a name for a conservative financial organization.

There is no question in my mind that the choice of the Wellington name was one of the cornerstones of our success. Since the name was easy to remember, it was well-suited to help us accomplish one of our major early objectives: to make Wellington a household word like "Cadillac," "Coca-Cola," or "Tiffany." Curiously, the timing of the Fund's name change was brought about by another of the lucky breaks that seemed to follow my career. Early in 1935, with our distribution efforts progressing surely—if slowly—I met a man who turned out to be one of the most remarkable, dynamic and able sales executives in the history of the mutual fund industry.

A. J. Wilkins walked into my office one day, introduced himself, and said he was interested in selling shares in our Fund. He knew of its fine record, he had a varied and successful background both in the general securities field and in the retail selling of mutual funds, and he wanted to set up a monthly purchase program for investors, using our Fund as the investment medium. No one had to be a genius to see the magical mathematics involved if thousands of individual investors purchased $10, $25, or $100 of our shares each month. Fortunately for us, several other fund distributors either hadn't recognized Al Wilkins' extraordinary ability or hadn't foreseen the intrinsic merit of his plan. However, we all were impressed with both the man and the idea, especially with his talent for salesmanship and his aggressive attitude. When I told him how many shares we had sold in the previous month (it was about 1,000) he replied: "Why, you're not even in business!"

It was Al Wilkins, too, who helped precipitate the change in the Fund's name. He shared our reservations about "Industrial and Power," and strongly urged that we choose a new name that would identify the Fund with the management company, as we had been doing to some extent in our reports and literature. He thus shared my enthusiasm for the Wellington name, and, with this meeting of minds, the decision was easily made: "Industrial and Power Securities Company" became "Wellington Fund, Inc.," on July 11, 1935.

The driving force of Wilkins soon made itself felt. Almost overnight, he created a retail selling organization, and sales moved sharply forward. Instead of the 10,000-shares-a-year pace of the early thirties, we were suddenly selling 80,000 shares a year, and then 100,000 shares. The distribution problem had been solved by the entry of Al Wilkins on the Wellington stage, just as Kulp-Barringer had appeared to help solve the investment management problem six years earlier. If it had not been for Al Wilkins, we would probably never have grown as fast as we did.

Fortunately, the basic decisions of the 1928-1935 period were sound decisions that favorably shaped the Fund's future. We had selected a sound form for it: the open capitalization, which permitted the constant issuance of new shares. We had chosen an unusual (for those days) philosophy that made it unique: the balanced concept. By the addition of able key executives, we had successfully attacked the two basic areas in which we needed to demonstrate competence: investment management and share distribution. We had established "a name to remember when investing," a name that would in fact be remembered by hundreds of thousands of investors: Wellington Fund. And as 1935 drew to a close, the first major milestone was crossed: Wellington Fund assets exceeded $1 million.

"Never look back. Something might be gaining on you." It is risky to ignore the obvious wisdom of this warning (generally attributed to the remarkable baseball pitcher Satchel Paige). Nevertheless, to complete the Wellington story, a brief review of a few major events subsequent to 1935 is necessary. For, although in many respects the nearly three decades that followed simply represented building on the sound foundation established in the pre 1935 era, the growth of the Fund from $1 million then to some $1.6 billion now is too large to be accounted for in "Topsy" terms. Indeed, on many a single day in 1963 investors purchased $1 million or more of Wellington Fund shares; in an average recent month purchases totaled $12 million, or greater than the Fund's assets in 1944.

Wellington Fund didn't "just grow." Its growth occurred in a healthy economic climate, as the nation rose out of the ashes of the Depression and climbed to a mature and healthy prosperity. Reflecting this prosperity, common stock prices continued a steady advance from 1935 to the current levels. To be sure, there were setbacks along the way, and the market was shaken by major declines in 1937, 1940, 1946, 1957, and 1962. Each of these drops was sharp, severe, and difficult of prediction, but none came close to matching the depth or duration of the 1929 holocaust. In each instance, stock prices (as measured by the Dow-Jones Average) recovered and matched, then exceeded, the previous high levels. As 1963 ended, the average had climbed to about 760. (You will recall that the 1929-1932 range was 381 high, 41 low. This 381 high was not penetrated again until 1954.)

The effect of the prolonged bull market lasting over three decades (1933-1963) was to give investors confidence in the merits of common stock investing, confidence that investing in American industry offered a potential opportunity for growth of capital and income. By the same token, each intervening market setback, however short-lived, served to convince investors that investment risk was more than illusory; it was something real to contend with. In other words, this long period in many respects provided the perfect climate for the growth of a balanced fund, a period in which its merits were tested and affirmed.

In our effort to build public acceptance of the mutual fund idea (and particularly for Wellington Fund), we recognized the need to continue the pioneering early efforts in the area of sales promotion. We worked to develop the good will of the press, in order to build public confidence. We always endeavored to be "first" in providing such things as attractive sales literature, a color motion picture about the Fund, and readable and interesting shareholder reports—all presented in crisp and accurate writing style and with the elementary idea that a simple chart or graph is worth a thousand words. We wanted investors to understand what investing was all about. One particular innovation—very advanced for its time (1940)—was our decision to print all of our literature in a deep shade of blue ink in order to differentiate it from competitive material. This, too, became part of our corporate image, and to this day investment dealers continue to refer to "Wellington blue."

The good fortune we enjoyed in having men like Abe Kulp and Brandon Barringer to head up the investment management group and Al Wilkins to lead the sales team also continued in the later years. By far the most notable example of this good fortune was our finding a man to spark our activities in the third key area of our company: general corporate administration, including representing Wellington at the industry conference table and before the federal and state governmental agencies. (These activities in the regulatory area became particularly important at the time of the Investment Company Act of 1940, and again as a result of the 1963 Securities and Exchange Commission study of the securities industry.) Like most of the "rugged individualists" of the early pioneering days of the mutual fund industry, I was probably too competitive and combative to play a key role as an industry spokesman. Instead, this vital job was handled for us by a man who is today generally acknowledged as the most respected figure in our industry: Joseph E. Welch. Welch came to Wellington in 1937 after experience and training with the Federal Reserve Bank of Philadelphia, and a local stock exchange firm. He served us first in a variety of routine financial duties, but soon his extraordinary ability, intelligence, integrity, and judgment became apparent—first to us and later to the industry. By 1949 he was executive vice-president of both the Fund and the Management Company, and in 1963 it was with great pride that I turned over to him my responsibilities as president and chief executive officer of Wellington Management Company. There can be no question of the invaluable contribution that Joe Welch has made to the development of Wellington Fund.

But, no matter how important looms the contribution of a large number of able individuals, a sound financial institution must be more durable than the individuals who direct its affairs during a given period, however long, in its history. It must maintain its basic character; in Wellington Fund, this meant a continued dedication to truly conservative investment principles, no matter how tempting the lure to abandon them in the search for even larger rewards. We have never deviated from our constant endeavor to achieve the Fund's three basic investment objectives: (1) conservation of capital; (2) reasonable current income; (3) an opportunity for possible capital gains without assuming undue risks.

We could not, of course, assure that these three investment objectives would be achieved in any given period: no responsible investment adviser can promise future performance. Nevertheless, these goals served as a constant guide to our investment decision-making, and we strictly adhered to them through an almost unbelievable variety of business and market conditions. In this connection, I am sure we have done a better job for the investor than he could have done for himself. The investors in the Fund know it, as witnessed by the fact that the rate of shares tendered to the Fund for redemption each year has traditionally been among the lowest of any fund in our industry. This "index of shareholder satisfaction" (so very important by reason of the open-end character of a mutual fund) has been a constant source of pride to us, and it will be a challenge to continue to maintain this confidence.

The thousands of investment firms all across the United States that have recommended Wellington Fund to their clients have also played a key role in the Fund's growth and success. These firms helped to bring to the American public the message that conservative investing offers the potential of real rewards. Not a one-way street to overnight riches, to be sure, for investment risk is always with us, no matter how it is moderated by diversification and balance. But these investment dealers helped millions of Americans to realize that absolute safety simply does not exist (for example, the rising cost of living has reduced the buying power of the dollar in a savings account by one third or more during many decades), and convinced them to take a moderate risk in the search for reasonable income and possible profit. By placing their clients' money in our hands, these firms have demonstrated their confidence in us, knowing that we are trustees and experienced managers, and that we will continue to carry on these duties with a high sense of fiduciary responsibility.

It has been this sense of responsibility, together with our constant belief in conservative investing, that has helped us bring Main Street to Wall Street. We have enabled the small or average investor to combine his invested savings with those of many others and own a share in American industry—not on the speculative and highly leveraged basis that Main Street came to Wall Street in 1929, but on a sound financial footing, with each investor's stake represented by a hundred or more stocks and bonds, securities generally chosen for their high and improving investment quality. Today's mutual fund investors—numbering more than three million Americans with some $24 billion invested in mutual fund shares—now include persons from all walks of life, from all over America, from all income levels. Included are both institutions which want professional management and diversification, and individuals who have little knowledge of investing and who have neither the time, inclination nor ability to "watch" the stock market. For them, Wellington Fund, and mutual funds generally, represent a sound approach to the problems of future retirement, children's college education, and income for today's rising living costs. The conservative policies of the Fund, as well as the conservative goals of its shareholders, are a far cry from the high leverage investing and "get rich quick" objective of 1929. The 1964 Wellington Fund investor is dramatically characterized by this letter we recently received:

> I am exceedingly grateful for the day a friend prevailed upon me to join Wellington Fund. I bought 5-10-15-20 and 25 shares when I could in the 1940's. I am a retired nurse who didn't know a big salary until the last six years of working, but through this welcomed suggestion and by reinvesting—I have enough from these dividends to pay my rent.
>
> I am not envious of the brains of this Fund. Instead, 1 count my blessings and am grateful that such men saw fit to start and do things so that persons like me can invest small sums which grow into a realization of future living.
>
> I well know that 15% of the world build and establish industries and give work for the rest of the world. While I could use more money, I simply thank God for such men who establish an avenue in which I have been able to travel more comfortably in my 67th year, and as a widow of thirty years who educated a daughter quite finely without borrowing, through knowing one can accomplish one's needs if one is not envious, if one applied oneself to honest work, and above all if one saves instead of squandering.
>
> My fervent hope and prayers are with the judgement of these fine gentlemen who have a grave responsibility, and a full thanksgiving for my 1,440 shares in Wellington Fund.

The Wellington Fund story, of course, is but one chapter in the extraordinary anthology of the mutual fund industry. Competitive firms, staffed by able managers, dynamic sales executives, and vigorous innovators, also share the credit for their equally good work and pioneering efforts in the development of the mutual fund idea. It was our industry in the aggregate—not any one company and certainly not any one man—that has been instrumental in furthering America's economic democracy by bringing Main Street to Wall Street. The concept of conservative balance that was pioneered when Wellington Fund was born some thirty-five years ago was simply one tributary in the river of mutual fund progress that brought to the average American family a modern method of investing. It is this investment method that will help to shape the financial future of millions of Americans in the years to come.

DAVRE J. DAVIDSON

WILLIAM S. FISHMAN

ARA Service

DAVRE J. DAVIDSON, chairman of the board and chief executive officer of ARA Service (Automatic Retailers of America), began his career thirty years ago by placing one-cent automatic peanut-vending machines in various locations in Los Angeles. Davidson Brothers, which he formed with his brother, Henry, became one of the leading regional vending firms, known for its innovations and services. In 1959, Mr. Davidson and his associates incorporated a new firm that was to be the nucleus for ARA Service, the country's foremost organization for providing food, beverages, refreshments and other products through automatic vending and manual services.

WILLIAM S. FISHMAN, president of ARA Service, with more than twenty-five years of experience in vending and food service, is a recognized leader in the field. He is a Phi Beta Kappa graduate of the University of Illinois, and a past president of National Automatic Merchandising Association and a member of its board of directors. He was formerly co-owner of Automatic Merchandising Company, operating in the Chicago and Detroit areas, and one of the first companies acquired by ARA.

Serving People—
Where They Are

Food for Thought about Vending

B Y

DAVRE J. DAVIDSON

and

WILLIAM S. FISHMAN

In retrospect, it proved to be an important highway marker along the road to what's become an $18 billion market. But at the time it looked to many like another dead end or costly detour in a business which is famous for them.

The year was 1959. The event was the formal bringing together of the two firms in which we were principals.

The business?

That's not so easy to say. In a way, defining the business and its directions is what this chapter is all about.

For one thing, it was not, is not, just vending. We can say this more certainly now than we could then, but by 1959 we had both realized that automatic merchandising—vending—was only part of the picture.

This isn't easy for two individuals who have spent the greater part of their lives at work in the vending field to say. But a lot of things are not easy to say. Part of the problem in grasping the truth about this business—this market—is that there are no easy, ready words to use.

To start with, it's a service business. It is based primarily on the provision of food and refreshment. Its consumers—and you probably either are or have been among them—are the millions of Americans in colleges or schools, offices, plants and hospitals who find it necessary to eat where they are, or who find it more convenient or pleasant to stay there to eat one or more meals or snacks every day, every week, throughout the year.

Such food and refreshment is sometimes provided manually, by personal service, in cafeterias, dining rooms, at bedside. Or it can be provided automatically, by machines. Or it can be offered by one of the many combinations of the two methods.

We warned you it's not an easy market to define. This is especially so if, as in our case, you keep your definitions broad enough to encompass growth and expansion into provision of additional services, such as operating bookstores, supplying landscape assistance, accounting services, et cetera.

Many have slipped into the mistake of overplaying the glamour and gee-whiz aspects of automatic service. Some of those are not in business today. Others, including ourselves, have made other mistakes, usually in misjudging either the direction of consumer wants or the timing in meeting them.

The most important thing to realize is that it is a "people" business. Success lies in giving customers what they want today and in correctly anticipating their wants of tomorrow. In turn, this translates into the recruiting, training, motivating and supervision of people who excel in customer service.

With our two backgrounds, each with an emphasis on vending, we've probably seen in the last few decades an interplay of man and machines that some day will sum up much of twentieth cen-, tury civilization.

In our book, man is winning over machines by a big margin. This fact underlies all of the successful companies in the institutional and industrial food service field today.

Our ARA organization, serving across the nation and recording a current rate of sales of more than 200 million dollars annually, has grown directly out of the bringing together of people-oriented people. Looking back, it was persistence in serving the wants and needs of customers, rather than in concerning ourselves with machinery per se, that helped us and other firms in the field to meet successfully two major periods of decision.

One was in the post-World War II period and consisted of finding ways to serve food—both hot and cold, and in variety— via automatic vending devices. The other was more recent, and consisted of the necessity to combine the entire structure of vending as we knew it with personal food service management to provide successfully what growing millions of consumers sought.

Figuring out customers was something we'd both been doing for years, as we grew up in the vending field in the thirties and forties. We had both had some rugged moments with customers.

Is "rugged" a strong enough word? Some examples of customer dissatisfaction were of the most drastic sort.

For instance, a young operator of vending machines named Davidson one day strolled upon a scene where four healthy, husky—and irate—longshoremen were literally at work heaving a recalcitrant beverage machine off a pier and into the ocean. Sudden recollection of duties elsewhere quickly reversed the young man's steps.

Similarly, this time at a landlocked spot, young Bill Fishman suddenly changed his mind about checking that day on a group of his machines at a steel mill. His was a vivid, mind-etching portrait of three burly customers hurling a large beverage machine of his into an open hearth furnace.

There had been another time when, displaying a bit more stick-to-it-iveness, a young fellow named Fishman came upon a scene in a Chicago airport that caused him to begin kicking a traveler's luggage with some force. When the traveler turned to demand the reason, he got this reply: "When you stop kicking that vending machine of mine, I'll stop kicking your luggage." The patron stopped.

It took time to get to know these vending customers of earlier days. In a West Coast establishment served by the Davidson firm, ingenious machinists devised a technique for triggering a mechanism and getting several chocolate candy bars for the price of one. When all attempts at blocking the technique failed, a complete refill of the machine, two hundred bars, was left outside, next to the machine. Two days later, knowing the basic fair play that marks Americans from coast to coast, it wasn't too surprising to find payment on hand for the full number of bars.

We had each learned many lessons in human nature before our companies were combined in 1959.

The early days of our two companies were parallel, although two thousand miles apart. To a large degree, they also reflected similar development on the part of many other firms.

The Davidson organization was launched in the mid-thirties on the proverbial shoestring and with borrowed capital. It was operated by brothers Henry and Davre on the West Coast, principally in the Los Angeles area.

Automatic Merchandising Company (AMCO) was begun about the same time in the Midwest. Founder Harry Winston, now deceased, was joined by the Fishman half of this by-line in 1941. Operations were primarily in the Chicago and Detroit areas.

The regional, localized nature of our companies was typical of the state of vending. A national company, Automatic Canteen, a pioneering organization in connection with many of vending's important developments, was the principal exception.

Both of this chapter's authors literally started with peanuts. The recollection may not strike many readers, but a good number will certainly recall the glass globes of peanuts which represented the heart of our sales in early days. Usually in or near candy stores, terminals, public buildings, et cetera, this type of machine would vend peanuts, gum or candy in fairly reliable style on the insertion of a penny.

The other main kind of vending activity of that period consisted of the sale of cigarettes.

The latter part of the thirties was a crucial time for vending and for our struggling companies. While public locations for our machines had advantages in usage through many hours of the day, reliable and fairly predictable demand, and continuity of machine placement, a number of firms such as ours envisioned the growth of another market, made up of service to people where they worked.

Until a number of developing factors converged toward the close of the decade, however, neither of our companies had much success when we called upon industry to discuss the placing of candy, peanut and cigarette machines.

Resistance was often unbelievably strong. "No. Those machines take up valuable space. They're a corridor hazard." "No. They just take our employees' time from their jobs, encourage loitering." "No. Those machines give us a big housekeeping problem." Almost always, "No."

Based on the state to which the vending art and vending machines were developed, maybe there was a bit of truth in earlier days about housekeeping. Vending maintenance men themselves got suspicious about supposed innovations after a while. One year a manufacturer came out with a multiple-flavor cold drink machine absolutely, positively guaranteed not to spill over or "run wild." When told this, one maintenance man said, "Fine, but when it does run wild, which flavor is it likely to pour?"

We encountered closed doors, frozen faces and frigid turndowns from many a businessman along the way. We actually smuggled small machines into some plants to meet the needs of some workers. We really felt we were right in our approach. Where employers let us show them, we proved that less time was lost from work by having machines right at hand than by forcing personnel to go to establishments off the premises.

Also, we offered with a good degree of effectiveness the results of a Harvard study of the mid-thirties showing the greater productivity through intake of energy-giving food such as candy throughout the day. Eventually, about 1940, other studies on personnel effectiveness appeared. The refreshment and rest period became a more accepted concept. Management attitudes were changing.

It was also a time of expanding production to supply Allies who were battling the enemy in the early days of World War II, before the U.S. entry into action. Production schedules couldn't stand employee trips away from the plant for refreshment items.

Also important was the opportune, simultaneous development, by the Stoner Company, of a truly reliable, selective-choice candy vending machine. Fortunately, there was enough volume production of these machines before the wartime ban on manufacture of all vending machines to permit wide usage in wartime plants.

Some companies and some individuals, of course, saw the light early. In the case of both our companies, the Douglas Aircraft Company, first on the West Coast and then in the Midwest, was the initial major industrial client to contract for our services.

In this connection, there's a very pleasant memory of the late thirties for the Davidson part of the by-line. Foiled by the complications of a new type of small vending unit at the Douglas installation in Los Angeles, vending entrepreneur Davidson was about to abandon trying to repair it and call for help when a distinguished-looking gentleman wearing a yachting cap strolled by and soon pitched in successfully to fix the unit. The repairman-for-a-day was one of the top executives of the client company.

Vending machines must have held a fascination for industrial leaders. A bit later, this time in Chicago, an AMCO vending repairman at Montgomery Ward reported getting impromptu but effective assistance from a courtly gentleman passing by his bank of machines. Less than fifteen minutes later the repairman watched this gentleman (Sewell Avery) being carried from the building in his executive chair—one of the more memorable tableaux of our wartime industrial history.

What really helped to bring most managements around to the acceptance of vending, of course, was World War II. The incredibly fast pace of production that was being established in plants all across the United States created a mass need for quick snack and refreshment services which only vending machines could supply on an around-the-clock basis.

By improvising, renovating old machines, and with some heroic maintenance by staffs of our companies and similar firms, the vending business pretty well met the demands. Actually, it crystallized the beliefs of ourselves and others that we were part of a vital and growing force that had a great post-war future in serving varieties of customers in a number of ways.

Statistics on vending volume help tell the story of post-war expansion. National Automatic Merchandising Association, the hard-working trade group which serves the vending field, reported the volume of vending in 1946 to be $600,000,000. By 1960 this figure was two-and-a-half billion and today it is more than three billion.

A good part of this growth revolved about one customer demand, that would give us headaches, yet precipitate a decision that has haunted us happily ever since—the decision to help work out ways of serving varieties of food and beverages, hot as well as cold, through automatic devices.

In the telling of this and other anecdotes, we should make it clear that we've never been in the business of vending machine manufacture. We've tried to relay back to manufacturers our views and judgments as they've been shaped in the direct service of customers, and we've been and are volume purchasers of vending equipment. But we've preferred to retain flexibility and complete freedom of choice in deciding which machine will do the best job of serving customers in particular situations.

At any rate, the scene this time, shortly after World War II, was the plant of an AMCO client in the Midwest, although roughly similar events were taking place for Davidson Brothers out West. Efforts to serve food via mobile carts to employees located at distant points in this manufacturing plant were not working out. Foods intended to be hot would arrive cold and vice versa. As the vending company supplying candy, milk and soft drinks, AMCO was called in to review the situation with a management group looking for answers.

Perhaps with more bravery than judgment, AMCO said it would do the job. Not starting too ambitiously, cold sandwiches were supplied. They were welcomed as an improvement over the past, but greater challenges were hurled. Could we get something hot? Like soup?

Of course. A few days later, while certain fingers were crossed behind certain backs, employees approached a machine with a new, if improvised, sign that read, "Hot Soup." To the practiced eye it looked very much like one of the nearby cold milk machines. That's what it was, except that the refrigeration unit had been taken out and a heating unit substituted. Also, soup had been placed in milk cartons. Hot soup was being vended from a cold milk machine, which was no longer cold nor offered milk. But it met the need.

In due course, after a disbelieving machine manufacturer had been dissuaded from pulling out his hair over the atrocity to his mechanism, some joint thinking took him along the route that has led to the successful vending of hot canned foods. Popular in many automatic cafeterias, these canned offerings—soups, stews, spaghetti, and so on—are kept piping hot in vending machines, safely and conveniently awaiting customer selection.

Not all of our efforts with our imaginative friends in the vending machine manufacturing business worked out as well. We almost completely missed the boat on several developments. In the mid-forties, with just about first crack at some instant coffee machines, we convinced ourselves that the time wasn't right. For three years we stayed out of the coffee vending business—while our competitors rolled up leads we found hard to overcome after we'd realized our mistake.

Today, the vending of fresh-brewed coffee is a mainstay of the coffee industry as well as of the food service industry in general. We do take some consolation in having later innovated techniques which led to methods still successfully in use in many coffee machines today.

The decisions that added up to more and more varieties of food offerings weren't at all easy. We had to learn the vitally important factors involved in placing food in a new and changing medium to meet new and changing needs and tastes.

Many previously prosperous vending companies and vending machine manufacturers went out of business during this period of transition because of inability to manage the complexities of food service. It was a capital-hungry business with a constant demand for new and more modern machines. It required the hiring of more people and new kinds of people. All of us, management and workers, had to demonstrate a willingness to serve, a sensitivity to consumer wants and a flexibility to change.

Competition, as keen if not keener in this field than others in our economy, made this a period of more and more innovations. Now that the customer had gotten a taste of progress, he wanted more. Like most of our confreres at this time, we decided we also wanted to eat. So we made the decisions that expanded our businesses, stretched our credit often to breaking points and, without realizing it, brought us closer to other decisions that were to radically change the course of what had been the vending industry.

The background here deals with the frequent over-stretching of resources and capital to try to keep up with still changing needs of the greatest innovation-causer in the world—the consumer.

As a life's calling, vending probably attracts more independent-thinking, poor but eager, self-made individuals than just about any other field that comes to mind. This is all well and good, except—as is very much the case with authors of this chapter—it creates financial crises of the roughest variety in early days of growth.

Each of us recalls separate days when, in each case, a telephone call arrived on a trip to let us know that coming back to our office might well be nothing more than a formality—that the cancellation of a key account had just about wiped out the business.

You could perhaps blame our persistence and bounce-back qualities on our relative youth. But we think it was more than that. It was almost a part of the business, a basic enthusiasm that told us the next step we were about to take would be a great stride forward—would really do a better job of serving our customers, would entice them into buying more and more of our wares.

We can recall how we talked each other into an all-out emphasis on a new type of ice cream vending machine. We proved to be wrong in judging our market's eagerness for the product. And the situation wasn't helped by the fact that the expensive ice cream machines—which we had bought in large quantity— were not the reliable, silent salesmen we thought they would be. For one thing, they offered no choice of product to the potential buyer. You had to like the one item offered. Many, many didn't. We wound up scrapping the whole effort and selling the cabinets to employees as home freezers.

The late forties and early fifties were really a prime time for companies like ourselves. Not in income or growth in all cases, but in the general air of enthusiasm and venturesomeness that prevailed. Many former servicemen of independent nature were attracted to vending, with its relatively low demand for initial capital as down payment on machines. They made this the field in which they could spread their wings as small businessmen.

Two machine manufacturing firms helped write a new chapter for the industry by working at—and eventually bringing to a stage of acceptance—vending machines that really produced appetizing, hot coffee. They made their development a spearhead for franchises set up in many parts of the country and operated by many an eager ex-GI. Many of the latter are key factors in the field today.

It was a field day for risk-takers. It was a rewarding time for those who claim that America's greatness stems from the basic courage and initiative of its people.

In a city in the East, a widowed mother with nine children literally mortgaged her sole possession, her house, in order to grant the well-founded belief of her eldest son that he could take a small, bankrupt vending business and make a go of it. He did, and today his division forms one of the successful arms of ARA Service.

Two other young men with a dream actually sold their cows in order to go into their own vending business which today forms another important part of ARA. Enthusiasm, optimism, competition all were going at full steam.

At a recent national conference of our top ARA management people, we happened to get on the subject of this period in our industry's history with three of our top executives. Each turned out to have a strikingly similar story. After the war, each had decided to try his hand in the vending-food service business. They did things by expediency. They devised techniques and ideas that—if they had realized it—were supposed to be impossible. They lined up organizations. They prepared for volume business. They had the courage to approach management of large companies and show a better way of serving customers. They got the important sales.

As these forces of enthusiasm and growth took hold in all parts of the country, the regional pattern of vending became more and more pronounced through the fifties. The need for new capital and other factors we'll note later inspired Davidson Brothers, AMCO and our associates to begin thinking of making ownership in our companies available to the investing public.

What was needed was an integrated corporate structure, the organization of specialized skills and a unification of formerly separate companies into a new team of corporate executives, management and operating personnel. This was accomplished by enlisting important groups of investors and the public into the ownership of Davidson Automatic Merchandising Co., Inc., incorporated in February of 1959. In September of 1959 AMCO was brought into this fold and ARA was on its way.

Other local and regional vending companies—the best in the land, we're naturally convinced—joined our company as we strove for growth through new ways to serve customers.

Our formerly local or regional firms found this banding together under the ARA banner a desirable step for other reasons.

beyond access to additional needed capital for expansion. For one thing, it assured corporate continuity and resolved problems of personal estate planning for men approaching their fifties. It helped to achieve balance and blend of geographical coverage. It widened the varieties of clients served, a good defense against a recession in a given field. Also, importantly, it enabled each of us to transfer our individual special talents—sales, finance, engineering, et cetera—over to a broader base.

And pervading all were the beneficial results to customers and ourselves of service that could continue to be rendered on a local basis but now even more expertly and well because of the centralized, back-up staff support our organization made possible. We knew that success would lie in correctly assessing the ways required in the years ahead to best serve this institutional-industrial market.

This kind of thinking naturally brought us to more intensive consideration of the service approach that represented a business that was also moving along, picking up momentum and, we realized, complementary to ours.

This business was made up of contract food service (sometimes called food service management) companies. Some were local, but a few had wide territorial coverage. These firms efficiently operated company cafeterias and executive dining rooms. And a few select ones were growing into expanding fields of college dining halls and cafeterias and of patient food services in hospitals.

An outstanding example was Slater Food Service Management, headquartered in Philadelphia. It was later to provide an Eastern accent to our Midwest and Western story.

Roots for the Slater organization were put down in 1926. That year John Slater was a graduate student at the University of Pennsylvania and living at the Delta Kappa Epsilon fraternity house. As was not uncommon in fraternity houses, there was a good deal of complaining about the food being served. When the protests became particularly loud one day, John Slater volunteered to take over management of the dining room.

His success at the job was almost instantaneous. He planned menus with imagination, engineered purchasing and streamlined kitchen procedures. It was not long before he was managing other fraternity dining rooms at other colleges and on his way to a growing business. Assisting in this growth was, among many solid Slater company citizens, the man who later became president of the company, James Hutton. He started working for the Slater firm when a student at Temple University in 1935, became a vice-president at the age of twenty-six and president in 1960. Today, along with Hy Minter and Harvey Stephens, two other outstanding executives, Jim Hutton is a senior ARA vice-president.

Difficult but necessary decisions were looming as expansion marked both food vending and manual food service companies. There was no doubt the two fields were interrelated.

The problem was to keep our focus on the customer in a period of time when technique and machinery were in the spotlight.

We were fortunate in having momentum at work as we moved into the sixties. It helped us meet the challenges of the decision that neither vending services nor manual food services alone represented the way of the future in providing a flexible alignment to meet those ever-varying customer needs and requirements.

The addition of the Slater company in 1961, with its national organization and capable executives who also believed in this kind of future, cemented that decision. In step with our action, whose logic is unassailable, are other leading vending firms who now have also realigned their organizations to recognize a new way of life.

Unfortunately not around as active top management men to make such a decision were some earlier exponents of change who had misjudged the tempo of events and consumer wants. They had believed that vending per se amounted to a magic formula for success.

In costly adventures the consumer was offered, and in some cases is still being offered, all manner of goods and services by way of vending machines. It's our feeling that consumer needs create vending and not vice versa. Some items, such as many soft goods, paperback books, and so on, are in our judgment not in demand via vending as yet.

It comes down to a sense of knowing how far and how fast to move with an innovation—of gauging that sensitive yardstick of consumer demand. Despite a number of errors in judging these factors in the past, our track record seems to stand up well.

An emerging market, for example, seems to be growing through experiments in automatic dining cars conducted for and with the Southern Pacific Railroad. Testing of the acceptability of the fully automatic public restaurant is being conducted by our company and by others. Again, the consumer will decide what kind of establishment he wants and when he wants it.

At the heart of the matter is the fact that ours is a service business. The customer—the consumer—will determine what new products we will vend, what new services we will offer, what new markets we will enter—and when we should do these things. Our real stock in trade is organizing and motivating people under circumstances where needs can be served at a profit to our company and with satisfaction for customers.

Flexibility will become even more important, as a recent ARA service installation indicates. Here, in connection with a university-hospital complex, our company is supplying the man and woman power to supervise, prepare and serve dietetic meals for patients, conduct classes for student nurses, provide around-the-clock employee food service by means of a large, combination manual and vending facility, operate vending machine installations at various points on campus and participate in the institution's nutritional research program.

This installation, the developing concepts, the people who make it possible, all testify to a sector of the American economy that has literally come a long way from peanuts.

CHARLES REVSON

Revlon

CHARLES REVSON is chairman of the board and a founder of Revlon, Inc. In 1932 Mr. Revson, his brother Joseph, and Charles Lachman joined a partnership under the name of Revlon Company. Martin Revson, another brother, became part of the enterprise in 1935. The firm grew quickly as a result of introducing a new concept in nail enamel, an opaque product made with pigments in a wide range of colors. In 1939 it consolidated its position as the leading nail enamel company by introducing lipsticks and nail enamels in matching shades. Revlon has broadened its product line and diversified into other retail fields, including acquisition of companies in the fields of shoe-care products, women's apparel and sportswear, artificial flowers and pharmaceuticals.

The Matter of Beauty

The Development of the Futurama Lipstick Case

BY

CHARLES REVSON

In the mahogany-paneled library of a fashionable home near Waterbury, Connecticut, there is a unique three-inch-thick book. Its creased, onionskin pages are typewritten carbons. Its covers are dull black hardboard. On the front is a paste-white label with two typed words, MANHATTAN PROJECT.

A few years ago this book was dynamite. The project described in terse, technical idiom was an industrial thriller. That accounts for its name. It was an explosive secret at Revlon for most of 1954, and it was to change the cosmetics habits of American women.

In that now-quiescent volume lies a record of tension and crisis, immense economic risk, and a saga of travels, exploration, industrial research and problems that at one time almost split the company in half.

Appropriately enough, Manhattan Project is shelved in the library of one Earl F. Copp, a gentle yet dynamic man, who little knew what he was getting in for on January 13, 1954, when I asked him to come to my office. It was his sixty-third birthday.

He was not surprised when I held a small object up between my thumb and forefinger and said, "Earl, take a look at this French lipstick case."

Earl was the chief operation officer of Risdon Manufacturing Company, which had been making most of Revlon's cases since 1947. Such a visit was routine. But his eyes narrowed slightly as he took the sample from me. He was a man who knew his business. One glance told him that the case was different from any then made in the United States. It was longer. It held a refillable cartridge that a woman could discharge when the lipstick was used up.

For a long time it had been bothering me that American women—so alert in many ways—had been content with that old smooth brass cylinder. It had no distinctive shape, color, finish or design. It looked like a cartridge case. They would buy them and discard them when they were used up, and then buy another. As for refills—there were no such things.

A number of cosmetics manufacturers had for years tried to make cases more distinctive. We had played around with the idea at Revlon. But all that any of us ever came up with was another version of the cartridge case. For one thing, all case manufacturers, including Risdon, had the same kinds of machines, with the same old limitations.

"Earl," I said. "Look, Earl, I want something."

He sat down suddenly, hunched forward. He knew me well enough to get the pitch. My look, my tone of voice meant one thing to him: a battle.

"I want a case, a *refillable* case. You have to make it different from this one. This is too much like the others, refillable perhaps, but not elegant enough. I want to see luxury, fashion, expensive jewelry. No more bullets. Can you see what I mean? I want a case that glows with fashion. That has such fashion magic it transmits right through the lipstick and onto the faces of women. Makes them feel the beauty touching their lips."

Earl was trying to say something, but I kept talking. "I don't want just one case, but a whole line. So that women will want one for morning, one for evening, one for special occasions—all suitable for refills with whatever different colors they prefer.

Finally Earl broke in, looking troubled. "This is a big order, Charles. It'll take a long time. It'll be way out of line in cost."

As Copp well knew, though we were the largest cosmetics manufacturer, our gross sales were only about $36 million. We couldn't afford a staggering bill for one product, lipstick. I could tell he was searching me out, trying to set up the most logical roadblock. Was this just another idea? How serious was I?

I didn't give him much of a chance. All I could think of was this fascinating little piece of metal and composition less than three inches long, and the kind of revolution it could start.

"One thing, Earl. You have to plan the design and production at your end so no other firm in the industry—*no one anywhere* —learns what we're doing." Earl knew as well as I that curiosity about what Revlon might be doing often gave rise to persistent, systematic searches by others. Security was no joke.

Then I suggested a plan. "Start setting up a schedule tomorrow. You'll work closely with the staff here. But let's get those cases designed!"

Copp was the logical choice to handle the project. Self-made, extremely efficient, he had the know-how and guts to carry through where other men would have quit. But even he, with his long experience in the industry, was not about to let me go away from the discussion with an easy mind.

"You know, Charles," he said with disarming softness, "we don't even have the kind of machinery you need for what you want. You can't make those cases with any tooling I've ever heard of."

"I know, I know," I quickly agreed, adding that he would not only have to find the methods, but that we had to end up with a finish that would last for at least two years, some kind of lacquer that would afford protection against scratches by hairpins and other objects common in every woman's purse.

"There is no protecting film in existence that will accomplish that," objected Copp.

"Well, there will be by the time we get finished with this project." Earl was right on every count, but the more objections he raised, the more I was determined to get the cases made the right way. As we talked, he made his first set of notes for the Manhattan Project record:

> The following projects are to start *immediately:*
>   a. Employment of designers—not less than five. . . .
>   b. Consideration of basic construction;
>   c. Review of present patent situation. . . .
>   d. Specific consideration for development of designs in different price categories;
>   e. Materials and finishes must be selected on the basis of durability . . . of lasting quality, up to two years if possible. . . .
>   f. Timetable to be established for performance;
>   g. Meetings to be held with Mr. Revson every thirty days. . . .

My colleagues know me as a persistent man. Some use the term "perfectionist." I don't mind the description. Not when there is meaning behind the motive. Not when there is a conviction, a philosophy about what has to be done. Something either is right or it isn't!

The idea for fashionable, refillable lipstick cases had been born twenty-one days before the meeting with Earl Copp. During a business trip abroad, I found myself at a stylish dinner at Maxim's in Paris. The candlelit room, the elegant service, the fine furnishings bespoke good taste and an appreciation of beauty. Next to me sat a chic and lovely woman. What interested me most about my dinner partner was not her beauty but a small object she had taken out of her purse. My eyes returned to it again and again, until finally, with an amused smile, she handed it to me saying, "I would not have expected an *American* man to be so interested in a lipstick."

The beauty of the case, hand-engraved and diamond-bedecked, was one outstanding feature. What really caught my eye, though, was that the lipstick could be removed with a single click-in, click-out action in just one section. And because the lipstick was contained in its own cylinder, removal of it was not only easy, but *smudge-proof.*

My dinner partner's remark kept goading me—"I would not have expected an *American* man to be so interested in a lipstick."

Of course not! All that an American man ever saw was one of those undistinguished brass bullets!

Do you see the philosophy here, the need to do everything *right*? Why should American women be denied the most fashionable lipstick possible within a modest price range? Why shouldn't she have different ones for different occasions—just as she has other accessories—refillable with the exact lipstick color needed to match her dress?

After twenty-two years in the cosmetics industry, I knew what American women wanted: to be caressed with luxury; to be chic, fashionable; to have lovely accessories. Every woman is an individual. She has different moods. This was the thinking behind much of our earlier success. It was behind our first big accomplishment, the introduction of different colors of nail polish. When all women wear the same colors in cosmetics, they feel alike. If each woman can find a color combination for herself, she is different, she can express her individuality. She can be daring or demure, conservative or conspicuous, as her mood dictates.

No matter what anyone says about education or talent or background, the way a woman *looks—the way she thinks she looks—* is the key to her personality. When she looks well, she thinks faster, works more effectively, behaves differently.

Long, long before that evening in Paris, my experiences at Revlon had proven the validity of this belief. We had started business in 1932 as a maker of nail polish. That year, we *grossed* about $4,000. Women used few cosmetics in those days. They timidly applied a few touches of natural gloss to their nails, leaving moons and tips white. But by the end of the thirties, as we daringly made a few colors available and more and more women saw our product as a way to express their individuality, they began to enamel their nails to complement a costume, occasion or mood.

No one ever *matched* lipstick with nail polish. Even if a woman had wanted to, it was all but impossible. Nail polish and lipstick colors came from different manufacturers. Most of the colors clashed.

Then, in 1938, I had an experience similar to my later one in Paris. I sat in a restaurant next to a woman whose lipstick and nail polish were completely incompatible. I had a feeling of real shock. Here was a supposedly attractive woman whose cosmetics were actually detracting from her looks! That experience put us into the lipstick business. Soon we were marketing the first *matching* nail and lipstick colors the American woman—or any other—was able to buy.

The more we linked fashion and color with cosmetics, to bring the American woman a new key to personality and individuality, the more she responded. Where once only the wealthiest of women could afford any kind of cosmetics at all, fashionable lips and nails now became an everyday sight.

By the late forties, our philosophy was proving itself so well that more women were buying Revlon lipsticks than were buying all other brands combined.

I had long been pushing and clamoring for bigger and bigger research programs—or as some put it, "indulging in the hobby of doing it right"—to develop new products. By 1954, when I had the idea for chic lipstick cases, we had already developed four new products that were helping to enhance the face of American womanhood.

The first—our liquid make-up—was introduced in 1950. Then our research and product development program moved into high gear. These were the first years of our great research-for-new-products push. We were changing from a maker of lipsticks and nail polishes to a maker of a full line of cosmetics.

Work began on other new products in 1951. Research facilities were expanded, chemists hired, plans made. Two years later, we were ready with three other new products—a compact make-up, a hair spray, and a twenty-four-hour lipstick.

And then in 1954, while we planned Futurama, we strove to develop still other products. Two—the pincurl hair spray and medicated skin lotion—were ready about the same time as Futurama. And in the next few years, we came out with a complete line of eye make-up, perfume, new make-ups, treatment creamer, aerosol fragrances, men's hair dressing, cologne, after-shave lotion, and many other things.

Throughout these years, I kept insisting on developing new lipstick colors, even though many voices kept repeating in my ear, "Charles, we already have so many we don't know what to do with them!"

"You have to get some *excitement* into colors!" I used to insist to my unhappy colleagues. "Women have a craving for romance and drama and a feeling they are part of it."

I drove our advertising agencies to distraction. I just couldn't see women getting all charged up over names like "Mrs. Miniver Rose" or "Sweet Talk" any more. So we gave them some real inspiration with "Pink Lightning" and "Cherries A La Mode" and "Honey Bee Pink."

By the end of the fifties, we were marketing about forty different shades. The most popular was "Fire and Ice."

Despite this record of success, and despite my firm pronouncements that I knew very well what women wanted, my return from Paris with the compelling urge to do something about revolutionizing lipstick fashions was not greeted with the enthusiasm I expected.

"Revlon is way out in front now," was a common reaction. "Why upset the apple cart?"

When I heard this several times a day, I was quick to let off steam myself. There were enough objections to keep my temper tuned for a long time:

"If you're wrong, Revlon's image of success will be KO'd."
"If you're wrong, we'll not only lose money poured into developing cases, but we'll lose out on sales."
"It'll be too complicated for women, confuse them. They're too accustomed to the old cases."
"Even if you're *right*, retailers will be sore, because they won't be able to unload all those old-style cases."

The trouble was—and that was why I kept climbing farther and farther out on my own private limb—that the arguments were put up by men of experience and ability.

As Manhattan Project began to limp along, with more and more problems and "bugs," I began to wonder whether I really was right after all. Why should I gamble with a deck that might turn out to be stacked against us in the end?

What convinced me that I should continue to pursue the idea relentlessly was this: every time I thought back in our company history to a successful innovation, I saw the resultant products directly related to the changing image of American womanhood. I kept dreaming about the American woman's reaction to a fashionable lipstick case and what it might do for that image—the personality, the individuality.

And don't forget, there was the challenge of a beautiful French woman expressing surprise that an *American* male could be interested in a lipstick case. I couldn't forget that.

I used to lie awake nights worrying about the slowness of the progress, as Earl Copp plugged away at the "impossible" program I had dreamed up for him. During the day, I was a bear to live with and work with. It got so the word would be passed around that "Revson was coming," and every one in the office would suddenly seem to have urgent tasks to attend to.

Few people outside our industry can understand the bitter struggle that takes place trying to maintain secrecy during the development of a new product. I was obsessed—I had to be—with the idea that there must be no security leak. As the leader in the industry, we had more to lose than any other company.

I told Earl Copp to be doubly careful. Records were to be locked up. No one in the company who was not directly working with me was to hear any mention of the project. Whenever Earl talked to outsiders, he could not tell the whole story. He had to talk to top designers—names like Lurelle Guild, Madame Majeska, Seaman Schepps, Schlumberger, Henriette Manville—but all he ever said was, "I want some lipstick cases that will look like expensive, custom-made jewelry."

He never mentioned refillable cases. What he wanted, he said, were just some special designs for a private customer.

When the designs started to come in, it was an exciting and stimulating experience. Many shapes were proposed: prisms, octagons, ribbons and bows, pencils, thimbles and countless others. But the most inspired was the hourglass, a shape that four designers suggested independently.

We experimented with many surface treatments, too: brocaded gold on silver, silver-plated with a gold spiral, wedding bands encircling the cylinder.

With Bert Reibel, our packaging designer, I selected two basic shapes by the end of March, 1954. One group of cases, shaped like hourglasses, would retail at $2.50 or more; the other group, thimble-shaped, would be less expensive.

The selection was deceptively easy. But we found we were completely stalled when it came to the matter of finish—the jewelry-like finish I had insisted was so important to the product. Of all the samples submitted, only *one* surface treatment resembled that of expensive jewelry. We had to make arrangements with Fifth Avenue jewelers and designers, visit art museums and study color photographs of good-looking jewelry from the archives. Almost every major jewelry shop in Manhattan was visited, to study expensive, hand-designed compacts and cases. But we were still little closer to our goal.

During the next eight months, we made up many thousands of designs and some five hundred actual models, each with a different surface or slightly modified shape. Parts were interchangeable, so we could produce still different combinations. We invented our own special language: "belts," "skirts," "balances," "waistlines." Which "belt" looked best with which "skirt"? Which "waistline" went best with which "collar"?

We could have produced the first acceptable design—or any other along the way. Time was getting important. Secrecy was becoming harder and harder to maintain. Already there were hints that the industry knew "Revson is up to something."

But I wasn't satisfied.

Not yet.

It got to be a joke that I was often awake all night worrying about a dimension of one-sixteenth of an inch. And it was true!

The search for new surface treatments inevitably brought us face to face with the limitations of machinery. I had become intrigued by one finish we found on expensive compacts—"Florentine" by name—which was a texture of minute, finely etched lines. In 1954 no case manufacturer had the facilities or know-how to produce it in volume.

"But that's what I want," I said.

"Charles, let's forget it," advised one of my closest associates. "You've got everything else you want. The expense won't be worth it."

"It's the only way I see that case," I persisted.

As it was, I might have lost the battle if it had not been for Copp. He finally, after long weeks of experimentation, had devised belts and grinding wheels that would simulate the "Florentine" finish.

To produce other finishes, he had to dispatch engineers to Switzerland and Italy before he could locate and buy the only turning machines on earth that could do a mass production job.

The battle was still far from over. I had specified that the finish *had* to be protected for two years.

"*One* year, Charles. We can do that."

"No, *two* years. If the surface won't hold out for two years," I said over and over, "the product will fail."

We contacted one of the leading testing firms in the country and experimented with lacquers of all kinds, from all over the world. Finally, it was proved that the best and most durable finish could be obtained by applying two coats of high-bake vinyl lacquer.

That still was not the end.

Our search for new finishes was accompanied by a search for a practical method of obtaining a *pavé* effect, in which small jewels are held firmly together, without any metal showing between them. I wanted *pavé* on the tops of some models.

"You have to hold the stones by metal prongs," jeweler after jeweler explained.

The problem caused one of the worst arguments that Earl and I had during the entire project. He was adamant in stating that the *pavé* effect could be created only at great expense and that he could not possibly meet my explicit guarantee using a cheap method of making these tiny prongs.

My guarantee was that the stone setting would last for the life of the case itself.

I harped on this constantly—over the phone, in meetings, by mail. There *must* be a method. Finally, a jeweler perfected a process of cementing the stones in place, and the fight was over— at least that one was.

Perfecting the refill was also a lengthy and taxing job, but the most important part of it relates, not to design difficulties, but to reaching a vital decision.

Once the case had been perfected, it was the opinion of some that the refill should be designed so that it would be useless without the case. My argument was that the refill should have a cap. "With a plastic cap," I explained, "women who do not have, or want, cases will still be able to take advantage of Revlon colors."

Despite stiff opposition from some quarters, I still felt that my overall business philosophy was sound: As the largest manufacturer, Revlon owed it to the consumer to make each product available, without complications. The American woman is very alert and perceptive. She would be the first to spot a "squeeze play" if we were to market a lipstick that was only usable after the purchase of a case. Besides, I was convinced that the market for the new, fashionable cases would suffer little from making the refill entities in themselves.

Finally, after eleven months of designing, modifying and developing, we began to manufacture nineteen selected styles of cases. Kay Daly, who was then with our advertising agency and is now a vice-president at Revlon, developed the advertising theme.

She revised the copy endlessly.

Early attempts missed the boat because they emphasized the fashion element, but did not adequately sell the "refillable" idea. The most frustrating task she undertook was the selection of a name for the cases. Hundreds were suggested, considered and rejected. I could not agree—no one could agree—on any of them.

Finally, she hit on *Futurama*. To my mind, this suitably brought home the newness, the excitement, the fashionableness of the product.

It was then that I was really shaken. A market research organization reported that Futurama "is not a good name. It is too masculine. It sounds too much like General Motors. . . ."

My associates and I spent many tense hours discussing this verdict. We were totally split in our opinions. In the end, I had to make the decision. There was, of course, only one way to look at it: from the viewpoint of the American woman herself. I decided to rely on my original reaction that the name was good, and that it would appeal to the consumer I knew best.

"Futurama it is," I said.

We immediately went into test markets. The results spelled a resounding success. Wherever Futurama was introduced, sales jumped by at least 35 per cent. America women purchased quantities of the refills, which sold at about twenty-five cents less than the old-style cases; but they also made heavy purchases of the new cases, in all price ranges.

We were ready for national distribution. The initial impact was so great that retailer complaints about getting stuck with old cases were almost non-existent. Overall lipstick sales went way up, and in the last few months of 1955 we sold more than 600,000 Futurama cases.

But again—controversy.

Advertising of Futurama and our other Revlon products went heavily into magazines in 1956, but our most notable campaign was on the quiz program, "The $64,000 Question." Sales continued their merry ascent. In the first half of 1956, women bought more than 2,500,000 Futurama cases, many of them with Florentine finishes. In the last half of the year, more than 7,000,000 cases were sold. And in 1957, the figure jumped to an astonishing 11,000,000.

Throughout the trade, there were cries that Revlon had "certainly hit a lucky break," with a TV program that caught on the way "The $64,000 Question" did. All kinds of stories were circulated to the effect that "Revlon growth was solely due to 'The $64,000 Question.'"

When I first heard that opinion voiced, in all seriousness, I was hit hard. This was distortion. The trade press has outspokenly, and not always too sympathetically, recorded some of my reactions.

Now, I am a great advocate of advertising, as is easily evidenced by the large sums Revlon puts into it each year. But I would like to make it clear, as I have in the past, that Revlon's growth (from about $34 million in 1954 to $96 million in 1957, the peak Futurama year) was the result of two basic factors: product research and development and our business philosophy in regard to the American woman. Advertising is meaningless unless the product lives up to the claims.

Futurama's success sparked Revlon's growth, but it did not do it alone. The other new products—the hair sprays, the make-up creams, the men's products, the skin lotions, the fragrances—fanned the growth flames.

By 1962, Revlon's sales were $163 million, and we had become a far more diversified company. In the intervening years, we had acquired interests in shoe polish, women's apparel, pharmaceuticals and shavers.

Futurama, with its unique Manhattan Project, has simply been the dramatic expression of a business philosophy and outlook. Its success was made easier by the earlier pioneering—in offering a whole color line of nail polishes, in developing matching shades for lipstick and nail polishes, in perfecting new beauty and make-up preparations.

The face of the American woman has been changed, along with her cosmetics habits. But the psychology of studying the needs and desires of the American woman has *not* changed. She is still looking for newer and better ways to express her personality and individuality. She still looks for that rich caress of luxury within her given budget. She still seeks the fashionable, the chic, the elegant.

What I understand in American women is what I seek in developing a product. And when I am rooted in the conviction that the product is what the American woman wants, then no one can shake me from the course of pursuing the ultimate—even when it leads me into technological byways dealing with specifications down to one-thousandth of an inch.

LEONARD H. LAVIN

Alberto-Culver Company

LEONARD H. LAVIN, president of the Alberto-Culver Company, has guided its meteoric rise from sales of less than half a million in 1955 to record sales of $80,000,000 in 1963. He graduated from the University of Washington in 1940, and after service in the Navy during World War II, resumed a successful selling career in the toiletries business. In 1952, he formed Leonard H. Lavin & Company, offering national sales service to cosmetic and toiletries companies. He bought the Alberto-Culver Company in 1955.

A Better Product Better Sold

A Winner in the Mass Market

LEONARD H. LAVIN

The American author J. F. Powers recently wrote a novel called *Morte D'Urban*. The novel, which delighted the critics, was given the National Book Award for Fiction in 1962.

Morte D'Urban was a spoof on success. It told the story of a Midwest order of priests who adhered to a decidedly secular motto.

The motto was: "Be a Winner!"

I thought of J. F. Powers and his book when I began this report on the Alberto-Culver Company, a successful, although mottoless, Midwest manufacturer and distributor of packaged goods for the mass market. I realized how difficult it was going to be to explain the success of the company without making the story, like *Morte D'Urban*, a work of fiction.

For we Americans love a winner. However, we insist the story of a winner be told in a certain way. It must end with the hero casting aside his disguise of common mortality and revealing that all the while he had a hot line to heaven.

It is as if in our fables of success we tell and retell the adventures of the ugly duckling, who of course is no duck at all, but really the Lone Ranger dressed up for a masquerade party.

What I am getting at is that the success of the Alberto-Culver Company, which I started in 1955, has not been due to spectacular secrets and insights. Perhaps we have worked harder at our jobs than some of our competitors. Perhaps we have pursued our convictions with more zeal and purpose. But have our business insights been peculiar to us? I insist not.

We are but one of many companies in the packaged-goods field. The growth of any company in this field, the solidity of any company, the well-being of any company, is dependent on the solid merchandising of existing items and the introduction of new items in markets where sizable volume can be obtained. Thus in the packaged-goods field you see companies constantly bringing forth new products.

We ourselves now market seventeen items. What may distinguish us most from our competition is the speed with which we brought out new items, the quickness with which we achieved their national distribution, and the pleasing alacrity of the public in accepting them. We expect that in time we will have seventeen more products, and then seventeen more on top of that. In other words, we feel that we have only begun to make our presence felt in the packaged-goods world.

It is not our record that makes us confident, but rather our conviction that our method of doing business is simple and sensible.

We introduce products we know the public will accept. We introduce products we know have mass appeal. Very simply, we take our cue from the consumer. We do not try to sell him products he does not want. It is so much easier selling him products that he does want. Of course one must know precisely what it is the consumer does want. You do not assume. You do not guess. You investigate. You research. You take nothing for granted. For the problems of selling packaged goods are sufficiently involved without further complicating them by not being dead certain

that what you intend to sell the consumer, the consumer, informed
and motivated by advertising, would be inclined to buy.

It would seem that we at Alberto-Culver work backwards.
But backwards is frontwards in the mass packaged-goods field.
Wasn't it Edgar Allan Poe who said that the way to write a short
story was to begin with the ending? It is like that in our business.
Make only what you can sell.

What I have said so far may strike you as obvious. And it still
does not explain what you might consider the precipitous success
of the Alberto-Culver Company. After all, we did start in business only in 1955.

I am getting ahead of my story, but let me say here that the
fact that we started so late was part of our good fortune. I am
sure that at first we looked like a pushcart peddler trying to steal
business away from the fancy supermarket just down the street.
Gutsy, but not so smart—I am sure that is what some of our big
and rich and established competitors thought of us for a long time.
What they did not know was that we had three things going for
us.

The first was that they had created some obvious markets for
us. Their very success told us what the public liked. At the same
time, it simplified our problems for us. In certain cases, all we had
to do was make better products. A better hairdressing. A better
shampoo. A better hair spray. The technical problems connected
with accomplishing this were and continued to be difficult, but
hardly insurmountable.

The second thing going for us—and it relates to the first—is
that at the very point in time when technology offered the promise of improving any product in the mass packaged-goods field,
we at Alberto-Culver were not committed to items that, although
enjoying mass acceptance, were doomed to extinction. We were
in a position to pick out the most vulnerable markets in the mass
packaged-goods field and in a deliberate and calculated and
cold-blooded way move against them. It is my observation that
the producer of successful items for the mass market is generally
reluctant to change a product once it has gained acceptance,

even when it means an improvement. And change when it does come more often presents itself as a nervous reaction to the claims of a competitor than as a genuine response to the public's demand for a better product.

Thirdly, we had television going for us. The exciting, enthralling, compelling one-eyed peddler. Storyteller and babysitter to children. Welcome distraction to the footsore housewife. Boon companion to the daddy of the family, who had swivel-chaired his way through another day, who only wanted a chance to shuck his shoes, punch a hole in a can of beer and forget overdue installment payments and yelling offspring.

Television by 1955, the year Alberto-Culver entered the packaged-goods field, had been received into most American homes. It was not a distraction, like most peddlers, it was an attraction. The chain was not on the door when it called. The era of true mass marketing had arrived. The pitch man was no longer an interloper—he was a friend of the family. And any friend of the family was a friend of ours. Our invasion of the packaged-goods field called for springing loose as many dollars as we could to buy television time. We felt that if the product was right, television was the medium for selling it. Eventually, we came to realize that what we were doing was creating products for the very advertising medium we had selected.

Perhaps at this point I ought to tell you something of myself. What was it that conditioned me to accept and appreciate the revolution in selling that had been effected by television?

It is quite easy to explain. I was a salesman. My confrontation with television involved a kind of conversion. It was as if television was something I had been looking for my whole career. Not that I knew it, of course.

When I was twenty-seven I was working for a toiletry company. I liked the field—it was the one I had gone into right after college—but my 1941-45 hitch in the Navy had left me with a permanent case of restlessness. It was the kind of restlessness that made you want to do things, not just change for change's sake. It turned into real discontent when I found out that the product I was selling was going to be milked—that is, no more money was going to be invested in promoting or advertising it. My job was to keep the money flowing as long as possible. It was a good item—a home permanent wave—and I knew it would be profitable for years before it ran dry. However, I wanted no part of the milking operation. My instinct was to run like crazy with any product that the public seemed to like. Besides, I had built the product up to the point where it was doing a volume of two million dollars.

One day I walked into my boss' office and told him I was quitting. He thought I was making a play for more money, an assumption that bosses are apt to make in such circumstances. He asked me how much money it would take to keep me with the company. I told him it was not a question of salary. He smiled and offered to double my pay. I smiled back and said I was not interested. I must admit that I had doubts about the wisdom of what I was doing: my wife and I were expecting our first child. Security did have its attraction. Nonetheless, I turned down the proposition, said goodbye to the boss, and cleared out my desk. I think both of us were surprised.

I went to work for a small Chicago advertising agency. I still cannot tell you why I did this. It just seemed like a good idea at the time. My function at the agency was to bring in new business. It was a frustrating experience. For while I was successful in landing new accounts for the agency, these accounts stopped being impressed by the advice I offered once they were in the fold. I would work hard at a presentation, make my pitch to a client, and end up without having had serious attention paid to what I considered reasonable marketing and advertising suggestions. I had one prospect tell me that I acted as if I knew more about his business than he did. It is only fair to report that this is how I did feel. I had made a serious study of his company and had arrived at the conclusion that he was making outrageous marketing blunders. If I learned nothing else during this period, I learned *not* to assume that simply because someone headed a company, there was not a great deal he might not know about his affairs. Or to put it another way, it was the job of the head of a company to know as much as he could about his affairs and he should never assume there was not more that he could learn. Even from an advertising man.

You can guess by now that I was not long for the advertising world. Parting was not such sweet sorrow. It was unalloyed joy. I figured I was on the wrong side of the fence.

I returned to the toiletry field. The company I worked for had just brought out a deodorant called Stopette. It was quite a product. Instead of dabbing the deodorant on, you sprayed it on. I was told to direct the selling and merchandising of the item.

What Stopette had in its favor was obviously its packaging. But how to exploit this innovation was the nub of the problem. I tried to build demand for it by advertising in magazines and newspapers. There was some response, but none that caused any excitement, least of all in my place of business.

My job involved a good deal of traveling. As I went from town to town, I asked questions of buyers and retailers. What I was looking for was advice on how to advertise Stopette. Everywhere I went the answer was the same. Toiletry items that were advertised on television moved faster than those that were not advertised on television. Nobody told me why this was so. Nobody had worked out an answer. But they could report the fact because they knew the fact. It was part of their daily experience.

I decided to give television a whirl. I recommended that part of the advertising budget be allotted to television and was given an OK. I shopped around for the cheapest buy I could find. And I found it.

The first Stopette television advertising was sandwiched between falls on a wrestling show!

I have never felt the same about this sport of sham and thuggery. I developed into as strong a rooter as that sweet little old lady called "Hatpin Mary." As you might guess from her name, this elderly woman used to sneak up to the apron of the ring during a match and hatpin the contestants. It was her way of showing enthusiasm for the sport.

My enthusiasm became pretty great, too. For this most improbable show sold Stopette, in greater quantities than ever before. It delivered a sizable audience, that was certainly one reason. But more than that—or rather, just as important—the medium of television allowed us to demonstrate Stopette's advantage over other deodorants. The advantage was, as I have said, the fact that Stopette was a deodorant you sprayed on.

Television had a new disciple, and his name was Lavin. My next move seemed obvious. We bought time on a network show called "What's My Line." Within months, Stopette was the leading deodorant in the country.

I decided it was time to go out on my own. I still thought of myself as a salesman, so the move I made seemed most logical. I formed a sales company to represent consumer-product manufacturers who did not have sales forces of their own. We handled everything from clothes hangers to room deodorants to ironing-board covers. In a year and a half we were doing more than seven million dollars' worth of business.

This episode in my career might be viewed as a turning aside from the field of mass marketing and television. Such was not the case. I had a plan in mind. It was to find and buy a product, preferably a toiletry item, that had true mass-market potential. I was on a sort of treasure hunt. Everywhere I went I asked questions. I questioned buyers in the drug chains, grocery people, retailers. Why do you think this item is selling? That item? What kind of promotions are the manufacturers running? What do you think of their advertising? Why is this product a success? Why is that one a flop? And then I would always ask: Do you know of any product around here that is on the market and for sale? I would follow the leads I was given. I checked out dozens of products. None of them struck me as the one I was looking for.

In March of 1955 I was having lunch in a Los Angeles restaurant with Alline Roth, a head buyer of Thrifty Drug Stores Company, one of the great drug chains. Alline was an old friend. I asked her if she knew of any products in the area that were for sale. She mentioned one. It was Alberto-Culver VO5 Hair Dressing. The name meant nothing to me. She said that the item had only limited distribution, but added that she thought it was the finest women's hairdressing she had ever come across. She explained that its owner had become ill and wanted to sell out.

I phoned the man—his name was Leonard Hoffman—and asked if I might see him. Later that day I visited him at his home outside Los Angeles.

Yes, he told me, he did want to sell out. But not just one product. He had a line of about a hundred small items, all of them meant for the beauty trade. He said that the backbone of the business was VO5 Hair Dressing, although any deal he negotiated would have to include all the products he owned. He was frank and pleasant. He showed me his books. I was impressed. The potential of VO5 Hair Dressing was clearly defined in them.

He explained that he already had a number of offers for his business. He was considering them, he said, but the drawback in each case was that the money was to be paid over a period of years. While he did not say it, it was clear to me that he wanted cash so that he could free himself quickly and completely from his business.

I told him that I would like to buy his business. The only catch was, as I explained, that I did not have the nearly half-million dollars he was asking. I said I would try to raise the money. He agreed to a short-term option. Within two weeks I was back with a certified check for $488 thousand.

Thus the Alberto-Culver Company was born. But instead of the one product I had been searching for, I had a hundred. This was an impressive number on paper, though only one of them appeared tailored for the mass consumer market. This was VO5 Hair Dressing. I killed off all but it and staked my future on its success.

It is not my purpose to chronicle the history of VO5 Hair Dressing. Let me just report, though, that the product was indeed successful. Our first year's sales were only a bit shy of half a million dollars. From the beginning we advertised as heavily as possible on television. I remember the first TV buys we made. They were in Philadelphia. I placed the order personally. The more we advertised, the more the product sold. The more it sold, the more we advertised. Within three years it was the leading women's hairdressing. Within five—and in a market that kept expanding because of advertising pressure—we were selling more women's hairdressing than all other manufacturers combined. Today the product commands sixty-five cents of every dollar spent by women on hairdressing. Today, too, VO5 Hair Dressing has a large share of the men's hairdressing market.

VO5 Hair Dressing did more than justify my judgment that it had true mass market potential. It supplied the capital (not to mention the encouragement) we needed for launching other attacks against the packaged-goods front. These attacks would be much more ambitious than the introduction of a woman's hairdressing. But VO5 gave us a toe hold on the continent. It was our private and personal Normandy beachhead.

Furthermore, merchandising the product refined our thinking on how to make these new attacks successful. We still weren't ready to develop our own items, so we kept an eye out for products we thought might have mass appeal. In 1956 I heard from a friend of mine named Ken Ault, who sold merchandise for me in Hawaii. He told me that a product called Rinse Away was for sale. I knew nothing about it. He assured me that it was the finest dandruff preparation he had ever come across. I investigated. Its distribution was quite insignificant, but it was clear to me that it had mass market potential. And so Alberto-Culver acquired a second product. In a short time it became the leading dandruff preparation. We were off the beach and moving inland.

Our first giant assault was held off until 1960. Meanwhile, we consolidated our hold on the hairdressing and dandruff-control markets. We built up our sales force, training each man we hired in a new kind of mass market methodology. We acquired a corps of executives who came to believe in the potential of Alberto-Culver as much as I did. We developed our own laboratory. And we probed and probed along the packaged-goods front until we found a major weak point. Then we launched our first giant attack. Our aim was to win control of the hair spray market.

The hair spray market in the United States came into being in 1948. A plastic spray bottle under the name Liquinet inaugurated the market. It was soon joined by a competitor, Spray-Wave. The two shared sales of a half million dollars, despite the fact that the spray nozzles became clogged with the lacquer that was used.

The market stood still until Helene Curtis created Spray Net, promoting it nationally with heavy advertising dollars. In 1952 the hair spray market jumped to $5 million. By 1955 the market had expanded to $49 million, with Curtis enjoying a 60 per cent share. At this time an aggressive and well-organized competitor challenged Curtis. This was Revlon, whose brand, Satin Set, claimed that it ended the nightly pin-ups. By 1957 Revlon was the market leader. Then Lanolin Plus and Colgate-Palmolive joined the field. During 1956 more than eighty million aerosol containers of hair spray were produced and sold to consumers.

May, 1957 saw the advent of Toni's Adorn. Before Adorn, women sprayed their hair *after* they had combed it to keep the hair in place. Adorn demonstrated convincingly, through television, that with its product, hair could be sprayed *before* combing as an aid in styling. With heavy television advertising and strong promotion, Adorn took the lead.

Nineteen fifty-eight through 1960 was a period of massive failures. Suicidal contests developed between low-priced brands of under a dollar and high-priced brands ranging up to $1.50 in price. The high-priced brands resorted to free premiums to help them compete. Important companies selling hair sprays lost heavily in this market—Max Factor with Curl Control and Natural Wave, Procter & Gamble with Winter Sett and Summer Sett, Richard Hudnut with Beauty Curl, and Helene Curtis with Tempo. In this period the hair spray market declined from $81 million to $75 million.

It was at this time that Alberto-Culver became interested in the field. Consumer research told us that women wanted—but could not buy—a hair spray that did not dull their hair. This was the vulnerable point we set out to exploit.

I felt sure that the hair spray market would shoot up phenomenally—if we could be innovators. I asked our researchers if they could perfect a hair spray with the qualities I felt the market needed. Our lab started work in early 1960. And then it happened: the Alberto-Culver lab came upon a resin formula that allowed the holding qualities of spray to function without leaving a film on the hair.

Working in conjunction with a large chemical manufacturer, a pilot operation was set up. We were the first nationally-distributed company to recognize the importance of this resin in the hair spray field. We were going to use it to create the best hair spray product the market had ever seen.

This was a critical juncture for us. Our enthusiasm was matched only by the negative reaction throughout the field.

A buyer friend of mine asked me, "Who needs another hair spray? Better a hole in the head." Buyers told me the market was overloaded. For the first time in my life I refused to take the advice of people in the trade. I was determined to launch our own hair spray. By late summer of 1960 our formula was undergoing changes, showing good results with half-head and full-head tests. (In half-head tests we compared hair which had been sprayed with our product with that sprayed with an existing brand.)

The first product batches of Alberto VO5 Hair Spray were ready in the fall of 1960. This hair spray was tested elaborately, using a "scoreboard" technique to rate our spray against all the leading brands.

Our spray showed exceptional holding qualities, yet *left no film*. It was moisture-resistant, was resettable without becoming sticky, and it was crystal-clear, permitting natural hair color to show through. This is how the scoreboard worked: Each spray was measured against every characteristic listed below and scored from zero to ten. A ten score was given when the individual characteristic was as good as it could possibly be. A zero score was given when it was extremely bad. The following is a list of product qualities that were screened:

1. Uniformity of film
2. Clarity of film
3. Drying time
4. Freedom from tackiness at low humidity
5. Freedom from tackiness at high humidity

6. Film clarity at high humidity
7. Ease of removal with shampoo
8. Ability to reset with water
9. Curl-holding qualities at low humidity
10. Curl-holding qualities at high humidity
11. Rate of film build-up after several applications
12. Resistance to flaking when combed or brushed
13. Dry combing lubricity
14. Reduction of static electrical charge when combed or brushed
15. Fragrance during applications
16. Fragrance when dry

All of the competitive sprays that were screened had as many characteristics that scored below five as they had that scored above five. The lab then attempted to develop a spray in which the lowest score for any value was seven. We were able to accomplish this. Of course, in addition to all of these screening tests, it was imperative that VO5 Hair Spray was completely safe to the consumer. Among the tests conducted by independent laboratories were tests for skin irritation, sensitization and inhalation.

The scoreboard technique showed that the qualities of Alberto VO5 Hair Spray were decidedly superior to existing brands.

In discussing our product with our agency, the lab had demonstrated the clarity of our product by spraying it on a mirror. The agency people decided on the spot that this was a unique way to present the major VO5 Hair Spray claim to the consumer. By the time they had taxied back to their office, the first commercial was written. It remained essentially unchanged from that moment on.

In preparing our launch we were also creating a full-blown market philosophy for Alberto-Culver. One aspect of the Alberto-Culver approach (of what to avoid, that is) is best expressed in lines attributed to John Ruskin: "There's hardly anything in the world that some man could not make a little worse and sell a little cheaper; and the people who consider price only are this man's lawful prey." We were going to make a product that was better than any premium brand on the market and we expected the consumer to pay a reasonable price for a better product. Thus, Alberto VO5 was to be launched at $1.50 for a seven-ounce size. This was at a time cut-price brands were offering larger sizes for 99 cents, but they weren't interested in creating a national market which would prosper. They were only interested in ambushing the market with an inferior product and running off with a quick profit.

We entered the field confidently, despite what everyone said, despite the cautionary words of friends. We were going to create a vital, responsive consumer market that would turn the whole picture about.

It is our philosophy to bring along the advertising dollars if the product begins to make sales. In this way, we fill in the weak spots in national distribution. What we did with Alberto VO5 Hair Spray was to introduce it as if the annual advertising rate were two and a half million dollars. The market leader, Adorn, was spending at a rate of three and a half million dollars.

We couldn't match this expenditure until we had started to build adequate distribution. But we were set to outspend Adorn if the market situation warranted. Since we believed in advertising (not to mention our product), we gave our hair spray every possible additional support at the first sign that it was doing well. At the end of the first quarter, our national advertising-to-sales ratio was 71.8 per cent.

We nursed our advertising budget along from the first week by holding weekly marketing meetings to review advertising and sales figures and to look for opportunities for increased investments. Our original intention had been to spend advertising dollar for sales dollar. As record sales rolled in, our budget rose to the three and a half million dollar rate and was increased again and again in the months to follow.

Our goal now was—market leadership for our brand, that same year.

Drugstores were unable to keep their shelves sufficiently stocked to meet the early demand. We knew beforehand that with a new product that takes off, wholesalers and retailers could be caught short. They fear to overstock. Any innovator brand that could take the market by storm could suffer. And suffer we did. An ugly out-of-stock condition hit Alberto VO5 Hair Spray.

We had launched our consumer campaign in January, 1961. By March 1, our major problem was coping with out-of-stock conditions. We had planned to leave nothing to chance. It was our goal to capture 20 per cent of the hair spray market in the first year, and not only reverse the downward trend of the market, but in fact add ten million dollars to its total size.

We estimated that our volume would be split equally between the grocery field and drug field. To get our product moving from factory to the consumer, we decided to offer special deals to distributors and consumers to maximize the potential market of our hair spray. We had introduced Alberto VO5 Hair Spray to the drug trade in a combination offer. When drug wholesalers bought ten-packages of VO5 Hair Dressing and Rinse Away in our standing consumer offer, plus six cans of VO5 Hair Spray, they received two VO5 Hair Dressing consumer offers free. This increased the cost of our product, but it was a necessary tack in view of the challenge we were facing.

Within the month we had 75 per cent drug distribution.

But it was another story in the grocery trade. The food trade moves at its own speed and it believes only in success. It will not support the innovator until his sales potential has been fully proved. It took us three months to establish to it that consumer demand for Alberto VO5 Hair Spray was really big. When such results began to register, the food outlets which had refused the brand began to demand it.

We had a special offer for them, too. Grocery wholesalers, rack jobbers, and chains had never responded well to the VO5 Hair Dressing offer we had made to the trade. This was because they had to disrupt their racks to find space for an offer that was only available for a short period. We found only 15 per cent of the grocery outlets accepted this offer, while drug distribution reached 80 per cent. Therefore, we created a VO5 Hair Spray offer which we felt better suited to grocery needs to help us get the distribution needed to jack up the hair spray market. We made a free-goods offer for orders of hair spray which achieved 25 per cent gross distribution in the first sixty days. This was good penetration of the grocery field. But it still wasn't good enough.

We devised a promotion for April 1 with large quantities of our standard seven-ounce hair spray plus a new fifteen-ounce $2.35 jumbo size. We began the pipeline of Hard-to-Hold hair spray in seven-ounce size. By introducing flankers, we hoped to get additional shelf space and beef up the impact of our in-stock displays, and also serve different wants among consumers.

We again offered new quantities of free goods to the trade to encourage increased stocking. This was successful in stepping up our distribution, but only momentarily. On April 21 I left for Europe to look over our business there. I was planning to supervise the introduction of Alberto VO5 Hair Spray in England, among other things. During my absence, orders began to overtax the capacity of our resin supplier. For two weeks, Alberto VO5 was on back order. Then the dike broke. We found we were unable to meet the demand.

I flew to New York from London. There were busy conferences, discussions, arguments. Our resin supplier said he would remedy the situation. He promised to put his plant on three shifts seven days a week; he went so far as to promise the construction of a new plant for the mushrooming sales of Alberto VO5 Hair Spray. He kept both promises. Our product was rolling again. By July, 1961, Alberto VO5 Hair Spray had cornered 10 per cent of the market as reported by Nielsen and was, if anything, beginning to show signs of even greater growth. We had passed the hurdle of initial sales and now we were getting repeat sales from satisfied customers. So good were sales that in the first quarter our advertising-to-sales ratio dropped dramatically. We decided to double our advertising again. And as sales swelled, the ratio came down again below 40 per cent.

Also encouraging was the fact that the flanker brand we had introduced, Alberto VO5 Hair Spray for hard-to-hold hair, was selling virtually as well as our regular brand, although we originally had estimated it would only sell at 20 per cent the volume of the regular. Obviously we had another winner.

Once again, in short order, we decided to insure heavy stocking of the hard-to-hold formula. We ran a July promotion, then introduced an aerosol can at $2.35 in the jumbo fifteen-ounce hard-to-hold spray, with free goods depending on ordering more of the regular product. Now, within seven months of introduction, we had at the same time four facings in the stores of four fast-moving brands.

October, 1961 was a double landmark for Alberto VO5 Hair Spray. It became the number one brand in the hair spray field; it was doing so well that we used it to get a new brand—VO5 Creme Rinse—sampled.

The second October landmark was the introduction of Alberto VO5 Hair Spray for gray hair, which was pipelined again in a combination trade offer.

In sum, we lived up to our estimates astoundingly, contrary to what the market prospect was when we started and contrary to what the experts predicted. In a year's time, we had captured 20 per cent of the market, become the market leader, and increased the size of the market by $10 million.

Today the hair spray market is over $140 million. VO5 Hair Spray continues to be the leader in the field. We still advertise and promote it more vigorously than our competitors advertise and promote their brands. And we continue to make a good deal more money, more profit, from our product than do any of our competitors.

Our success was followed up by attacks against other areas of the packaged-goods front. We introduced a hand lotion called Derma-Fresh, a regular shampoo called VO5, a medicated dandruff shampoo called Subdue, hair coloring called New Dawn, and a spray-on powder deodorant called Calm. In each case our attack was patterned after our assault on the hair spray field. In each case our assault was successful. The pattern—and the success—has been repeated in other fields, too.

And we expect to repeat the pattern time after time in the years ahead. For the pattern works. It works because it is based on the realities of the packaged-goods business. It is a pattern that began to take shape when I made the first sales call of my life. It is a pattern whose definition became greater when, at twenty-seven, I instinctively rejected the idea of not promoting and selling a good product as hard as possible. It is a pattern whose definition became greater yet when I worked for Stopette and, confronted with television, realized the one-eyed peddler was my passport into every living room in America.

From that point on all I needed was just one product with mass appeal to break into the packaged-goods field on my own. I found the product in VO5 Hair Dressing. It and Rinse Away supplied me and my company with the everyday experience and the capital to launch our first massive attack on the packaged-goods front, as we did when we introduced VO5 Hair Spray.

The pattern of which I speak has these elements:

Take your cue from the consumer. Sell him what he wants, whether it be an entirely new product or a new and improved type of product that he has already accepted. When you tell him that you have what he wants, use television as your medium, since it is inherently the most effective mass communications tool for mass market goods possessing clear and demonstrable advantages. Finally, if you know that your product and your advertising message are right, go all the way. Spend as much as you can on advertising. If your product is in fact one with mass appeal, if it is truly and demonstrably superior to competing products, then it must succeed.

It is obvious that the key point in this pattern is the advertising message. It must communicate. It must motivate. Looking back, I would say that the message is fully as difficult to create as the product itself. I would almost say *more* difficult. It is not possible to really succeed in the mass market with an inferior product. On the other hand, it is quite possible to fail in the mass market with a superior product. If the message is wrong, the possibility is far from remote. This is precisely why we at Alberto-Culver never launch a product unless we know the commercial used to advertise the product is as superior in its way as the product. Sometimes it has happened that we have perfected our message before perfecting the product. This was possible because we knew the exact advantages we would build into our products. We knew what they *should* be from consumer research. And we assumed—we *knew*—that we had the skills available to produce what the consumer ordered.

A learned friend of mine once called this the art of interchanging technology and advertising. He spoke of this as a phenomenon unique to our age. Even now I am not sure that I understand what he meant. I suppose he was saying that I believed successful mass marketing involved the perfecting of both product and message and that I treated them as two distinct tasks to be worked at simultaneously.

Indeed, I would say this *is* mass marketing.

WILLIAM S. BEINECKE

S & H Green Stamps

WILLIAM SPERRY BEINECKE is president and a director of The Sperry and Hutchinson Company. He received his A.B. from Yale University in 1936, and then went on to Columbia Law School, earning his LL.B. in 1940. Following Navy service in World War II, he practiced law before becoming general counsel to The Sperry and Hutchinson Company in 1952. He was elected president in 1960. He serves as a director and trustee of a number of companies, banks and schools.

Save as You Spend

The Rise of Trading Stamps in Retail Promotion

BY

WILLIAM S. BEINECKE

The year 1954 was drawing to a close.

Business was good, with an increasing number of merchants using our S & H Green Stamps. Over a half century before, we had established our position of leadership in the trading stamp field. We were number one then, as we are today, and regarded as the Tiffany of the stamp business.

Consumer acceptance of our service was strong, and daily growing stronger. Our profit return was satisfactory, our financial position sound. We were blessed with a solidly harmonious internal organization.

It was a good way to greet Christmas.

It was, that is, until we accepted an appointment with a very special visitor. He was a distinguished person—a leader in the U.S. food retailing industry, the head of a national chain of food stores. But he had not come to wish us a Merry Christmas.

I remember the visit well. We were gathered—my uncle, E. J. Beinecke, chairman of the board; my father, F. W. Beinecke, chairman of the executive committee; and I—in my father's office to meet our visitor.

He came quickly to the point: We were to stop providing our trading stamp service to his competitors, or he would ruin us.

How did he propose to do this? Not knowing our business, our visitor either believed or had been led to believe that our economic survival hinged on issuing many more S & H Green Stamps than we would ever be required to redeem for our merchandise.

Apparently unknown to him at that time was the fact that the actual redemption of our stamps is extremely high. (The Internal Revenue Service, for example, in its audit of our income tax returns, recognizes the fact that at least 95 per cent of all the stamps we issue are redeemed.) Our operations for each year are based on projections for high redemptions, with provision for the value of the small amount of unredeemed stamps being represented in better service to accounts, improved redemption stores, and higher redemption values for savers.

Our caller warned that if we did not comply with his directive to get out of the food business, he would have the value of our unredeemed stamps declared "public domain." This, he must have assumed, would be a death blow to our company. And well it could have been, for there *was* no "kitty" of windfall profit in our bank account. As mentioned above, to the extent that a small number of stamps do go unredeemed, we spend more on service to customers and merchandise values to consumers. Windfall profit from any source at all does not persist long in an industry as competitive as trading stamps.

So it was that, according to his way of thinking, we were faced with two grim alternatives: Get out of the food business, or face ruin!

E. J. Beinecke is a soft-spoken man, known for his self-composure. He quietly informed our visitor that we had other ideas. I still remember the look on our visitor's face. There was nothing in it of the Yuletide spirit. He left our office with one purpose in mind—to destroy The Sperry and Hutchinson Company and remove trading stamps from the market place.

Our decision was of course to protect ourselves against whatever might be visited upon us. We were not worried in any fundamental sense about his threat to introduce so-called "escheat" efforts (a state's right to recover "abandoned property") against unredeemed stamps. We would win such a case. Moreover, as honorable people, we had no choice about what we had to do. We had contractual obligations with a great many fine merchants across the nation—men who had strengthened their businesses through the use of our promotional service. Some of these were owners of local and regional food chains who were apparently competing very effectively against some of our visitor's stores.

There was another factor, too—the most vital of all—which this visitor neglected to consider. If, as he thought, he had forces on his side capable of putting us out of business, we had even more powerful allies of our own. We had the consumer.

Most people liked the extra value of trading stamps, and to an ever increasing degree consumers were voting for them—by patronizing those stores where stamps were given. Consumer reaction had reconfirmed a conclusion that objective observers of the retailing scene regard as axiomatic: when prudent housewives decide collectively that they want something, they usually get it.

The pattern of commercial opposition to the competitive effectiveness of trading stamps was not new. Years ago when the large department store came into being, a great ruckus was raised by local merchants. They organized into militant groups and called upon their legislators to help squelch what they referred to as a "frightening menace." But the department store concept survived, and for a very good reason: housewives liked department stores, and patronized them.

The same story was repeated when mail-order houses started to make their impact on the market place. Legislators were flooded with appeals to ban their operation. Some merchant groups organized "catalog bonfire parties" and offered ten cents for every catalog brought in for destruction. But mail-order houses were successful, too, because once again the consumer had cast her vote in their favor.

Next it was the turn of the food chain store. Again groups were formed to destroy this newest alleged "threat to the economy." Again legislators were appealed to by merchants who feared competition. And again the American housewife, by virtue of her patronage, decided the outcome.

Perhaps it's human nature. Whenever a competitive activity is successfully launched, a storm of protest arises from what my uncle, E. J. Beinecke, calls the "vested interests on the receiving end of the competition," and every effort is made to destroy the new or better way of doing things.

Ironically, the interests opposing trading stamps were, in part, some of the large food chains. But once again the consumer's voice was heard and respected. She liked stamps, just as she had come to like department stores, mail-order houses, and food chains. And we at The Sperry and Hutchinson Company were going to do our utmost to oblige her. One thing was sure: if we didn't meet the public desire for stamps, *somebody else would.* We had been in a leadership position far too long to allow this to happen—since 1896, as a matter of fact.

Mr. Sperry and Mr. Hutchinson first conceived the idea of trading stamps as a discount to the housewife for paying cash or for paying her bills when due. The reasoning was, and still is, quite simple. The manufacturer receives a discount for what he buys. So do wholesalers and retailers. Why not the consumer as well? Now, by means of trading stamps, the consumer would be able to receive—as she has every right to do—a discount for payment of cash on even her smallest purchases.

For each dime spent she gets one stamp. After filling an S & H collector book with 1,200 stamps, she can exchange one or more books for any of 1,700 different quality items at one of S & H's 860 redemption centers.

Trading stamps actually serve a dual purpose. To both the consumer and the retailer, they are a form of discount. But to the retailer they are a promotional tool as well—just as are advertising, "loss leaders," consumer contests, or the offer of credit, free delivery, and other "extras."

Our company's founders first introduced this service in Jackson, Michigan. Gradually, consumer acceptance of the concept spread to the East and within the next few years trading stamps were adopted by retailers throughout the United States. Growth, though steady for the most part, was relatively slow until the mid-forties and early fifties, when the number of savers, and competing stamp companies as well, began to mushroom dramatically. To the increasing distress of retailers not offering stamps, consumers by the millions made it clear that, all other things being equal, they preferred to shop where stamps were given.

Consequently, when our caller left our offices on that eventful day, we decided to roll up our sleeves to do whatever might prove necessary to protect our business.

I might add that there was no lack of vigor or indignation in our reactions. The spirit of self-preservation is strong in all of us. And it may be worth noting that in the process of protecting ourselves we were, incidentally, protecting some pretty fundamental American rights. In addition to our own right to do business in a free society, there was the right of the consumer to seek the best possible value, including trading stamps or anything else. There was also the right of the retailer to use, or not use, any legitimate promotional tool he wished in order to win customers from his competitors. It takes a great deal of presumption to tamper with rights as basic as these.

Stamps have proven over the years to be a powerful promotional tool in the hands of the merchant who knows how to use them as an "extra" to supplement competitively low prices, quality products, good service, effective advertising, and other fundamentals of retailing. We have always told our customers that neither stamps nor any other promotional tool can compensate for poor management or the failure to be competitive in the basics of store merchandising.

Trading stamps had performed an outstanding job in increasing sales for thousands of stores and fulfilling the needs and desires of millions of consumers. The competition was understandably aroused. My father has often said: "The virulence of the opposition is a measure of our success."

The very nature of our position as a minority or "franchise" enterprise and as "champion of the underdog" had always invited attack. Large interests, particularly, had traditionally opposed stamps. Here is why:

In order to use stamps most profitably a merchant must have a good potential of business to draw from—a substantial number of customers capable of being attracted to his store. Now, if you take a situation where two stores are competing, with the large store drawing 90 per cent of the customers and the small fellow only 10 per cent, the small fellow obviously has far the greater potential for increasing his business.

Such was the state of affairs in the early fifties. Although S & H had many grocery and supermarket accounts, the total sales of stores offering stamps were still small compared to the total volume of the large food chains. But an important change was taking place in the food business in the United States. The supermarket revolution was reaching maturity. More and more, the level of competition became supermarket against supermarket, with consumers finding less and less difference among stores in such basic merchandising attractions as price, convenience, quality and service.

In this kind of environment, where there were a growing number of competitors with little difference among them, promotional tools like trading stamps were becoming more important than ever in the so-called "merchandising mix." One of the factors that made trading stamps a particularly attractive promotional device was its "co-operative" aspect; namely, the extension of its service on a franchise basis to a limited number of non-competing retailers in a given trading area. This meant that each member of the co-operating group helped to share the cost of the joint promotion, and helped strengthen the pulling power of the stamps for the others—and, in the end, for himself.

Someone once said that the worst thing about trading stamps is their effectiveness. Just how effective trading stamps can be was illustrated by our experience with Thorofare Markets, Inc., of Pittsburgh, a well-managed though relatively small local chain. We believed Thorofare could use our service effectively, but encountered a certain skepticism. So we said, "Give us your toughest market, your biggest problem store."

The test store was located in Clarksburg, West Virginia. It was barely holding its own, with gross weekly sales of $11,000. Within *three weeks* after the introduction of our stamps, sales rose to $31,000, an increase of 182 per cent. Four months later, the store was doing $42,000 per week, an increase of 282 per cent.

This sort of activity did not go unnoticed.

Nor did the experience we had with Eberhard's, a small local chain in Grand Rapids, Michigan. Here, too, unprecedented growth had been recorded. In an amazingly short time the chain went from a small enterprise struggling desperately to stay out of the red to a solidly profitable operation.

The head of the chain couldn't get over it. He praised stamps to anyone who would listen. He made speeches to retail and business groups. George Schirer, a veteran of more than fifty years with our company, occasionally referred to him as the best salesman we ever had. And he's still a very favorite account.

The pattern started to repeat itself all over the United States. More and more food chains took on S & H stamps. The effectiveness of trading stamps was becoming increasingly apparent to the retailing industry.

In Chicago, for example, there was a thriving independent department store. The owner of that store used to say: "I'd gladly pay ten cents a head for each customer I can draw off the street —just to get her inside my store."

This shrewd and successful businessman had two main drawing cards: trading stamps, and a huge aquarium which he maintained at an annual cost of $250,000. One day the biggest department store chain in the Midwest made this man an attractive offer for his store, and he sold it. The big chain was fanatically anti-stamp. The first thing it did was to drop stamps. The second thing was to dispose of the aquarium. The third thing was to get rid of the store, after trying unsuccessfully to make a go of it.

Consumers wanted trading stamps, and the opposition was growing restless. More and more chains were going to stamps; in the Midwest, in California, Texas, New Jersey, New England, the South—all over the United States.

One day, shortly after the visit from the food chain head, we were approached by some representatives from another of the larger chains. They had made exhaustive studies of the value of trading stamps, and saw stamps as a powerful competitive tool. They came to us, they said, because S & H was number one in the field. After weighing their offer carefully, we had to turn it down. As a result, this chain helped institute a very successful trading stamp company which is now one of our leading competitors.

However, had we sought to serve this chain, we would have had to provide our stamp service to all or most of its stores. This would have meant conflicts with some of our existing franchised accounts. It has always been our policy never to cancel a smaller store in favor of a large one. We believe in repaying loyalty with loyalty.

Returning now to our visitor, it soon developed that his threats had not been idly made. Within a month of his visit an escheat suit was brought against us, ostensibly by the State of New Jersey. This suit, which was silly on its face, was to be carried out at the expense of New Jersey's taxpayers.

Two New Jersey attorneys had proposed to the State of New Jersey that it claim the value of all unredeemed S & H stamps on the basis of New Jersey's abandoned property, or escheat, laws. S & H is a New Jersey corporation. The suit therefore laid claim to all unredeemed stamps—whether issued in New Jersey or not— dating back to 1900, the year of our incorporation.

At that time I was chief legal counsel for the company. I went down to Trenton to ascertain from the Attorney General just why the State had started such a flimsy suit against us. Among other things, I wanted to know why, without so much as a previous visit, a phone call, or a letter from his office, we were suddenly summoned to court. This was one of the astonishing parts. We were a good New Jersey corporate citizen, and good citizens just aren't treated like this in their home states.

We also felt it would be of interest to the Attorney General to know that the lawyers who had persuaded him to bring suit against us were listed in the law directory as counsel for the chain headed by our visitor. We felt, too, that the Attorney General should be apprised of the effect that this suit was having on us in far-off places. For example, it had by then been seriously asserted in Montana's legislature that the State of New Jersey had already collected $500 million from The Sperry and Hutchinson Company!

The Attorney General said he was shocked by this information. It came, he said, as a complete surprise. He explained that one day he had been approached by two attorneys who had in mind what appeared to be a good way for the State of New Jersey to realize some millions of dollars. Bring an escheat case against The Sperry and Hutchinson Company, they suggested, claiming the value of all stamps that had been issued but not redeemed—going all the way back to the company's incorporation in 1900. They also suggested that one of the members of their firm should represent the State of New Jersey, and the appointment was so made by the Attorney General.

Now all the facts were in the open. But, because of the publicity the case had already received, the Attorney General believed it was too late to withdraw it. So it ran its expensive course through the courts.

Without getting into a technical discussion of the law, suffice it to say that the suit was legally ludicrous. We won the case three separate times: first when the trial judge dismissed; next when the three appellate judges unanimously affirmed this dismissal; finally when all seven judges of the New Jersey Supreme Court again unanimously affirmed the dismissal. Eleven judges had considered the case on its merit. *We did not lose a judge.*

Soon after the initiation of the New Jersey escheat suit, double-page advertisements began to appear in newspapers in many different parts of the country. They were sponsored by the food chain headed by our Christmas visitor. They made the baseless charge that stamps raised the price of food.

It quickly became apparent that the ad campaign was merely a prelude to something far more serious—the introduction of a flood of anti-stamp legislation throughout the country. Charges that were cunning, ingenious, and in most cases preposterous, were hurled at us from all directions. Consumers were financing a fight that belonged in the market place.

Bills were introduced in state after state. Almost all of them were similar; many were identical. It seems fair to assume that many of them had a common source. In 1955, fifty anti-trading stamp bills were introduced in twenty-five states. It soon became obvious that every imaginable legal and propaganda resource was being mustered against us. Accuracy seemed of little consequence. The anti-stamp allegations were false, far-fetched and irresponsible.

In addition to state-wide legislation, federal probes were instigated. One was a House Agriculture Committee investigation. Here the anti-stamp counsel righteously quoted the opinion of a distinguished Court that because of an excessive number of middlemen, prices to consumers were ballooning and that much of this was caused by trading stamps.

Rising to my feet, I asked *when* this opinion had been given. The counsel seemed reluctant to answer. When he finally murmured, "Nineteen-ten," he was practically laughed out of the hearing room.

The Federal Trade Commission also decided to take a look at our operations. For more than two years all our files, records and correspondence were subjected to detailed scrutiny. This was by far the most searching examination ever conducted of a trading stamp company.

The outcome was highly gratifying. Normally it is the Commission's custom, following an investigation of this type, to either file a complaint or do nothing. On this occasion the FTC took the unprecedented action of issuing a press release, opening with this paragraph:

The Federal Trade Commission announced today that it did not consider trading stamp plans in themselves to be an unfair method of competition under the laws it administers, and concluded not to issue any complaints at this time prohibiting the use of trading stamps.

So it went, case after case, probe after probe, charge after charge. The facts were laid on the table. Legislators and others looked at the facts and were usually quick to recognize that the fuss represented an attempt by commercial interests to achieve favorable legislation as a relief from a competitive situation. One by one the charges were made, met, and exposed as distorted or ludicrous.

One of the pet notions peddled was that consumers lose when stamps are introduced because they force prices to go up. The U. S. Department of Agriculture made an exhaustive study of this charge, and their report should have disposed of this issue of whether consumers come out ahead in areas where stamps are used. Relying on U. S. Bureau of Labor Statistics data, the Department traced the price trend of supermarkets before and after their introduction of stamps in twenty-one cities. Price trends were compared to those of supermarkets which made no use of stamps over the period of investigation, November 1953 to March 1957.

In very nearly half of the cases, the prices of the supermarkets which adopted stamps either remained the same or fell, compared to the stores which did not use this type of promotion. When the entire group of stamp-using stores was considered, a small price gap of about six-tenths of one per cent opened up in favor of those not using stamps. The Agriculture Department pointed out, however, that "the difference in price trends observed in this study may have been caused in part by non-stamp stores lowering food prices to meet the competition of stores adding trading stamps." We took this as evidence that, as usual, some stores were responding to competition from trading stamps by reducing prices; so all consumers gained.

The Department went on to point out that the merchandise value of redeemed stamps was several times greater than the minor price differential between the stamp and non-stamp group.

The Department concluded: "It would appear that, on the average in the 21 cities studied, consumers who save and redeem stamps can more than recoup the relative price difference between stamp and non-stamp stores."

Meanwhile, the proponents of the so-called "fair-trade" laws had revived the notion that stamps *cut* prices and thus violated fair trade agreements. *Here, at one and the same time, one group was contending that stamps* raised *prices, while another was charging that stamps* cut *prices.*

It was suggested to the press that trading stamps cut advertising revenues. The contrary is the case. Trading stamps actually stimulate advertising, and proof was presented.

We were hit on all sides by ridiculous and baseless charges: we were guilty of unfair competition; we were unfair to farmers, unfair to retail trade associations, unfair to just about anyone the anti-stamp propagandists could conjure up, from the sons of the Napa Valley grape pickers to the Daughters of the American Revolution.

There were bills to tax stamp-giving stores at punitive rates. There were bills imposing prohibitive taxes against stamp companies. There were bills applying gambling regulations to trading stamps; bills forbidding the issuance of stamps with specific products ranging from eggs to gasoline; bills denying the right of stamp companies to offer exclusive franchises; and bills forbidding the issuance of stamps with fair trade items.

You know the size of a trading stamp. One of them just about covers your thumbnail. In Orlando, Florida, in 1955, a city ordinance was adopted requiring that the face of each stamp be imprinted with the name of our company, the address of our company, the name of the Florida merchant issuing our stamps, his address, and the information that the stamps would be redeemable in cash. The courts threw this out as a completely unreasonable regulation.

This year of 1955 was our baptism under wide legislative fire. Our opponents succeeded in passing two lone bills of the fifty introduced. One, in North Dakota, imposed a prohibitive license tax. It never went into effect. It was repealed by a popular referendum in 1956. The other bill, a minor regulation in Utah, has never been enforced.

Not many state legislatures were in session in 1956. It was a so-called "off year" for them, but not for those feeling competitive pressures from trading stamps. They made the most of even their limited opportunities for harassment, and were able to introduce fifteen hostile bills in eight different states. We emerged, however, with only superficial scratches.

The next year, though—1957—was a year we would choose to forget. This was another "on year." Even federal agencies had come under strong pressure from special interest groups to scrutinize our operations.

An even hundred bills were introduced that year in some thirty-five states. But only two were passed that affected us in any way. Of particular significance was the one in Tennessee which, among other things, imposed a prohibitive tax on stamp-using merchants. A storm of consumer protest followed, with *Life* magazine covering the story. Although the legislators were persuaded that the elimination of trading stamps was in some vague way related to the public welfare, the courts did not share this view. The law was promptly held unconstitutional by Tennessee's Supreme Court in July of that same year. It never became effective.

So, as 1957 ended, we remained very much alive—and, in fact, stronger than ever.

It is an interesting sidelight that today *all three* of the large food chains that were originally opposed to stamps are now giving them in their stores.

The A & P is actually an "old friend" of trading stamps. Prior to World War I, it happened to be S & H's biggest customer. This largest chain of all at that time confirmed the growing popularity of stamps by an extremely kind letter which is still in our files.

"Having carefully investigated the value and character of the premiums given by The Sperry and Hutchinson Company," Mr. John Hartford wrote, "and having found them satisfactory in every respect, we take pleasure in announcing that we have renewed our contract with said Company for a term of years, and will continue to give the famous 'S. & H.' Green Trading Stamps to our customers as heretofore."

The letter is dated August 7, 1912.

In retrospect, I can say now that in spite of the legislative onslaught I have described, I firmly believe that our company gained from the experience. We developed a strong, flexible, loyal, and superior organization. Many of our middle management people crowded years of experience into a span of months.

More important, we learned to appreciate fully the truly critical role being played by the consumer in the economy of the nation. We learned in North Dakota, New Jersey, Oklahoma, Tennessee —all across the country—that where any "vested interest" group has the temerity to attempt to deprive the consumer of her rightful freedom of choice, she can be counted upon to strike back.

In Nashville, Tennessee, 75,000 women with our help organized themselves in one week in opposition to the anti-stamp lobby. Women filled the house galleries during hearings. They flooded law-makers with mail protesting anti-stamp legislation. One group filled clothes baskets with pro-trading stamp post cards and presented them personally to legislators.

The massive legislative attacks of these years made another basic point unforgettably clear. It was that our company, while privately owned, was public in character. As such, we had become obliged by our scope of operations, our leadership position, and our obligations to an increasing number of accounts and employees, to keep the public more fully informed of our objectives and our actions. We had to abandon forever and entirely our patiently held hope that sound performance alone would speak for itself. We decided to encourage, energetically, a continuing public scrutiny of the trading stamp business.

Our reasoning was simple: Not only had we nothing to hide; we were performing a positive role in the American economy. Each day our system of free enterprise was moving increasingly in the direction of greater efficiency in the distribution of goods, increased savings for the consumer, and constantly improving values in return for dollars spent. It was a working principle at

S & H to participate as fully as we could in attaining these objectives. We believed, therefore, that if more people understood our operations and motivations, we would receive broader public support for our activities, and be permited the luxury of going about our business.

As a result, we decided, among other things, to co-operate more fully with press media by volunteering information. We expanded the production and distribution of booklets, leaflets, speech reprints and other materials to help acquaint the public with our business. We encouraged marketing students, economists and others to investigate all aspects of trading stamps. And we put down for our own guidance, as well as for external use, what we thought to be the key factors about our operation.

These factors were and are as follows:

—A trading stamp company has the same inherent right as any other American company to offer its services freely. This right, along with the right of any consumer or merchant to accept or reject such services, should be inviolable under our economic system.

—Struggles over the use of trading stamps generally reflect a controversy initiated among business competitors. As such, they belong in the market place, not in legislative halls or in the courts, at the ultimate expense of the taxpayer.

—Since trading stamps are primarily a promotional tool, an attack on stamps is essentially an attack on the concept of all promotions and, in a sense, on the economic system itself, because the distribution phase of our economy depends heavily on effective advertising and promotion techniques.

—While a successful operation, S & H makes no more than a modest profit. On the basis of our total sales over the past ten years, 1953-1962, our profit after taxes has been 5.2 per cent.

—Trading stamp redemption rates are at least 95 per cent and we make every effort to encourage maximum redemption. It is in our own best interest. The housewife becomes an enthusiastic stamp saver only after she has redeemed her stamps for merchandise which will be valued and remembered. Without enthusiastic stamp savers, our business would collapse.

—There is no evidence whatsoever, after years of experience with trading stamps, that they necessarily bring about an increase in prices. In fact the sum of all existing studies to date would suggest that the competitive impact of trading stamps is such as to tend to bring about, if anything, a downward pressure on price structures.

—The value received by consumers saving S & H Green Stamps is greater than the total cost paid by merchants for the company's stamp service. On the average, the company sells its service for considerably less than the three dollars represented by the 1,200 stamps that fill an S & H collector's book. The average retail value of merchandise acquired per book runs $3.00 or higher. S & H derives its profit from the fact that it pays wholesale, not retail, prices for redemption merchandise.

Having set down these factors, we commenced the burdensome job of communicating them to the public. We staffed ourselves with a national network of persons trained in public information work. Concurrently, better to understand and articulate the impact of trading stamps on consumers, merchants, and the economy as a whole, we engaged a professional economist of unusual talents, who had made exhaustive studies of the trading stamp business as a University of California professor.

He mapped out areas of company activity requiring research and, for assistance, retained outside organizations such as Louis Harris & Associates, Benson & Benson of Princeton, and a Harvard Business School group.

S & H had long been a consumer-oriented organization, but we had always kept our thoughts and beliefs pretty much to ourselves. Now, research gave us new information to share with the public. A 1963 Benson & Benson survey discloses, for example, that S & H trading stamps are being saved in some thirty million U.S. households, or 55 per cent of the total households.

We also documented through research why stamps are so popular. To begin with, stamps afford people a way to save as they spend. There is only one thing a consumer can do with his stamps. He can't, in a weak moment, shake them out of the piggy bank and fritter them away. Therefore, stamp saving becomes a relatively painless process for achieving the desirable things every consumer likes to have, but ordinarily wouldn't, or couldn't, go out and buy.

Our child's rocker, redeemable for only one-and-a-half books, is a good example. This is a useful addition to any home with children, but one which many families might hesitate to buy, not liking to lay out cash for what might be construed as a luxury item. But it is an important number in our catalog. In 1962 we distributed no less than 184,000 such units. This is evidence of the nation-wide impact made by the issuance of some 30 million illustrated S & H catalogs.

We could point to a host of other products, too, which developed into major sources of manufacturing income and employment as a result of our catalog distribution. These range from pinking shears and card tables to room dividers and sets of sterling silver. Everyone loves to receive a gift, and trading stamps enable people to fulfill this human desire. Add to this the natural collector's instinct shared by so many Americans, the satisfaction of actually receiving the merchandise at the redemption center and, most important, ownership and use of the merchandise, and it's easy to see how stamp saving adds a new and happy dimension to the role of the consumer.

Our research shows that stamp saving has been registering new gains with consumers in every age bracket, as well as on every occupational, financial and educational level. Trading stamps, it appears, have a kind of universal appeal to people from nearly all walks of life. These surveys have also substantiated our belief that the consumer takes a dim view of legislative attempts to hamper merchants who give stamps. Statistics show that only six out of one hundred would favor government action to eliminate trading stamps.

Our research revealed something else that would interest the public; namely, the effect of trading stamps on the country's economy. Distribution, not production, is a principal problem in our economy today. An overriding national need is for solutions to this distribution problem that will fall within the framework of the profit economy, yet will preserve its precious elements of individual initiative and individual freedom.

We feel we are contributing toward this end. Trading stamps stimulate retailing and improve its efficiency on the one hand, and increase the distribution of goods through redemption on the other.

Our industry is on the threshold of becoming a billion dollar business. Through more than 2,000 redemption stores across the nation, over a million units of each of the following product categories are distributed annually: wallets and billfolds, luggage, blankets, sheets and pillow cases, bedspreads, towels, clocks, cooking ware, furniture, lamps, glassware and garden tools.

Bear in mind, too, that these are largely *extra* sales, ones that ordinarily would not have occurred without trading stamps. Some merchants used to complain that merchandise distributed through redemption stores deprived them of sales. Such complaints have all but vanished because it has been documented that the redemption process actually stimulates a great deal of new buying. Permit me to cite a recent personal experience in this area.

Recently my son saved enough S & H Green Stamps (what other?) for the product of his choice, an Eastman Kodak motion picture camera. So, off he went to pick it up. But that was just the beginning. Next he had to have a projector, screen, film, and carrying case—all of which were purchased from the local merchant.

The pattern is a familiar one, and applies to a host of products. Stamp redemption touches off the initial desire. Then the local retailer reaps the benefit of follow-up buying to complete sets, provide accessories, match luggage, and the like.

Conventional outlets also realize extra business as a result of the exposure given their merchandise in the company's 860 redemption centers and in its widely circulated catalog.

There is another thing about the S & H operation that is not widely known, but affords us a good deal of satisfaction. This is the progress we have made in the last ten years in improving our operating efficiency through the introduction of technological improvements and close scrutiny of costs. In point of fact, our operating costs per 1,000 stamps a decade ago roughly matches our revenue per 1,000 stamps today. So, had we not succeeded in sharpening our operations and reducing costs, we would now be ranked among the country's largest non-profit institutions.

Putting this improvement in efficiency another way, a consumer redeeming S & H stamps in 1953 received merchandise worth about $1.04 for stamps, the use of which cost the merchant $1.00. In 1963, the consumer's merchandise value was about $1.16 for every $1.00 of stamp cost to the merchant. These figures are based on what the consumer would have had to pay for our catalog items in regular retail stores. (On the basis of manufacturers' suggested or list retail prices, the merchandise value figure would be about $1.25 rather than $1.16.)

It is a foregone conclusion that over the long haul the popularity of trading stamps will continue to be dependent on the performance of stamp companies, not what is said about them, or what they say about themselves. And there is little doubt that one of the unsung chapters in our own company's recent history has been the superb performance of our operating people in overcoming the demands imposed by rising costs and rapid growth. In the last ten years, our sales multiplied almost six times. This brought on a staggering volume of problems requiring prompt but thoughtful solution if the company was to maintain its reputation for service to accounts and stamp savers.

Inventories were vastly expanded; new warehouses built and almost immediately enlarged; hundreds of new redemption centers constructed, relocated, stocked and staffed (during one year we opened an average of one redemption center every four days); a multimillion dollar data processing center and telecommunications system was installed; a continuing national advertising campaign was launched; the entire internal organization was revamped; salary and sales compensation systems were overhauled; recruiting and training programs were expanded—all this, and more.

Now the fifties are gone and we are well into the sixties. While some of the extreme forms of opposition continue, our problems in this area are in competent hands and well under control. The situation we had faced was of course far from unique. It was the familiar story of a business success producing a swift and sharp response—and controversy. The pattern is by no means confined to the stamp business. In any event, now and in recent years our efforts have been focused, as they should be, on finding new ways to increase our value and service to accounts and consumers.

It must be increasingly difficult today for our opponents to reconcile their contention that trading stamps are undesirable with the fact that S & H alone has more than 75,000 loyal stamp-giving outlets, or with the fact that we issue more stamps than the United States Post Office Department.

We know the part—small as it may be—that we are playing in the nation's economy. We know we are helping to stimulate production and employment, and to expand the distribution of the nation's goods. We know we are contributing many millions to the tax revenues needed to operate governments at all levels.

We know, too, that the service we offer is a good one; that the value received by the consumer is fair and just; and that the mere existence of trading stamps as a promotional tool tends to sharpen retail competition—to the benefit of all consumers, whether they save stamps or not.

Still, we often wonder how much *greater* value the consumer might have received if, in the last decade, all the millions of dollars and all the human energy employed in trying to stop trading stamps had been diverted into competing more effectively against them—in the market place.

It's something to think about.

ROY ABERNETHY

American Motors Corporation

ROY ABERNETHY, president and chief executive officer of American Motors Corporation, has spent his entire adult life in the automobile business. He started as an apprentice mechanic in Pittsburgh in 1925 and attended Carnegie Institute of Technology at night, studying highway and bridge engineering and later, automotive engineering. In October, 1954, Mr. Abernethy joined American Motors as vice-president of Nash sales. A year later, when the Nash and Hudson sales organizations were merged, he was named vice-president of distribution and marketing for the Automotive Division. In 1960 he was elected a director of the company and promoted to executive vice-president. Following the resignation of George Romney as president and chairman on February 12, 1962, he was elected to his present position. From his first association with the company, he has been instrumental in bringing American Motors to the high position it now holds in America's automotive community.

A Car Is a Car Again

The Story of the Rambler Concept

ROY ABERNETHY

America in the mid-fifties went on a big car binge. In the following years, tailfins soared to monumental heights and the family sedan grew to Gargantuan dimensions with a fuel appetite to match. Dazzling in lavish chrome and four-tone colors, cars sprouted massive metal projections fore and aft which defied the capacity of home garages and public parking facilities.

This was the era of excess in car design—a period when quality and usefulness took a back seat to size and ostentation. Lights burned late in automotive styling studios as stylists outdid themselves in devising new frills and furbelows to advance the philosophy of forced obsolescence. The buyer had little choice. He could buy a big car or a bigger car. His alternative was one of the cramped foreign makes which were beginning to invade the domestic market.

From a product standpoint, American Motors was in much the same position as others in the industry. We were building some of the biggest cars on the road—the large Hudson and Nash models—which could be classed with other "gas-guzzling dino-saurs" of the time. The difference was that our share of the market was diminishing rapidly. In 1955, the industry's first seven-million car year, our sales amounted to less than 2 per cent of the market. Added to this, American Motors was a newly formed corporation fighting a grim financial battle to stay alive. We were heavily in debt and our credit lines were exhausted. The bankers were beginning to measure us with the air of an undertaker sizing up a prospective client.

The situation of the independent car manufacturer in the fifties was not a happy one. The easy selling years had vanished as production caught up with the heavy post-war demand for cars. Now, travel-hungry Americans were enjoying the return of a buyer's market, and the big volume producers were going all out to attract their favor. Competition was intense as the industry giants joined in a fierce struggle for first place in sales. The pressures of their competition and vast factory output ate heavily into the independents' share of the market. Further, the larger manufacturers had developed a high degree of interchangeability of components which permitted them to build a wide variety of makes utilizing a common body shell. This gave them the advantage of frequent styling changes at a cost no independent could match.

George Mason, president of Nash-Kelvinator Corporation, believed the independents' only hope for survival was in combining their assets and facilities and in gaining some of the advantages of interchangeability enjoyed by the larger companies. He began a series of talks with other independent producers which culminated in the merger of Hudson Motor Car Company and Nash-Kelvinator in May, 1954, to form American Motors, with Mason as president. Plans for implementing the physical merger of Nash and Hudson facilities were still on paper when Mr. Mason died suddenly and unexpectedly October 8, 1954. There was little question about his successor. George Romney, the company's young and enthusiastic executive vice-president, was named chairman, president, chief executive officer, and general manager.

When I joined American Motors in the fall of 1954 as vice-president of Nash sales, I was fully aware of the many problems facing the fledgling corporation. After many years with Packard and later with Kaiser-Willys as sales vice-president, I had no illusions about the independent car maker's position, especially that of a new company facing the complex job of integrating the facilities of two struggling operations while fighting the powerful competition of Ford, General Motors and Chrysler. The problems were immense, and the odds against success were mindful of the fifteen hundred companies which had perished in the automobile business.

Any doubts about the company's critical position were quickly dispelled in my first meeting with George Romney in Detroit. The facts confirmed my conviction that the company would scrape bottom before it could begin to move up. Obviously, a large measure of faith in American Motors' future was needed by anyone joining the company at that time, and this was the fundamental management attitude Romney was seeking. Examining the situation in its most formidable aspects, we found we shared a mutual belief in the opportunities open to American Motors if we could move expeditiously to correct basic deficiencies in the sales organization. This would be my area of responsibility.

Our discussions established certain facts on the company's situation. The field sales organizations of both Hudson and Nash were sorely in need of a general overhauling. Field sales personnel had grown rusty and apathetic; the dealer bodies were weak and ineffective and, with few exceptions, unable to step up to the competition of a tough buyer's market.

Public acceptance of Hudson and Nash cars—once proud names in the automotive world—was declining rapidly. Understandably, few buyers were interested in cars that were potential orphans, and many industry observers were already writing American Motors off.

Badly needed design and styling changes, other than minor face-lifting, were still far down the road in view of the company's precarious financial position. Moreover, American Motors had no meaning to the public. It was a new name in a field dominated by old-line companies which had achieved a high degree of product identity. American Motors needed to stand for something before it could gain product acceptance.

On the other hand, American Motors was a big company with total annual sales of about $400 million in the appliance and automotive markets. Its predecessor companies had exceptional records of accomplishment and were widely respected as leaders and innovators in their fields. It was a classic American business situation with multitudinous problems paralleled by unlimited opportunities. Time and meager resources were against the company's chances for reversing its downward trend. At the same time, the half-century history of the automobile business recounted a typical story of struggle against formidable odds for each company that persevered to win success.

The challenge was exciting. The first objective, we knew, was to build a hard-charging management team—one that could take twelve-hour work days in stride and compensate for limited financial resources by expending extra effort and determination. My initial major effort was to be the revitalization of the Nash sales organization and the creation of a dealer body competitive in ability and attitude. We knew the company had no hope for a future without an effective dealer organization. It was a big order, but my decision to join the team gave me a role in events which were to revolutionize the automotive industry's product approach and have a profound impact on the transportation choice of millions of American motorists.

To put the American Motors story in perspective, an understanding of two earlier consumer-dictated revolutions in the automobile industry is necessary.

Early in this century, Henry Ford saw the need for high-volume, low-cost cars that would provide basic transportation for the average American at a price within his means. Until then, the motor car was built and priced on the premise that it was a rich man's luxury. Ford's famous Model T, introduced in 1908, met with overwhelming public response and forced other manufacturers to revise their production and marketing practices. More than fifteen million of the historic "tin lizzies" were built over a period of nineteen years. In 1924, they accounted for nearly 50 per cent of total U.S. industry sales.

The era of bare, basic transportation gave way to another revolutionary idea in the thirties when General Motors moved to capitalize on the fact that cars could be glamorized and merchandised as symbols of the status of their owners. Other makers saw the success of the GM market approach, and the size and horsepower race was on. By 1940, the "bigger means better" concept had increased the average overall length of the three most popular makes to more than sixteen feet, compared to the Model T's modest twelve feet. Up to then, 60 per cent of the industry's business had been accounted for by cars in the under-sixteen-foot class.

The "big car" concept gained fresh impetus following World War II, expressing itself in the form of even larger, gaudier and more costly cars. Advertising and merchandising put heavy emphasis on the symbolism theme and the public was conditioned to accept the motor car as evidence of the owner's status in life, economic and social. Along with rising prosperity, growing acceptance of the idea that chrome and impressive car size denoted success pushed the sales of medium- and higher-priced cars to more than 40 per cent of the market in 1955.

In the face of such factual evidence, it was easy to accept the theory that the American car buyer was irrevocably committed to satisfying his ego with the most lavish land yacht he could afford. Market reports, surveys and all devices for measuring consumer buying habits gave overwhelming support to the big car philosophy. To run counter to the industry pattern appeared on the surface to be a suicidal move. Yet this was the carefully calculated decision of American Motors in late 1956 when we committed our product approach to the compact car idea, a move which precipitated the third major automotive revolution.

Behind this bold decision was the cumulative thinking of minds which reached beyond the ordinary in vision and resourcefulness. The genesis of the compact car began with George Mason's experiments with smaller, light-weight vehicles before World War II. Mason believed the unitized body construction principle which the Budd Manufacturing Company had developed offered excellent possibilities for automotive application. With his product engineers, he began an experimental project which resulted in the Nash "600," a car of conventional size but one which weighed five hundred pounds less than the average for similar vehicles. The "600" enjoyed only modest success when introduced in 1940, but it established the design principles which led to the development of the first compact car, the Rambler.

Mason continued his small car experiments with the resumption of passenger car production following World War II. He was convinced that the American public would eventually turn to more practical and convenient forms of personal transportation. But he also recognized that the American car buyer would not accept austerity or stripped-down, low performance vehicles which sacrificed comfort for functionalism. Others in the industry had driven down this road to a dead end.

Mason's goal was balanced design—a car which provided economy and performance with acceptable American standards of comfort and operating convenience. He believed this balance of features could be obtained in a six-passenger car in the overall length range of 170 to 200 inches. Below 170 inches, his research showed, some compromise must be made on one or more desirable characteristics, including interior space. Above 200 inches, superfluous weight and bulk set in. Nash engineers targeted on the lower end of the range, and the first modern Ramblers introduced in 1950 to test the market were convertible and station wagon models 176 inches in overall length. Four-door Rambler sedans appearing in 1954 were nearer the top of Mason's specified range. They were 186 inches long, with interior space comparable to cars a foot and a half longer.

The debut of the first compact Ramblers generated little excitement. To a public enchanted by big cars and rising horsepower, the Rambler was a novelty best suited to low-income buyers and eccentrics. Size, flash and breath-taking acceleration were the popular criteria of car value. Rambler's sensible design and exceptional features were scarcely noticed in the industry rush to produce bigger and more powerful highway Juggernauts. Mason's idea was right, but too advanced for the time.

The tenuous position of the independents worsened in the industry's record year of 1955. Sales for all independents dropped below 5 per cent, the lowest in history. American Motors' share was 137,000 cars, of which 72,000 were Ramblers. On net sales of $441 million, the company lost $6.9 million. In 1956, the company sold only 115,000 cars. Losses totaled $19.7 million on net sales of $408 million. The price of American Motors shares dropped to a low of $5.25. Business writers contributed to the gloomy outlook with frequent predictions of the company's early demise.

Convincing the public that American Motors would stay in business was a pressing need. While I concentrated on the formidable sales problems and organized field sales personnel into an efficient, competitive team, Romney followed a back-breaking schedule of speeches, conferences with bankers, press interviews and meetings with union officials and others concerned with our position. Over and over, to all who would listen, we repeated: "We have not one idea of uncertainty in our minds about the future of American Motors." In time, this expression of faith generated a note of optimism among employees and associates—prevailing against the cold, hard facts of our situation. By stressing our opportunities and displaying a solid, unwavering front to those who questioned our position, we gained valuable time in which to attack our vital problems.

We launched an aggressive information program to tell our product story to the public and to gain corporate identity. One of the most effective projects was a touring road show which displayed our products under the slogan, "American Motors Means More For Americans." It was viewed by thousands in major cities from coast to coast in a year-long tour. Digging deep into its slim advertising funds, the company invested in a popular network television show, "Disneyland," which presented our product lines to millions of viewers.

To strengthen the company's management, an extensive reorganization and decentralization program was begun, with the accent on youth. A new policy board was created which represented a wide range of experience and youthful vigor. The average age of its members was only forty-seven, but they represented unusual management ability. Its chief purpose was to establish the overall operating policies within the general corporate decisions of the board of directors. Each member had clearly defined responsibilities and authority in his particular area, with open-door access to the president's office.

The total result was a new look in American Motors' management—a lean, hungry team with an evident fierce determination to succeed against all odds. Its most valuable asset was its flexibility and capacity to initiate changes at top speed. As one industry observer commented: "At American Motors, major decisions are made and put into action while those at the other companies would still be looking for the right person to say 'yes.'"

Meanwhile, my detailed investigation of the sales organization confirmed the seriousness of our competitive position at the retail level. Dealers generally were poorly financed and unable to meet the stiff competition. To strengthen their financial position we established a unique Dealer Volume Investment Fund. Some retail operations were obviously beyond help by reasons of mismanagement or inadequate facilities. These were terminated. Others with a chance for rehabilitation were given every possible assistance. New business management procedures were instituted through zone offices. Work teams studied each dealer point and established a market potential for individual dealerships. A long-range dealer development plan was charted and we began the task of rebuilding a strong, competitive dealer body.

Even as we were putting our house in order, we continued to weigh our product position against the might of Big Three competition. Our discussions led to the conclusion that we were courting disaster in attempting to meet the larger makers head on. We needed to take a different approach—to find an undeveloped segment of the car market on which we could concentrate exclusively.

Was there a part of the market which was not being fully exploited by our competitors? Exhaustive studies of all available market data failed to provide the answer. Finally we turned to the consumer himself and examined his position in the light of the industry's current product offerings. Despite his apparent dedication to big cars, were his true needs being adequately served? We looked closely at certain changes taking place in the way people were living. Slowly, some significant facts began to emerge.

The population shift from the inner cities which began in the early fifties had expanded beyond the outer cities. Suburban communities were mushrooming around metropolitan areas at a tremendous rate.

The automobile was providing a new way of life for millions of Americans in spacious suburban areas. Churches, schools, and shopping centers were relocating nearby to serve them. With all this, dependence on the automobile was increasing. Cars were no longer mere status symbols; they were a necessity for travel to and from work, to take children to school, for shopping, and for the many personal transportation demands attendant with suburban living. There was a great increase in short-trip driving and new intensity of car use. Parking was fast becoming a major problem in heavily congested areas.

Multiple-car owning families were on the rise, which meant that initial car cost and total operating expense were becoming important budget considerations.

Most important, we noted a significant change in consumer buying habits. There was increasing competition for the dollars that formerly went into the purchase of long, showy and costly automobiles. Back yard swimming pools, boats, winter vacations and higher education for children were diverting disposable income into new channels. Further, the psychology of car ownership was undergoing a change. The automobile was, virtually unnoticed, losing its pre-eminence as a status symbol. Increasing prosperity had brought new cars within the reach of virtually all income groups.

Adding up the facts, we concluded that a gap was developing

in the car market. It was obvious that the standard-size cars could no longer qualify as low-cost transportation. The time appeared right for a new car concept, one which could serve the new needs of the American consumer. Surveys confirmed our conclusions. We had the car to drive into the gap—the compact Rambler— and a once-in-a-lifetime opportunity to gain a competitive lead on our rivals. In the fall of 1956, after careful deliberation, the company decided to stake its automotive future on the Rambler.

The decision was not enthusiastically endorsed by all in our management group. Some of our executives clung to the thinking that the way to meet competition was to match them in product concept. And as the plan included the ultimate phasing out of the large Hudson and Nash cars, they questioned the wisdom of putting all our eggs in one basket. Why not, they argued, put extra merchandising effort on the Rambler but keep the big cars to give broader market representation? In their thinking it was foolhardy to abandon what business we had to gamble on an unknown and unproved product idea.

We had to change this thinking within our central organization, as well as with the dealers, before we could make real headway with the public.

A few of us felt that our road to success lay entirely in the direction of outflanking our giant competition, rather than in continuing to try to meet them head on. Dropping the larger cars from our product line, we believed, was a key move, under the circumstances. This would permit us to do an all-out job on merchandising the advantages of the compact Rambler. With the large cars in our model lineup, we would be in the difficult position of selling one size against the other. Our sales argument for the Rambler would be weakened if we were forced to walk a tightrope between big and small. In addition, our slender advertising funds were woefully inadequate and if our message was to be heard, we needed every dollar concentrated on the Rambler.

Dealers also registered strong opposition to the idea that the Rambler could be our volume car, the general consensus being that the "factory" had lost its mind. Some angrily threatened to cancel their franchise agreements. The reaction was understandable. Historically, they had enjoyed lush sales years with the large Hudson and Nash cars, and while they were disturbed by shrinking volume and low profits, they generally believed the setback was temporary—that all we needed was fresh styling and more competitive engines to get back in the race. With few exceptions, they had given the Rambler offhand merchandising effort, if any. Their attitude was typical of the period—that size was directly related to value, and anything less than the biggest was inferior.

Our marketing strategy was clearly defined. Before we could hope to move Rambler up to higher sales levels we needed to crack the prevailing myth that car value was related to size—that bigness in itself was a virtue.

We prepared our campaign carefully, our basic strategy being to present the true facts of car design to the consumer for judgment. For years, the public had been accustomed to automotive advertising in stereotype form—usually a pretty picture surrounded by ego-titillating copy which held forth a promise of greater social acceptance. Few facts on the car itself were offered. Rambler advertising took a fresh approach. It offered comparative facts on big car versus compact design—pointing to the sensible advantages of the compact car for modern living. The copy actually named other cars, which was in itself a revolutionary automotive advertising approach. However, this was not intended to be just another advertising campaign conceived by clever agency people. Instead, it represented a total management approach which, by virtue of its sincere dedication to consumer interests, encouraged the car buyer to take a close look at his position in relation to the industry's current offerings. Rambler advertising posed a fundamental question: Are you, the car buyer, receiving true value for your dollar? Without making excessive claims, it offered factual evidence of the normal full-size passenger space and superior convenience and economy provided by compact design. It attacked the wasteful doctrines of excess and forced obsolescence. It refocused public attention on the basic function of the motor car.

Even the format of our advertising expressed American Motors' different approach to the consumer. We used full-page newspaper ads with news-type headlines and bold drawings and sketches of Rambler features. We carefully avoided catch phrases and clever slogans. By accepted advertising standards, our ad copy was far too lengthy, but it was factual and informative in every line. The most important difference, however, was the basic approach that marked all our communication efforts—an approach that recognized the customer as an intelligent person capable of making an intelligent decision when given the true facts about cars. In itself, this was a unique experience for the American car buyer, long accustomed to the emotion-charged, psychologically contrived copy that characterized most automobile advertising.

Response to the Rambler campaign was even greater than our best expectations. Readership studies showed that our assumption was correct—that the American public, surfeited by a bland diet of superficial automotive advertising, was indeed hungry for facts about cars. We accelerated the campaign, working with every available communication medium to reach the car buyer. One of the most effective tools was an "X-ray" booklet which presented a comprehensive study of comparative car values with diagrams and specifications of leading makes that permitted the reader to draw his own conclusions. Thousands of these booklets were distributed.

The campaign intensified on a person-to-person basis. George Romney expounded our product philosophy from every available platform, often making two or three speeches in a single day. One of his best-received talks was titled "Dinosaur in the Driveway," a humorous treatment of big-car ownership which attracted wide editorial attention and support.

Mixed in with the humor, however, was a serious assessment of the industry's direction:

> The automobile industry is noted for its super-salesmanship. It has demonstrated it by selling people on the idea that big, heavy, bulky cars are safer and more comfortable.

However, the innate intelligence of the American people usually manifests itself, particularly when informed.

What's the excuse for such heavy concentration on the production of big cars? Why, even the smallest cars of the Big Three are as big as the biggest cars used to be! The average American family today consists of only 3.5 members, and only half that number (1.7) comprises the average payload of the average car on the average run. Yet the average sedan body in use today—if its interior space were fully utilized— could carry two average families. This means that the American driver whether driving alone or carrying passengers is at all times paying for the transport of two families. And he has enough engine power under the hood to pull a ten-ton truck. How long would you have a job if you bought transportation on the same basis?

Yet most of you spend your own hard-earned money for extra bulk and weight on the highway.

Do you think it's safer? It isn't.

Do you think you get more comfort? You don't.

Do you think such cars are easier to drive? They aren't.

Do you have an inferiority complex that makes you buy much more car and bulk than you need just to make you look successful? Pierre Martineau, research expert of the *Chicago Tribune,* says the desire to look successful is a top car buying motive. Of course it's true. But why not have others think you're *smart* as well as successful?

And certainly smart buyers buy *today* what others are going to think is smart tomorrow.

Cartoonists picked up the theme, and there was a rash of newspaper and magazine cartoons lampooning tailfins and seriously questioning excessive size. It was encouraging evidence that public opinion was bending in our direction.

Another significant development about this time gave added support to our position. Sales of foreign cars, which had been a mere trickle, began to assume flood-tide proportions, further evidence of growing consumer disenchantment with U.S.-built cars. Before the compact car successfully stemmed the tide, the imports were taking a healthy bite out of the domestic market— as much as 10 per cent of total registrations in their peak year of 1959.

In developing co-ordinated dealer effort and a genuine partnership spirit, I know of no substitute for personal contact. My personal approach to dealer problems had always been on an "eye-to-eye" basis, and I elected to follow this procedure in convincing dealers that our product position was sound. The company planes having been sold in the interests of economy, I became a familiar customer of the commercial airlines. Crisscrossing the country with executive teams, I met with dealers on a round-the-clock schedule. At the same time, we thoroughly revamped our zone and field organization and procedures. It was a formidable task, and we knew we were in a battle against time to gain adequate sales strength before we were crushed with financial losses.

By 1957, the weeding-out process had reduced our retail outlets to some nineteen hundred dealers, and this was the nucleus from which we developed one of the industry's most prosperous and able dealer organizations. The personal, frank discussions of our plans had aligned a satisfactory number of key dealers behind the compact idea, and it was this group that brought us to the first stage of Rambler's rise. It's interesting to note that some of the most compact-resistant dealers eventually became our biggest volume retailers.

The car market took an encouraging turn in the spring of 1957. Rambler sales began a steady rise, and by the end of the model year were up 30 per cent over 1956. With confidence gained from more than 90,000 Rambler sales, the company reaffirmed its dedication to the compact concept by dropping the large Hudson and Nash models from the 1958 product line. The 1958 lineup included a 100-inch, a 108-inch and a 117-inch wheelbase Rambler—all within the compact range of 170 to 200 inches overall. Whereas Hudson and Nash together had five basic bodies, the 1958 Ramblers used only two basic bodies, which simplified tooling and reduced costs to a more competitive level.

The upturn in Rambler sales was reflected in growing dealer

confidence. They became noticeably more aggressive in merchandising the Rambler, aided by factory-sponsored economy runs which brought more prospects into their showrooms.

Interest in the Rambler franchise increased and by the end of 1957 our dealer count was more than twenty-three hundred. More important, apathy had given way to an attitude that Rambler was on the move—that we had an exclusive product position in a growth segment of the market. Any doubt about the soundness of our market approach evaporated in 1958 when Rambler took 4.6 per cent of industry sales. In the face of adverse economic conditions and a decline in automobile sales generally, Rambler more than doubled its 1957 sales. The building of the retail organization continued with a net gain of 425 new dealers in 1958, and this growth continued against a background of a steadily increasing dealer mortality for the industry as a whole.

Despite the growing evidence that there was a strong market developing for Rambler-type cars, our competitors remained largely unimpressed. Import makes continued their inroads on the market, rising to more than 400,000 units in 1958. Still, rival company officials persisted in their contention that there was no sizeable market for smaller, more practical cars. Their dedication to the big car philosophy was expressed in such public statements as:

"Americans still want only the biggest and fanciest cars they can buy. Tailfins are here to stay!"

Or: "Our surveys indicate that the type of product we are now offering represents the desires of a major portion of the car-buying public, and it is my opinion that it will continue to do so for the foreseeable future."

Customer letters crossing my desk told a different story. We were winning attention for our superior quality and our emphasis on providing an obviously better value. The general theme of customer letters was: "Thanks for building a sensible, easy handling car that fits my garage." Invariably, the writers praised Rambler fuel economy and low operating costs. Some of these letters were used in a series of "Love Letter to Rambler" ads in national magazines.

The full impact of changing consumer attitudes and preferences hit the industry with explosive force in 1959. Rambler sales soared to 368,000, representing 5.8 per cent of industry sales, an increase of 85 per cent over sales in the previous year. Bypassing many of the most popular makes, Rambler moved up to sixth position nationally in sales and to third place in twelve states. Orders exceeded the company's productive capacity, and an extensive expansion program was initiated at our Wisconsin plants. Further underscoring the American car buyer's revolt against extravagance, import car sales climbed to more than 650,000 in 1959.

The overwhelming evidence of a major consumer trend could no longer be ignored. Other manufacturers pushed the panic button to convert plants for compact car production. The 1960 model year brought the first of our large competitors' compacts into the market. Aided by their massive advertising budgets, the compact market expanded rapidly. Rambler sales in 1960 totaled 435,000, the highest sales mark ever attained by an independent manufacturer. For the first time, American Motors' net sales topped the billion dollar mark.

By 1961, nearly one third of all U.S. car production was allocated to compact makes. The revolution sparked by Rambler was in full swing. Compacts were accounting for 36 per cent of sales and swiftness of the transition in the market forced an extensive realignment of product lines and models throughout the industry. Compact sales made heavy inroads on the standard makes, which had long abandoned any claim to their former "low-price" classification as they grew in size and opulence. The so-called "medium-price" cars suffered the sharpest decline due to the upward pressure of compacts, dropping below 20 per cent of the market from the lofty 38 per cent they commanded in 1955.

The transition continued in 1962, with the compact makes strengthening their market position with an increasing variety of models which gave the buyer a wide range of choice. For the first time, the "volume" segment of the market was shared equally between the compacts and standard cars. By 1963, there were more than 8 million compact cars on the road, of which nearly 2.3 million were Ramblers.

Of greater significance to the American motorist is the return to functionalism and usefulness in car design which accompanied the compact revolution. The exorbitant growth in car length was arrested, making cars easier to handle and park. Overall length of the average 1963 sedan was nearly a foot less than the average 1959 model—the year U.S. cars reached their postwar peak in size. At the same time—also reflecting the compact influence— average interior dimensions were noticeably improved.

By restimulating the competitive resourcefulness of the U.S. automobile industry, the compacts have given the consumer a greater choice in personal transportation and cars more closely tailored to his needs. The budget-shattering costs of car ownership of the pre-compact era have been reduced by new emphasis on economy of operation and features designed for less maintenance expense.

Above all, the compact movement helped to restore industry attention to the need for better quality and value. Safety, economy and dependability have replaced chrome and frivolous gadgetry as measurements of car value. Today's automobiles are vastly superior in quality and durability, as evidenced by the extended warranties offered by most manufacturers.

Without the sales stimulation of the compact cars, it is doubtful if the industry would have moved as soon as it has to a new platform of seven million-plus car sales a year.

American Motors' spectacular rise from near oblivion to a position of automotive leadership is, I believe, a dramatic restatement of the great opportunities inherent in the American competitive system. In finding and satisfying a new consumer need, our company became a financial success, created thousands of jobs, and redirected the product trends of a giant industry which importantly influences the way of life for millions of Americans.

With annual sales of more than one billion dollars, American Motors now ranks among the top fifty of the nation's largest corporations. Employment has risen from 16,500 in 1957 to 30,000, with annual payrolls totaling $250 million. In addition, the world-wide production of more than one-half million Ramblers in 1963 provided new stability and prosperity for the vast network of supplier firms serving the automobile industry.

The Rambler dealer body has grown to thirty-one hundred soundly based, profitable and highly competitive business operations, with an aggregate net worth of more than $200 million. The affinity with our dealers is closer than most because of the life-or-death struggle we shared in our early days, and this is reflected in a unique "partnership" relation between factory and dealers.

More cars are produced in our Kenosha assembly plant than in any other single U.S. automobile production facility. The completion of a multi-million-dollar expansion and modernization program in 1964 will increase capacity to nearly 700,000 cars annually—almost triple the 1957 level.

Rambler cars are now appearing throughout the world in countries where rising prosperity has created a rich market for American-type cars of compact dimensions. Rambler exports account for 18 per cent of new car shipments from the United States, and our overseas markets are served by 110 distributors around the world. Rambler manufacturing-assembly plants are located in Canada, Mexico, Australia, New Zealand, South Africa, Belgium, Argentina, Uruguay, the Philippines and Venezuela. Just as the domestic market was reshaped by the compact car, Rambler-size automobiles are altering world markets by creating greater acceptance of American cars abroad. Large American cars of post-war vintage were too big, too costly and too expensive to operate for motorists of other nations, and the export market was virtually nonexistent until revitalized by the availability of compact cars. Thus, the scope of Rambler's influence since our historic decision in 1956 has been world-wide.

When George Romney resigned from American Motors in 1962 to make his successful bid for the governorship of Michigan, I became president and chief executive officer. The consumer-oriented policies we established as guidelines for our approach to the automotive market and which were basically responsible for Rambler's success have remained pre-eminent in product planning and research and in the overall conduct of company affairs.

We are ever mindful that it was the consumer who validated the Rambler idea in the market place and refuted the motivationists who believe appeals to human irrationality are more likely to be profitable than an appeal to rationality. When we began to look beyond the cold statistics of market studies and approached the consumer as an intelligent, rational individual rather than an unthinking cipher, we found the key to success in one of the world's most competitive businesses. It bears repeating that the ultimate boss of every business endeavor is the customer. As a constant reminder, Rambler cars are assembled under signs in our plants which read: "Build every Rambler as if it were your own."